M

SOUND MATTERS

SOUND MATTERS

Essays on the Acoustics of
Modern German Culture

Edited by

Nora M. Alter

and

Lutz Koepnick

Berghahn Books
NEW YORK • OXFORD

Published in 2004 by
Berghahn Books

www.berghahnbooks.com

Library of Congress Cataloging-in-Publication Data

Sound matters : essays on the acoustics of modern German culture /
edited by Nora M. Alter & Lutz Koepnick.
    p. cm.
   Includes bibliographical references and index.
   ISBN 1-57181-436-1 (alk. paper)
    1. Music—Philosophy and aesthetics. 2. Sound. 3. Music—Social
aspects—Germany. 4. Music—Acoustics and physics. I. Alter, Nora
M., date–. II. Koepnick, Lutz P. (Lutz Peter)

ML3845.S6835 2004
780'.943—dc22

                                                        2003063625

British Library Cataloguing in Publication Data

A catalogue record for this book is available from
the British Library.

Printed in the United States on acid-free paper

CONTENTS

ACKNOWLEDGMENTS

The editors would like to acknowledge the University of Florida Scholarship Enhancement Fund, the Graduate School of the University of Florida, and the Graduate School of Washington University in St. Louis for their generosity, which facilitated the research, organization, and editing for this project. In addition, the editors would like to extend their thanks to all of the contributors in this volume, who provided original and exciting texts with which to work.

Thanks also go to Alexander Alberro, Keith Bullivant, Gerd Gemünden, Sander Gilman, Anton Kaes, and Eric Rentschler for their encouragement and support for this project, and to the anonymous readers at Berghahn Books for their helpful comments on the entire manuscript.

We are indebted to Leah Chizek, Gwyneth Cliver, and Patience Graybill for their help in editing individual contributions and preparing the manuscript for publication.

We would like to express our gratitude to the entire staff at Berghahn Books and in particular to Shawn Kendrick for her careful copyediting and typesetting of the manuscript. Last but not least, thanks go to Marion Berghahn for her support of this project.

NORA ALTER   LUTZ KOEPNICK

SOUND MATTERS

INTRODUCTION
Sound Matters

Nora M. Alter and Lutz Koepnick

I

First published in 1992, Rick Altman's *Sound Theory: Sound Practice* and Douglas Kahn and Gregory Whitehead's *Wireless Imagination: Sound, Radio, and the Avant-Garde* broke new ground in cultural studies.[1] Both volumes, by investigating the role of the acoustic across a broad spectrum of genres and media, spearheaded a virtual explosion of work on sound that took place during the second half of the 1990s. A decade after Altman's and Kahn and Whitehead's anthologies, sound has come to figure today as a viable space of critical exploration, a productive register of social and cultural analysis in various academic disciplines. One often hears that we live in an age dominated, and even overwhelmed, by the visual image. But we merely need to close our eyes for a moment to realize just how much sound matters in late modernity as well—to those involved in scholarly writing as much as to those participating in the arena of cultural production itself.

In the area of film and media studies, the examination of sound has become one of the primary fields of interest and analysis. Numerous recent monographs have drawn attention to the manifold ways in which filmic music, noise, and dialogue can shape cinematic meaning and direct the viewer's perception.[2] Additionally, sound itself has been thematized in recent years by a number of filmmakers who have sought to increase our awareness of the acoustic dimension of the medium. German director Wim Wenders, for instance, in his 1994 *Lisbon Story*, centers the entire narrative on the efforts of a soundman, Philip Winter, to produce a soundtrack of a film in the making. Following Winter's expeditions through Lisbon, the viewer soon loses sight of the images of the city as its sounds and noises come to predominate. Wenders's work of the 1990s—in films such as *Until the End of the World* (1991), *Buena Vista Social Club* (1999), and *Viel passiert—Der BAP Film* (2002)—is also indicative of another sonic turn that has occupied the cinema of the last decade and a half, namely, the unprecedented success of soundtracks released as separate compact discs. In many cases, Wenders's soundtracks during the 1990s were commercially much more lucrative than their filmic sources, a development that is symptomatic of a fundamental shift in what we may define as the cinematic experience today. In the wake of the soundtrack mania and revolution of the 1990s, it has become difficult to further uphold one of the most basic tropes of classical film theory and criticism, namely, that the visual is the primary site of meaning, identification, and spectatorial pleasure. As it decenters the conventional unity of sound and image, Wenders's work of the last decade suggests that acts of listening might be as creative and pleasurable as those of viewing—an insight that has also found ample resonance in recent academic studies of opera, radio, and contemporary music, on the one hand,[3] and in analyses of newer phenomena, such as MTV file sharing through the Internet, on the other hand.[4]

Yet even more ambitious and challenging is the entry of sound into the visual arts and art criticism. Recently, there has been an abundance of works, and not just video or filmic ones, that can be called "sound pieces." A prime example is Sylvia Kolbowski's *an inadequate history of conceptual art* (1998), which consists of a sound installation of the recorded responses of forty artists to the request that they "Briefly describe a conceptual art work, not your own, of the period between 1965 and 1975, which you personally witnessed/experienced at the time."[5] Kolbowski was particularly interested in those manifestations of conceptual art that are the most ephemeral and transitory and the least likely to leave a concrete trace, the ones that exist only in memory and oral history. Sound sculpture also defines German artist Marcel Odenbach's *As If Memories Could Deceive Me*, which creates an audial history of the twentieth century played out on the keyboard of a piano. Here it is worth emphasizing that the linkage of history and sound breaks new ground, for it postulates that history needs to be heard as well as read and replayed. Odenbach's point is echoed by some of the most innovative cultural studies of recent years, such as Adrian Rifkin's *Street Noises: Parisian Pleasure 1900–1940*, an alternative history of Paris told through the popular songs and operas heard throughout the city during those years, and Greil Marcus's *Lipstick Traces: A Secret History of the Twentieth Century*, which chronicles the 1970s and 1980s through an investigation of the twentieth-century strands of negation that culminated in punk rock music.[6] In a particularly bold move, Jean-Luc Godard recently distributed his monumental videotape, *Histories of Cinema*, separately as a soundtrack, prompting the possibility of an entirely new art form—one in which vision has been entirely abolished and the sonic emerges as a principal conduit to history and memory.

One of the central questions that led us to the compilation of this volume seeks to determine why sound has become so important today. Our working hypothesis is that we cannot discuss the increased prominence of the acoustic as a field of production and investigation without also speaking about a number of important technological breakthroughs and developments. Modernity has usually sought to master the visual prior to the audial[7] (e.g., the advent of photography mechanically reproduced the image decades before the phonograph could record a voice; silent cinema preceded sound film by three decades; even computers were silent until recently), resulting in a certain lag—conceptually, materially, practically, and theoretically. One of the significant developments in audial recording devices was, for instance, the portable audiotape cassette, which entered into the general market in the 1960s. These cassettes soon made the older, bulky reel-to-reel tapes obsolete, while at the same time providing the average person with the means of custom-making sound recordings. With cassette decks, even children could record whatever sounds they chose at will. Thus, the portable cassette tape technology was to audial recording what the Polaroid camera was to image production. The importance of the new technology was located in the potential it offered for individuals to master the medium and produce their own sounds. The advent of the portable video camera (Sony's Portapak) in the late 1960s along with digital editing programs developed in the 1990s have revolutionized sound and image production. Within the discipline of music, easy access to sound technology has led to new forms of contemporary music, such as "scratch," "rap," "dub," "hip-hop," and "techno," all of which depend on the active manipulation of recording and playback devices. Indeed, this very ability to separate and remix sound and image tracks has produced new video art installations, such as Julie Becker's *Suburban Legend* (1999), which replaces the original soundtrack of MGM's *The Wizard of Oz* (1939) with the rock band Pink Floyd's *Dark Side of the Moon* (1973) in order to enact the popular myth that Pink Floyd's album is completely synchronized with the film. Another example is Christian Marclay's *Up and Out* (1998), which pairs the visual track of Michelangelo Antonioni's *Blowup* (1966) with the soundtrack of Brian De Palma's *Blow Out* (1981), thus altering the interpretation of these well-known feature films while commenting on the role of recordable media in our culture. In short, sound is today more easily produced, distilled, manipulated, and controlled than ever before, and it is this unprecedented proliferation of sound production technologies that, in many respects, accounts for the growing fascination with the acoustic.

Writing about this invisible medium, however, poses an unusual challenge. Though pervasive, and indeed at times invasive, sound is also by its very nature ultimately evasive. Unlike the visual, sound has been

thought of as ephemeral, leaving no trace, to the extent that its early the-
oreticians lamented about the "ghastly impermanence of the medium."[8]
But perhaps the greatest challenge in writing about sound is the lack of an
established critical language. This is in stark contrast to the visual, with its
abundance of terms such as "looking," "visualization," "focus," "regard,"
"view," "see," "observe," and so forth.[9] A brief detour into the etymology
of the word which signifies one of the major components of sound, "volume," might be a productive starting point in theorizing how we can
begin to talk about the acoustic. The word came from the Latin *volumen,* to
roll, designating a scroll. With time, it came to signify volumes of *written*
production, and later still, bulk, such as the represented mass in art or
architecture. Only in its most recent meaning does "volume" refer to the
degree of loudness or sound.[10] Thus, the word evolved gradually from a
term defining a textual referent, to a term with a visual implication, to one
with an aural connotation. Perhaps the increased critical interest in the
problem of sound will shift the meanings (even if ever so slightly) of other
key words and terms to make them operative within sound studies. But
for now we are still limited by a sparse critical vocabulary and the need to
borrow metaphors from the other senses, particularly from vision.

    While a number of books have recently been published on the relation
between German classical music and national identity, most are stuck like
the skipping of a scratched record on two well-worn grooves: Wagner and
Adorno.[11] This is not to imply that these studies have been unproductive,
but the aim of *Sound Matters* will be to extend the analysis of the sonic construction of German nationhood beyond the relatively narrow confines of
the practice and theory of these two individuals. The uniqueness of this
anthology, however, is located in the way in which its contributors combine historical, theoretical, and interpretive lines of inquiry in order to trace
the role of sound in ongoing negotiations of high culture and mass entertainment, of cultural particularity and international influence. Informed
by a diverse spectrum of contemporary theory, the essays consider the
sonic as a pivotal site where notions of individual and collective identity
are constructed and contested. Sound is understood as a primary medium
through which the boundaries of shared meanings, ethnic differences,
political representation, codes of gender identity, and the organization of
private and public spaces are constituted. It is the task of the following
pages of this introduction to map out in further detail the historical, theoretical, and analytical dimensions of our interest in the acoustical.

II

Sound, as we present it in this anthology, is a distinctly modern and historically variable category. It is inseparably bound up with the organs,
instruments, environments, and machines that produce it, and it cannot be

isolated from the media that record, disseminate, and transform it. Sound links human subjects to each other. It communicates power or utopian fantasy, passion or critique. But it always does so with the help of historically contingent tools of articulation and mediation. That sound, in the course of the nineteenth and twentieth centuries, has been increasingly subjected to processes of technological transmission and reproduction does not simply alter some external features of the acoustical field. Rather, it revolutionizes our whole understanding of that field and of its effects on the human subject. Every successful technological innovation in the realm of modern sound recording and circulation—the gramophone, the telephone, the radio, the sound film, the tape player, the compact disc, and now the Internet—has activated pleasures, perceptions, and cultural practices that have overthrown earlier conceptions of sound production and reception. Once symphonies were broadcast over the radio waves, the same performances in the concert halls had a fundamentally different ring to them. Voices recorded on tape upset the rhetoric of corporeal presence, the here-and-now, traditionally attributed to the speaking body. Internet calls may sound similar to customary phone calls, but they involve cultural practices that differ from former conventions and that cast light on what we normally do when listening to and speaking into a telephone. As sound, with the advent of the second industrial revolution in the late nineteenth and early twentieth centuries, became mechanically transmissible and reproducible, nothing concerning the place of sound in society could be taken for granted any longer. Once sounds were able to travel freely through space and time, the relation of this medium to other modes of sense perception—the visual, the haptical, the olfactory—underwent irreversible transformations.

According to Jacques Attali, sound represents the social organization of noise, a source of political control as much as of subversion. By channeling noise into manageable shapes and formations, sound is a "tool for the creation or consolidation of a community, of a totality."[12] Yet as John Cage has theorized, nothing would be more foolish than to think of noise as a primordial matter, as a timeless substance requiring the mediation of a human voice, a musical instrument, or a recording device in order to enter the arenas of human experience. Noise might often be perceived as a rather intractable, and hence mythical, source of disorder and disruption, but it, too, is a product of history, of human activities and interventions. Nothing about noise, in other words, is natural. On the contrary, the concept of noise as we know it was a product of the industrial revolution, and what it indicated was a precarious loss of what previous ages had considered as the organic identity of sound and source, the acoustical and the visual, the voice and the body. In the factory and on the metropolitan street, in the mine and at the train station, nineteenth-century industrialization introduced itself with "a constant din of construction and pounding, of the shrieking of metal sheets being cut and the endless thump of press machinery, of ear-splitting blasts from huge steam whistles, sirens, and electric bells that beckoned and dismissed shifts of first-generation urban laborers from their unending and repetitive days."[13] Although the sounds of rural life had, of course, by no means always been pleasant to the ear, they had been relatively predictable and identifiable. Preindustrial sounds could be traced to their origins—an animal, a hand-held tool, a cloudy sky—and hence made meaningful. In the newly rising metropolis, by way of contrast, the multiplicity of sonic stimuli challenged the individual's senses and triggered a curious splitting of aural and visual perception. Urban noise ripped sights and sounds apart. It overwhelmed the urban dweller with experiences of shock and discontinuity. Unchained from their sources, industrial sounds traveled randomly and connected the incommensurable. Like train travel, they collapsed former boundaries of perception, connected dissimilar spaces, and thus upset traditional demarcations. Part of a curious dialectic of modernization, cacophonic sounds haunted modern life like a specter, relentlessly troubling the drive to reorder and rationalize the world. Though itself a product of modernity, noise disturbed modern articulations of meaning and community with seemingly meaningless clamor.

Jürgen Habermas has famously defined the modern as that which breaks with sanctified traditions and must create its norms and values out of itself. Modernity no longer borrows its models of orientation and meaning from earlier epochs. It is self-reflexively cast back upon itself without the possibility of escaping its peculiar and highly unstable position in time.[14] The story of modern sound reflects this logic in many ways. In the age of mechanical reproduction and transmission, sound lost the aura of the here-and-now. The soundscapes of modern life confronted the individual with an overload of sensory input and heterogeneous stimulation. They decentered traditional categories of perceptual synthesis and inaugurated an unprecedented sense of simultaneity and contemporaneity. Industrial noise and sound radically shrank the temporal and spatial coordinates of human experience. They put distant realities on a single plane of availability and thereby created a new consciousness of worldly immanence. In the face of overabundant sonic distractions, all that had once seemed solid now melted into the air. Because industrial sound prompted a fragmentation and atomization of the perceptual field, the issue of how to (re)organize attentiveness and maintain identity became one of the most pressing questions of modern life. But as the contributions to this volume show, the historical answers to these questions, as proposed during the nineteenth and twentieth centuries, were by no means unambiguous. Some sound practitioners and ideologues suggested strategies intended to reconstruct perceptual synthesis and halt any further diffusion of sounds, images, and identities. They hoped to rearticulate a subject whose attentive capacities were able to discipline sonic overstimulation—a subject able to isolate certain contents of the acoustical field and convert fragmentary sounds into stable meanings and uncontested orientations. Others, by way of contrast, explored the modern profusion of sound as a means to question unified notions of perception, subjectivity, and cultural identity. They embraced the inherent tenuousness of sound in modern life—its potential to transgress traditional boundaries and diffuse the subject's sense perception—in order to subvert hegemonic constructions of order and stress the transitoriness of modern experience. Rather than reinforce stable boundaries between self and other, sound for them served the purpose of bridging differences or of recognizing the Other as a potential source of self-critique and transformation.

Whatever long-term responses it may have triggered, the arrival of modern sound can best be described through the figure of shock. Industrial noises and mechanically reproduced sounds disrupted the working of the subject's perceptual apparatus. They often elicited fear, pain, or horror, and prompted the development of sensory protection shields that could cushion or even parry traumatic intrusions. This threat of sonic trauma has perhaps found its most instructive allegorical portrayal in Hans Christian Andersen's tale, "Den lille Havfrue" (The little mermaid), published in the eleven-volume edition, *Eventyr, fortalte for børn* (Fairy tales, told for children, 1835–1848). In Andersen's fairy tale, the material realities of modern life are, of course, nowhere mentioned in either word or phrase. And yet the whole story hinges on a peculiarly modern anxiety about corporeal and perceptual disintegration, a fear caused by the shock-like separation of sights and sounds in industrial culture.

Andersen's immortal mermaids, we read in the beginning of the tale, are equipped with the most beautiful voices. Their words sound like sheer music, more charming than those of human beings. But such vocal talents are of little use in achieving what the mermaids desire most, namely, to bridge the gap between their mythic world and the historical world of the humans. They sing lovely songs in order to seduce passing sailors into coming down to the bottom of the sea; yet the sailors are unable to understand these songs and mistake the mermaids' primeval hum for the noises of approaching storms. Unable to link the archaic and the modern, the timeless and the mortal, the mermaids turn into voyeurs who gleefully consume the ephemeral sights and sounds of human life as spectacles of first rank. They position themselves at the surface of the sea in order to gaze "at the large city on the shore, where the lights twinkled like hundreds of stars; to listen to music; to hear the chatter and clamor of carriages and people; to see so many church towers and spires; and to hear the ringing bell."[15] In their distanced perception, and in the absence of meaningful contact and exchange, the city emerges as a figure that fascinates—a site of never-ending distraction and stimulation. Look and listen, but do not touch or intermingle, is the mermaid's melancholic motto.

Enter the Sea King's youngest daughter, the Little Mermaid. She falls in love with a handsome prince during a stunning festival of sonic and visual attractions, staged on the sea in order to celebrate the Prince's six-teenth birthday. With the help of a witch, the Little Mermaid acquires a human body and hence the ability to immerse herself in the spectacular scenes of city life. But the price of her admission ticket is more costly than she can afford. It is her most precious gift, her voice, that Andersen's mermaid has had to barter in order to obtain a pair of legs. Silence thus marks her entry into the world of the other and bars her from communi-cating with the very object of her desire, from bridging radical alterity. Yet speechlessness is not even her greatest torment. Every movement of her new body is purchased with intense physical pain, causing the for-mer mermaid to choreograph her own appearance: "Every footstep felt as if she were walking on the blades and points of sharp knives, just as the witch had foretold, but she gladly endured it. She moved as lightly as a bubble as she walked beside the Prince. He and all who saw her mar-veled at the grace of her gliding walk."[16] To enter modernity means to stage one's own body according to dominant expectations and shared aesthetic standards.

The modern, in Andersen's tale, is a realm of inauthenticity and non-spontaneity, of loss and fragmentation. This sense of artifice and impos-ture is further amplified when the witch makes use of the Little Mermaid's voice to win the Prince for herself. Andersen's witch thereby embodies the dark side of capitalist modernization, namely the mystifying law of com-modification and reification. Under the witch's spellbinding influence, voices travel from one owner to the next like merchandise. They become things among other things, mobile and endlessly exchangeable. Liberated from tradition, individual identity here reemerges as a construction site: you can put your self on and off like a mask, you can re-dress your body with traded sights and sounds. But even though, in the Prince's modern world, nothing concerning the relation of sounds and sights seems stable anymore, no one is able—or willing—to notice that nothing might be as it appears to be. The modern spectacle excites perception but silences the mind. It presents itself as a phantasmagoria, as a self-producing and self-contained universe. In this world, he or she who rules over the relation of sights and sounds rules over the world.

Andersen's mermaid is unable to bear the burden of modern life. In sharp contrast to the Disney incarnation, the original heroine literally dies from the dissociation of the visual and the sonic that structures modernity. The Little Mermaid's trauma, this anthology argues, is that of sonic modernism. Yet what amounts to her downfall—the unfixing of sound and image from tra-dition—marks modernism's point of departure. Her torment designates an experience of rupture that nineteenth- and twentieth-century modernism will, in so many different genres and ways, persistently work through or act out and hence turn into a source of aesthetic creativity and political concern. Wagnerian modernism, for instance, will seek nothing less than to restore expressive and perceptual synthesis. It embraces advanced materials and techniques so as to resynchronize the fragmented registers of modern sense perception, to re-fuse image and sound into affective unity, and, in so doing, to redeem both the recipient's body and the body politic. What we can call Brechtian modernism, by way of contrast, explores the fragmentation of sight and sound in modern life in order to draw our attention to how we perceive the world in the first place and endow it with meaning. It emphasizes and, in fact, intensifies dissonance in the hopes of enabling self-reflection, nonidentity, and political critique. Whereas the Wagnerian modernist tries to reinvent the innocent pleasures of the mermaid's undersea realm, Brechtian modernism wants to do away with anything that may constrain the self-creation of meaning and identity in the Prince's city.

The essays gathered in *Sound Matters* trace the productive legacy of the mermaid's trauma in nineteenth- and twentieth-century German sound culture. They discuss competing practices of modern sound production in the fields of concert music, popular culture, song, radio art, filmmaking, literature, and poetry. According to the following contributions, sound mattered immensely to the articulation of meanings, identities, pleasures, and communities in modern Germany. Whether Wagnerian, Brechtian, or other in orientation, the sound practitioners discussed in this volume considered the sonic as a powerful means to question the modern unbinding of perception and representation, and to address the problem of attention in industrial culture. They perceived the audiovisual spectacle of modern life—the Prince's city of attractions—as a site not of cultural homogenization but rather of social disintegration. Modern spectacular culture, as several essays in *Sound Matters* explicitly point out, was less concerned with orchestrating operative communities than with "the construction of conditions that individuate, immobilize, and separate subjects, even within a world in which mobility and circulation are ubiquitous."[17] The spectacle of modern sights and sounds reunited the separate as separate,[18] whereas sonic modernism embraced the acoustical in order to construct subjects and communities that could supersede experiences of cellularization and isolation. Whether they sought simply to reverse or to refunction the decentering drive of modern sound, most of the composers, artists, writers, intellectuals, and filmmakers discussed in this book employed their medium as a means with which to heal what they recognized as the pathologies of modern life. Even though—as some contributors will show—neither Wagnerian synthesis nor Brechtian dialectics should be seen as the last word on modernist sound, sonic modernism in all of its different manifestations shared the dream of reconstructing expressive authenticity and sensual pleasure as the grounds of community. In so many ways, sonic modernism hoped to re-form the body politic by recuperating some sense of corporeal immediacy, and it did not hesitate to reinstate the desired state of spontaneity through calculated acoustical effects, through instrumental reason.

III

After seeing the first film shown with synchronized sound in German theaters, Lloyd Bacon's *The Singing Fool* (1928), future Minister of Propaganda and Popular Enlightenment Dr. Joseph Goebbels noted in his diary of September 1929: "I was surprised about the already far advanced technology of sound film. Here is the future, and we are wrong to reject all this as American bunk.... The content was dreadful, New-York-style, sentimental kitsch. But nonetheless ... we have to recognize [that] here is the future and coming opportunities."[19] Less than four years later, Goebbels converted opportunity into practice. In their efforts to produce and control modern mass culture from above, the Nazis embraced the advent of sound film as a highly welcome technology of fantasy production. Synchronized sound helped to link Nazi entertainment cinema to other arenas of organized leisure and mass communication, in particular, to the emerging record and radio broadcast industries. Although actual practice often contradicted theory, cinematic sound was seen as a viable means to disseminate the timbre of the German language and German musical traditions, and, in doing so, to integrate diverse viewers into the national community. Synchronized sound, in the perspective of many Nazi film practitioners and theorists, had the power of stimulating Dionysian ecstasy. No matter how modern in origin, it carried individuals beyond themselves and the immediate moment so as to experience a sense of the elemental. In the view of Nazi film officials, sound thus not only constituted the modern mass as mass, but also naturalized the community of viewers/listeners into something primordial. Though a product of advanced technologies, synchronized sound could provide mythic experiences of continuity and homogeneity.

Goebbels's commitment to sound cinema indicates the extent to which the acoustical in modern German culture was caught up in political struggles over the contours of identity, tradition, and community. Whether before, during, or after the Nazi era, German artists, composers, and ideologues in fact often considered the modern sound of music or of linguistic expressions as inherently political. It articulated a way of seeing the world as much as it defined one's affiliations in the present. It could cement the given order as much as it could launch subversive attacks on dominant institutions of power. To name only a few examples of sound politics in twentieth-century Germany: Nazi cinema often stressed regional accents in order to feature the nonrepresentational aspects of language as icons of national identification; American jazz, in the German cinema of the 1950s, earmarked urban culture as decadent and chaotic so as to promote the rural homeland as the sole site of authentic meaning and social order after Hitler; throughout the 1960s and 1970s, rock-and-roll gave vent not only to generational conflict but to struggles over the legacy of Nazi authoritarianism in postwar Germany; and hip-hop today serves as a mouthpiece of minority discourse and self-pride, giving voice to a new kind of multicultural sensibility that seeks to escape the putative boredom of the everyday.

Goebbels's emphasis on the politics of modern sound urges us to explore how modern German artists, composers, filmmakers, and audiences have used the sonic in order to address issues of power and subjection, solidarity and dissent. We cannot speak about the role of modern sound without also examining the dynamics of modern mass culture and its relation to aesthetic modernism. As several contributions to this volume show, the study of sound as one of the primary media of modern culture begs us to rethink conventional oppositions of high and low. It asks us to revise the standards according to which previous generations of scholars have classified and evaluated the products of cultural activity, for to speak of sound means to draw our attention beyond the arena of textual encoding and expression, beyond the realm of aesthetic artifacts. Instead, it means to pay heed to the ways in which sound—whether produced in the sphere of aesthetic autonomy or that of commodified mass diversion—elicits diverse pleasures and historically specific acts of signification. As the essays in this volume inquire into the relation of texts and contexts, meanings and practices, institutions and appropriations, they systematically crisscross what has often been considered the boundary between the aesthetic and the popular. Sound, as we present it in this collection, cannot be reduced to a text, a circumscribed set of symbols, a stable work. It is a form of practice, of intersubjectivity, of symbolic exchange and material transaction. Its meanings are in constant flux, its manifestations inherently performative. By investigating the changing construction of the sonic in nineteenth- and twentieth-century Germany, the essays encourage the reader to conceive of modern culture not in terms of a Manichaean struggle between cerebral modernism and vulgar mass culture, but as a location of various and often competing public spheres in which people have sought to voice their perception of the industrial world, including experiences of blockage, displacement, and speechlessness.

The modern age has often been described as an excessively visual one: a time of spectacle, of optical surveillance, of scopophilia and perverse voyeurism. *Sound Matters* balances this stereotype by illustrating the importance of hearing and sound production in the making of modern German culture since around 1800. To be sure, we are not claiming that German culture, in its devotion to the pleasures of sights *and* sounds, followed a special path of development; after all, there is no "normal" way of negotiating the relation of the visual and the acoustical in modern life. However, what this volume hopes to do is to contribute to a richer understanding of the nexus between power and culture, between perception, pleasure, and political domination, in German history since the age of reason. Sonic material was often essential to the foundation of authoritarian rule and the segregation of cultural identities in modern Germany. But not every sound served this purpose, nor did the history of modern German sound production teleologically culminate in the ear-numbing performance of German music and speech during Nazi Party rallies. While correcting a long-standing academic bias against the sonic, this volume suggests at the same time that the politics of modern sound are necessarily plural and ambivalent. Though *Sound Matters* does not disregard the despotic legacy of sound in modern German culture, this anthology reveals the role of other sonic traditions in Germany—traditions dedicated to individual emancipation and democratic transformation, as well as to a recognition of other cultures as sources of self-critique and political intervention.

It is interesting to note in this context that the scholarly bent against the sonic has been perhaps most striking, and symptomatic, in the field of German film studies. Following the well-known rejection of synchronized sound by intellectuals around 1930, postwar German film scholars by and large overlooked the pivotal role of film music and dialogue and instead focused entirely on the visual aspects of the filmic medium. In so doing, they not only ignored the rich legacy of sonic experimentation in German art cinema, but also failed to develop critical categories with which to assess the popular appeal of film sound since the early 1930s, symbolized not least of all by the fact that Germany's most popular television magazine of the postwar era continues to carry the imperative name *Hörzu* (Listen!). Prior to the 1990s, the field of German film studies, particularly in the United States, focused primarily on the feature productions of the 1920s and the 1970s—on the masterpieces of expressionist filmmaking and the muted visual designs of the New German Cinema. As a result of this scholarship, German cinema was primarily constructed as an art cinema. Seen as a medium in search of a nationally specific and aesthetically compelling language, it was celebrated as an intellectually challenging counterpoint to Hollywood, a robust alternative to popular filmmaking. As a consequence of this normative quest for the artful and nonpopular, little room was granted to the study of sound practice, for sound seemed to spoil the artistic expressiveness of the visual. The sonic was seen as connecting cinematic works to the vernacular, the popular, or the transnational; its analysis moved German cinema closer to Hollywood than many scholars were willing to admit. Throughout the foundational decades of German film studies, sound thus represented a bad object: an incursion of the popular over the boundaries of both the aesthetic and the national. It was only during the last years of the 1990s that German film scholars on both sides of the Atlantic discovered film sound as a viable and instructive object of scholarly analysis. As represented in this volume, the emerging field of German film sound studies today puts the former definition of German national cinema under severe pressure. It is part of a new literature that maintains that German cinema has always been a cinema of cultural transfers and transcultural fusions, of border crossings and transgressive identifications—a cinema of sights *and* sounds in which the local and the global, the experimental and the popular, stand side by side.

Much more willing to recognize the creative possibilities of film sound than many of his contemporary colleagues, film theorist Béla Balázs underscored in 1930 the unique potential of sound to restructure the film viewer's spatial experience. Sound itself, he argued (long prior, of course, to the arrival of stereophonic and Dolby Surround Sound systems), cannot build space. Yet in combination with the visual, it is able to articulate spatial depth and texture in ways unsurpassed by any other medium of representation. According to Balázs, nowhere does the power of sound to model spatial experience become clearer than in cinema's staging of silence: "Silence is when I am listening far. And as far as I am listening the space belongs to and becomes my space. Noise surrounds us with narrow walls of sound; it confines us to a cell of noise, similar to a prison cell. The life afar is drowned, and we merely see it, as if looking through a window."[20] Following Balázs's argument, cinematic silence allows us to experience the world—in Michel de Certeau's terms—as *"a practiced place,"*[21] as a room we perceive as meaningful and structured because we have managed to inhabit and appropriate it according to our needs and desires. Noise, on the other hand, embodies spatial heteronomy. It does not allow us to build a room of our own. It regulates agency, blocks creative forms of occupation, and controls the body's movements and sense perceptions.

Whether or not we agree with his prioritization of silence over noise, Balázs's linkage of sound and space helps to explicate one of the central ambitions of this volume, namely, to remap the dimensions of modern experience and reconsider the political meanings of modern German culture. Modernity has often been understood in merely temporal terms, as that which breaks with the authority of sanctified traditions and instead privileges novelty and transitoriness. Just as importantly, however, modernity also deals with the reorganization of spatial experience. The modern age inaugurates an unprecedented separation of time and space from the premodern rule of static place.[22] Under the sign of industrial culture, the premodern identity of the spatial and the temporal became fluid; the former solidity of both space and time melted into the air. In Anthony Giddens's words, the modern "severance of time from space ... provides the very basis for their recombination in ways that coordinate social activities without necessary reference to the particularities of place."[23] Modern institutions of communication, transportation, and information emancipated subjects and societies from the preeminence of circumscribed places and local times. They allowed people to live in often highly mediated elsewheres and elsewhens. In fact, what made modern societies essentially modern was their power to connect and transform dissimilar spaces and times, to enable shifting spatial arrangements, and hence simultaneously to shrink and expand the horizon of individual experience.

This volume proposes that sound was deeply mixed up in the modern dialectics of space and time, of here and there, of now and then. As we understand it, sound has both a temporal and spatial dimension. On the one hand, the sonic must be theorized as a medium shaping or incorporating time. A musical melody, a spoken sentence, the rattle of a machine—they all unfold along a temporal axis and literally need time in order to come into being. Moreover, sound can work as a form of memory as much as it provides a source of anticipation, enabling us to recall forgotten pasts or envision utopian futures. Equally important, however, the acoustical—as Balázs argued more than seventy years ago—may also be seen and experienced as inherently spatial. It plays a fundamental role in how individual or collective agents traverse their social geographies and inhabit the places provided for them. Whether disseminated in the cinema, the concert hall, the urban street, or the seminar room, sound marks territories. At once symbolic and sentient, sound structures spaces in which we construct meanings, take on or refute prefabricated identities, and stake out a place of our own amid the topographies of the present.

Speaking schematically, premodern societies experienced sound as being organically tied to a particular location and a specific time. It was only under the pressures of modernity—the intertwined emergence of capitalism, industrialism, urbanism, bureaucratic centralization, and the territorial nation-state—that the two dimensions of sound separated from the former preeminence of place. Modern sound traveled ever more freely through space and time. It no longer followed the dictates of linear chronology or simple geometry, but instead allowed embodied subjects to inhabit highly incongruent realities at once. However, it would be wrong to think of this process of unfixing merely in terms of a loss. Once severed from the burden of the here and now, sound became recognized as something whose meanings and pleasures were not simply given but rather constituted through human action and contested through intersubjective exchange. It was the very separation of sound from the premodern identity of place that provided—to modify Giddens's insight—the basis for the ability to recombine sounds and sights actively and, in so doing, to shape new, post-traditional architectures of community.

It is this view of modern sound as a makable and malleable space of human interaction that demonstrates most clearly the extent to which this volume participates in the academic project of cultural studies. In its various inflections, cultural studies—in our understanding—explores how people use symbolic materials in order to mark history and establish the possibilities for agency. What unifies the various branches of cultural studies is the interest in demonstrating that nothing concerning the creation of meanings, pleasures, identities, and forms of agency is natural. Cultural studies dismisses the concept of a single, unified, and text-produced consumer; rather, the goal is to investigate how diverse constituencies, at the intersections of the private and the public, creatively form and transform cultural materials. Rather than extracting stable meanings from the past, cultural studies highlights the fluid and contextual character of categories such as meaning, identity, perception, and pleasure. It destabilizes the seemingly natural by reconstructing how acts of articulation and negotiation produced historical experience—even when people did not act under conditions of their own making.

As discussed in the following essays, modern sound is precisely this: a transitory space of articulation and negotiation. Once sound lost its tie to the premodern rule of place, it inhabited or even opened a variety of public spheres in which principles of nature or tradition per se no longer seemed to provide cultural legitimation. And yet historical irony has it that even the modern understanding of sound as articulated was rarely seen as something given. Modernity emancipated sound from place, but it also produced many forces that hoped to reconnect the sonic to particular times and locations. The most potent attempt to reterritorialize sound was nothing other than the nineteenth-century idea of the nation.

IV

Over the last four decades, a vast number of theoretical texts and analytical studies have emphasized the constructed and orchestrated character of categories such as nationality and nationalism. In the wake of this recent literature, we have learned to recognize the modern nation as a historical and social imaginary; as a creative process of articulation and intervention; and as a space in which ideology, fantasy, and memory produce politically effective notions of community. Unlike late eighteenth- and nineteenth-century formulations, the template of the nation is no longer seen in terms of timeless values and transcendental meanings, of organic coherence and essential belonging. Nations, we have come to understand, are neither something that is simply out there, nor something to which we could ever have unmediated access. The national might continue to present itself as a primordial form of social bonding. It might claim to be a primary structure of shared identifications prevailing over all other markers of identity such as class, religion, gender, or sexual orientation. But there is little academic controversy today about the fact that nationality is a distinctly modern and hence historically contingent category. National identities require ongoing and mass-mediated processes of sustenance and reproduction. They provide symbolic orders in which people construct and contest collective meanings, norms, traditions, and utopias. While many post–Cold War nationalisms once again sanctified nationality as absolute, stable, nondiscursive, and homogeneous, the dominant tenor of recent scholarship has been to explore national identity as a relational category inevitably linked to the vicissitudes of modern representation. Like modern culture itself, the national is understood to be necessarily plural and differential. It is seen as a sign of difference whose meaning is multiple and diversified, fluid and contextual.

The category of modern nationality emerged as part of the formation of territorialized political cultures in the aftermath of the French Revolution. In its projective nineteenth-century sense, the idea of national integration "imagined a desirable future of harmonious living and collective self-determination within the sovereign space of a well-integrated and soli-daristic social and political order."[24] In some general sense, the national served as a panacea for the modern world's drive toward formal rational-ization and disenchantment. As imagined in the course of the nineteenth century, nationality seemed to offer a viable space to transfer religious sig-nifiers of love, fear, sacrifice, and the sacred to an increasingly secularized world. National communities represented themselves as "chosen ones," as civil religions, even if this implied intermingling conflicting vocabularies of theological universalism and ethnic particularism.[25] More concretely, however, nineteenth-century visions of nationality were meant to counter-balance the multiplicity of semiautonomous and often bureaucratically organized centers of domination in modern industrial society. Much more than a mere political doctrine or—in Marxist terms—an expression of false consciousness, the idea of the nation helped legitimate the modern state's move toward political centralization and economic intervention. It pro-vided a means with which to control and contain the emergence of various competing institutions of power in modernity. Post-1800 narratives of national identity therefore aspired to (re)center the state by bonding diverse publics to exclusive notions of territorial identity, popular sovereignty, or constitutional rule. They desired to reduce internal complexity and conflict by creating stricter boundaries between imaginary spheres of sameness and difference.

The ideas of nationality and nationalism, in their nineteenth-century conceptions, described a general condition and overarching project of the modern body politic. They might have served various political agendas, but they cannot be separated from the grounds on which their meanings were developed in the first place: the terrains of culture. Material pres-sures and cultural factors were of equal importance in the formation of the modern sense of nationality; both were crucial and in fact often "appeared in indistinguishable ways."[26] To explore the emergence of modern nation-ality therefore always also means to explore how cultural resources have elaborated fictions of common destiny or have sought to recast history as nature. Because, as Etienne Balibar has argued, no modern state or nation ever really possessed a particular ethnic basis, the creation of a fictive sense of ethnic belonging and national specificity became one of the pri-mary functions of cultural materials. Cultural expressions staked out the territories in which the political institutions of the modern nation-state could be inscribed. Language standardization and popular education were important component in this process. They served the purpose of homogenizing regional dialects, canonizing a corpus of written texts, and engineering a normative sense of the "mother tongue." They created the tessitura of the spoken word and the texture of poetic expressions as objects of self-identification, as seemingly natural wells of national commonality. Inculcated through school curricula as much as the literary public sphere, the love of the language assimilated differences in class and region, aligned diverse linguistic practices, and produced ethnic particularity as the basis of national integration.

The adoration of linguistic properties has no doubt played one of the most important roles in the cultural production of modern German identity since 1800. Romantic philosophers such as Johann Gottfried Herder and Johann Gottlieb Fichte embraced the German language as the nation's most palpable common ground. They hailed its inner structure not simply as a catalyst to but as an essential predicate of what it meant to be German. Subsequently, this equation of language and nationhood became a steadfast trope in discourses on German nationality. It informed Jakob and Wilhelm Grimm's monumental conception of the *Deutsches Wörterbuch*—the first volume was published in 1852—as much as Wim Wenders's 1991 gloomy declaration that, after Hitler and in the face of Hollywood dominance, "The German language is everything that our country no longer is, what it is not yet, and what it may never be."[27] And yet linguistic properties by themselves were never quite sufficient to warrant the national imaginary, to territorialize modern political culture, and to secure stable frontiers between self and other. Nineteenth-century language experts designed the German mother tongue primarily on the paragon of the written word. Often divided about how to reconcile the abundance of regional dialects with the idea of the linguistic nation,[28] they elaborated a purified idiom that sought to discipline difference but could never fully subdue the vernacular sounds of local linguistic practices. Likewise, what made—and makes—language into an unreliable engine of national identification is the fact that nothing can really block its ability to transgress geographical boundaries and bridge alterity in the medium of mutual translation and appropriation. To tie language down to the territory of a particular people means to block the quintessential telos of speech, namely, its inherent capacity to connect nonidentical particulars and liquefy borders between self and other. As they converted the mother tongue into an icon of national autochthony, nineteenth-century ideologues stripped language of its communicative infrastructure; they ignored the fact that language cannot function without its power to enable cultural transfer and slippage.

Linguistic ethnicity, in its nineteenth-century invention, remained haunted by a constant return of the repressed. It was unable to contain the persistence of class-specific idioms or the differential sounds of regional accents. Dominant ideology may have suggested that the language community had always existed, but due to the principal openness and provisionalness of linguistic expressions, the language engineers of the nineteenth century did not succeed in erasing all traces of inner divisions and particularities, let alone define a common destiny for all future generations. Language worked both ways: as a source of territorialization as much as deterritorialization. For language—written or spoken—to produce a sense of homogeneous ethnicity and nationality, an additional measure of exclusion was required, and as Balibar has argued, this additional measure was found in the principle of race. Race appeared more powerful than language as a means to naturalize internal differences and generate a harmoniously integrated body politic. Compared to language, the category of race was seen as a more radical equalizer, a stable and predictable denominator uniting individuals across divisions of class, religion, gender, and age into the national community. Race needed language in order for it to be constructed and proliferated, but at the same time it enclosed and arrested what language had left precariously open. One could thus not do without the other: the production of modern ethnicity and nationality involved "the verbalization of race" as much as the "racialization of language."[29]

One of the tasks of this collection is to show that in the developing symbolism of modern German nationality, sound and its mass-cultural dissemination played a role similar to that of language. It has become commonplace among scholars of modern German culture to point out that German composers and intellectuals since the late 1700s conceived of musical dispositions as direct conduits to national identity, to the deepest recesses of the German soul. And yet as a number of essays in this volume suggest, the relation of music to the nation often turned out to be at least as slippery and ambiguous as the construction of linguistic ethnicity. Like perhaps no other medium of artistic expression, music—whether popular, classical, or avant-garde—has always traveled well within and across geographical boundaries. Musical sounds might have elicited a high degree of affective identification and sensual pleasure, but they also have proven to be a highly productive catalyst of cross-cultural transfer and transnational deterritorialization. Bach's work relied on French and Italian models; the Austrians Haydn and Mozart were heavily influenced by Italian music of the time; Wagner celebrated his greatest successes in Paris; German-Jewish composers in exile defined the shapes of Hollywood film music in the course of the 1930s; German students embraced the Rolling Stones in the 1960s in order to protest the lingering shadows of the Nazi past; American hip-hop became an important idiom of articulation in the early 1990s for Turkish minorities in Germany; and Detroit techno, infused with German lyrics, made red-haired Berliners run, not just across their own cityscape, but through movie theaters world wide. Rather than providing some kind of explanation, the oft-mentioned link between German identity and the sound of music raises more questions than it can answer, for musical sounds have always had the power to transgress rigid boundaries and connect different cultures, to absorb the foreign and engage in unpredictable acts of appropriation. Hence, even a nationalist such as Richard Wagner was hesitant to define exactly what makes German music German. Puzzled by the international character of German musical traditions, Wagner ended up explaining the Germanness of German music by pointing at the ability of German musicians to rework foreign sources and unlock the true meaning of other aesthetic traditions.[30] Sound, for Wagner, had the ambiguous power to carry us beyond or inside ourselves. At its worst, music could decenter identity, dissolve territories, and stress the provisional and negotiated character of modern life; at its best, it could recover identity as something fixed and absolute and reterritorialize the body in the ethnicized spaces of the nation.

Exploring the echoes of Wagner's dilemma in modern German culture, *Sound Matters* adds to recent scholarship about the role of music and musicology in the construction of German identity since the late eighteenth century.[31] In its modern and often technologically mediated form, sound—this anthology suggests—provided meanings and pleasures that either legitimated the modern drive toward political centralization or articulated difference and dissidence. It amplified fantasies of national fixity and hierarchical segregation as much as it bridged cultural boundaries and initiated processes of cultural adaptation, translation, slippage, and hybridization. But to speak of sound as merely a tributary to the formulation of modern German identity ignores the complexity of modern representation and experience. In contrast to earlier examinations, the contributions to *Sound Matters* shed light on what we understand as the modern dialectics of sound and nation. According to the essays of this anthology, sound was deeply implicated in the dramatic expansion of modern industrial culture. It by no means evaded the ways in which modern technology, urbanization, and media culture changed former categories of perception, experience, and creativity. In many instances, sound may have bonded the individual to competing notions of the nation. But the developing idea of the modern nation in turn often helped to silence the overwhelming noises of modern life, to discipline sonic distractions, and to restore what premodern societies had considered as the unity of the visual and the acoustic. The modern discourse of nationality, then, was one moment within the larger reorganization of attentiveness and perception in industrial society. It cannot be separated from certain experiences of loss and perceptual rupture associated with the rise of modern industrial culture. Sound mattered to the formation of modern German nationality, but ongoing debates about the contours of national identity also redefined the matter of sound itself. In many cases, the idea of the nation served the attempt to contain the distracting presence of sounds in the modern lifeworld, to gloss over experiential discontinuities, and to synchronize sights and sounds into mesmerizing spectacles of consumption and imagined harmony. In other instances, however, the quest for nationality also encouraged people to recognize experiences of lack,

disjuncture, and nonidentity as sources of meaning and creativity; dissonance and discontinuity were endorsed as integral elements of modern
subjectivity and community.

V

Part 1 of this volume, "Sound Nation?" explores the symbiotic relationship
between sound and nationhood, and the role each plays in constructing the
other. Nicholas Vazsonyi's essay, "Hegemony through Harmony: German
Identity, Music, and Enlightenment around 1800," explores the Enlightenment legacy of German nationalism by revisiting Mozart's *The Magic
Flute* (1791) and Beethoven's Ninth Symphony (1824). Vazsonyi performs
a double-edged critique which challenges, on the one hand, the theory
that music in Germany became important only after German Romanticism and, on the other, the assumption that German nationalism developed only after 1806. Historically tracing the connection between culture
and national identity to Schiller's 1801 poem fragment, "German Greatness," in which Schiller proposes that the German language produces a
world of enlightened citizens who overcome conflict and national difference, Vazsonyi shows how both *The Magic Flute* and the Ninth Symphony
parallel Schiller's formulas in their use of musical structures. Vazsonyi
demonstrates that the success of the Enlightenment project in producing
universal harmony also has a negative outcome, for it cannot exist without separating the world into friend and foe. As Sarastro asserts at the
conclusion of *The Magic Flute*, whoever cannot rejoice at his teaching
"does not deserve to be a human being." Similarly, Beethoven's symphony engages in the formal rationality of the tonal system in order to
unify minds and mollify unruly thoughts and emotions.

Carl Niekerk's essay, "Mahler contra Wagner: The Third Symphony and
the Political Legacy of Romanticism," discusses the subtle ways in which
the production and reception of musical harmony or disharmony inflected
discourses of nationalism in the nineteenth century. Niekerk calls for a
reconsideration of the work of Gustav Mahler, who, though popular at the
time and as frequently performed as Wagner, has been largely neglected by
contemporary scholars who favor Wagner's work over that of other composers. This elision, Niekerk provocatively argues, is due not only to the fact
that Mahler (unlike Wagner) did not produce a large body of writing for
scholars to access, but also to the habit of German cultural studies to reproduce hierarchies that reflect the cultural interests of the German middle
class in the late nineteenth and early twentieth centuries, interests that
include Wagner but decidedly not Mahler. Niekerk thus examines Mahler's
Third Symphony, which, under the influence of Nietzsche, the composer
initially wanted to call "The Gay Science," and demonstrates that whereas
Wagner dismissed "chaotic formalism" and "confusion of styles," Mahler

embraced the fragmentary in a conscious effort to find a musical language that would stress the indisputable fissures of the modern experience.

The third contribution to this section takes us into the twentieth century, to a time when fissures, fragments, and disharmony were abandoned altogether in favor of a totalization of the acoustic sphere. Frank Trommler's essay, "Conducting Music, Conducting War: Nazi Germany as an Acoustic Experience," examines the importance for the Nazis of encoding a political agenda through music. Reading the enormous role that the Nazis attributed to music through Thomas Mann's *Doctor Faustus,* Trommler goes on to outline the state-sponsored administrative institutions that were designed to align German music and musicians with the Third Reich's national mission. He argues against dominant theories in German cultural studies that have privileged the visual sphere over the acoustic, proposing instead that participation in musical activities—singing in the Hitler Youth, taking part in music education in schools, performing in parades, attending innumerable musical events, and, above all, listening to the radio—led to a dominance of acoustics in the construction of a national soundscape. Trommler also stresses the extent to which the National Socialists were merely following a strong tradition, established in the nineteenth century, that saw German music as the expression of national identity.

Part 2, "Dissonant Visions," returns to the idea of disharmony, especially as it is accentuated and exaggerated in the complex relationship between sound and visual images. All three chapters in this section focus on film sound and deal with conscious alterations and manipulations of the audial track in order to produce alternative narratives. Nora Alter's essay, "The Politics and Sounds of Everyday Life in *Kuhle Wampe*," examines Brecht and Dudow's collaborative 1932 film, paying special attention to the relationship between fiction and nonfiction and its correlative on the soundtrack. Examining both the early reception of *Kuhle Wampe* as well as Brecht's own theory of film, Alter challenges dominant Brechtian film theory and criticism as it was formulated in the late 1960s and 1970s in the film journal *Screen.* Whereas previous film scholars and critics turned to Brecht's theory of theater—especially his distanciation effect and the foregrounding of the cinematic apparatus—when interpreting *Kuhle Wampe,* Alter grounds her analysis in Brecht's theory of sound in film. She concludes that while distanciation certainly played a significant role in this film, identification—achieved on both the audial and visual tracks—was equally important. The distanciating contrapuntal compositions of Eisler were repeatedly contradicted by the inclusion of popular, easily recognizable tunes that set the audience in the cinema at ease.

Twenty-five years later, in the shadow of Hollywood and conventional restrictions on visual experimentation, sound offered West German filmmakers a realm for cinematic play. Sound could be manipulated in unconventional ways without fully alienating spectators long accustomed to focusing in the first instance on visual imagery. Hester Baer's essay, "Sound

Money: Aural Strategies in Rolf Thiele's *The Girl Rosemarie*," examines the controversial German hit film of 1958. The use of "cabaret" music in this film resuscitates a genre associated with Weimar cinema and theater and is consonant with the film's revision of the motifs of the modern metropolis, the street, and the body of the female prostitute. Like the Weimar "street films," *The Girl Rosemarie* thematizes anxieties about urban decadence, class mobility, sexuality, and women's social roles—anxieties that were as pervasive in the postwar period as they had been in the 1920s. In creating a cinema tailored to the demands of the domestic market, Thiele used the appeal of popular music as the sugarcoating on the bitter pill that is the sordid tale of the rags-to-riches transformation of the Federal Republic in the late 1950s. However, at the same time that the film's popular core attracted audiences and facilitated a space of aural reception that promoted close listening, Thiele included significant passages replete with a sonic distortion that indicated the deep fissures and cracks lying beneath the veneer of the "Economic Miracle."

In a similar fashion, Fassbinder employed sound, and the human voice in particular, as a decentering device. In her essay, "The Castrato's Voices: Word and Flesh in Fassbinder's *In a Year of Thirteen Moons*," Brigitte Peucker reads the 1978 film's "voices," or codes, through several specific instances of the human voice and delineates the material and symbolic aspects of exchange in the film through the multiple relations it establishes between sound and image, word and flesh, self and other. The film's strategy, she argues, is to collapse the binary oppositions that structure these relations, transforming the "either/or" of exclusion into a "both/and" of mutuality or simultaneity. According to Peucker, the erosion of the distinction between self and other that is registered acoustically in Fassbinder's film takes on the ideological task of imaging German-Jewish relations. In particular, Peucker focuses on the slaughterhouse scene in the film, linking it audially to the famous abattoir sequence in Fritz Hippler's Nazi propaganda film, *The Eternal Jew* (1941). Her analysis of the slaughterhouse sequence suggests that for Fassbinder there existed a cultural continuity between idealism and Nazism. Peucker then demonstrates that whereas Hippler's film exemplifies the Nazi strategy of utilizing a paternal voice in order to reinforce purity and organic wholeness, Fassbinder resorts to a multiplicity of voices and soundtracks that are specifically not harnessed to visual images or bodies. The result is a film that severs itself both stylistically and thematically from fascist aesthetics.

Part 3, "Sounds of Silence," concentrates on the absence of sound as a signifying practice whereby—à la John Cage—it is silence that speaks to us. Lutz Koepnick opens this section with a meditation on Walter Benjamin's seminal 1936 essay, "The Work of Art in the Age of Mechanical Reproduction." Koepnick discovers a striking aporia in Benjamin's text, namely, that although written almost a decade after the introduction of sound film, this essay still approached film as a silent—and therefore primarily *visual*—art form. The theoretical and practical implications of Benjamin's neglect of sound in film are vast. Koepnick contrasts this silence on sound to Benjamin's earlier writings in which his encounters with sound systems such as telephones, radios, and the general cacophony of the city, are described, indicating that he was very aware of the potential of sound as an important signifying system. Koepnick then demonstrates that Benjamin's shunning of sound in film was a strategy that at once allowed him to conceal critical disjunctions between his political and aesthetic agendas and to uphold his thesis of the interdependence of artistic innovation and political reform. By remaining in the realm of silence, film would not sever its ties to fine art, nor would it become a popular form of mass entertainment, replete with music, noise, dialogue, and other acoustic interferences. The enormous power and potential of sound film to unify a public was already firmly in place at the time Benjamin was writing his essay, leading Koepnick to conclude that by ignoring this metamorphosis of film into a propaganda machine, Benjamin sought to redeem film as a potentially politically progressive artistic medium.

Elizabeth Hamilton picks up where Benjamin leaves off. Her essay, "Deafening Sound and Troubling Silence in Volker Schlöndorff's *Die Blechtrommel*, is concerned with the uses and abuses of sound, specifically in the political appropriation of the voice in the service of National Socialism and again in the postwar era's struggle to "come to terms with the past." Hamilton demonstrates that notions of the voice and hearing, informed by social and linguistic Darwinism during the Nazi years, continued to thrive in the postwar years. She deftly shows how Schlöndorff utilized sound in *Die Blechtrommel* (The Tin Drum, 1979) in order to convey the historical trajectory and legacy of National Socialism. By exploiting the tension between the sonic and the visual, through the juxtaposition of extremely loud sequences with silence, Hamilton argues, Schlöndorff creates out of silence a critical voice of resistance, opposition, and healing. In addition, Hamilton reveals how Schlöndorff recuperates a language of signs and visual symbols in order to confront postwar cultural silence; his film incorporates techniques reminiscent of silent film to recall the past and enable mourning.

The third contribution to this section moves from the postwar era to the present Germany and its new capital, Berlin. Berlin's visage has been a relatively silent one, all the more striking given the cacophonous sounds of construction that permeate the entire city. Christopher Jones's essay on the crime fiction of contemporary writer Pieke Biermann, "Silence Is Golden? The Short Fiction of Pieke Biermann," demonstrates how sound plays a vital role both in the crimes depicted and in the tapestry of contemporary Berlin. Jones traces the link between Biermann's fiction and John Cage's practice of using noise as a concrete building block of music. Heavily influenced by Cage, Biermann assigns a vital role to sound in her novels, especially the manner in which sound evokes contemporary Berlin life. Jones systematically unpacks Biermann's attempt to translate and transpose

Cage's composition theories into a written, narrative piece of fiction. Biermann's decision to investigate the two extremes of noise pollution—represented by the desire to employ it on one hand as a concrete medium for capturing one particular essence of the city in an art form, and on the other as a source of sheer stress and irritation that can literally drive someone mad—requires that the stories be treated as antithetical companion pieces with a message about noise that can be synthesized only from a reading of both texts. Biermann thus questions Cage's rarified aestheticism and gives it a more worldly application.

Part 4 of this volume, "Translating Sound," features essays that problematize sound as a contained entity enclosed by linguistic and national borders. All of the contributions expand the field, giving free rein to the invasive, uncontainable, and almost fluid-like characteristics of acoustics. This section also addresses the issue of what happens to sound texts when they are produced and received in cultural and national environments that differ from their place of origin. Tom Cohen's "The Big Wagner Broadcast: Transmission, Dissemination, Translation," raises important questions about what it meant to program and broadcast Wagner in the United States on the eve of World War II. Using a *Walküre* sequence from the popular 1938 movie *The Big Broadcast of 1938* as a springboard, Cohen outlines the problematic involved not only in the geographical displacement of Wagner's music from Bayreuth to New York, but also in the translation to radio and filmic broadcasts of a music designed for live transmission. His essay examines the clash between two rival communication networks: the American motion picture industry (including the media for unlimited wireless transmission and communication) and Wagner's more archaic orchestrations. The first mode of communication sought to market culture as a cosmopolitan phenomenon free from those racial associations and national interests that the second, Wagner's productions, considered essential for an authentic art of the people. Cohen concludes that certain "defense mechanisms" spring not from the psychological struggles of individual human consciousness but from the interaction between different communication networks.

The second contribution to this section, Russell Berman's "Sounds Familiar? Nina Simone's Performances of Brecht/Weill Songs," examines how the American performer transforms and translates into the African-American tradition the songs of Brecht and Weill. Berman, while maintaining Brecht's theory of nonidentification, proposes that any oral performance necessarily moves from the unrealized potential of the written text to a very specific rendition by an individual performer in a particular context. Simone's performance is therefore interpreted by Berman as a project of translation: moving the reception of the text from the silence of the page to a new and concrete historical and cultural venue (in this instance the United States during the civil rights movement). Thus, Berman examines how a Brecht text travels from German verse to German voice, and from a

German performance to an African-American one. Berman's essay not only demonstrates the importance of cross-cultural exchange, but also seeks to problematize the way in which traditional German studies have to date been deaf to the African-American reception of German culture. Simone's reworkings of two classic texts of German modernism—"Seeräuber-Jenny" (Pirate Jenny) and "Moon of Alabama"—represent a significant cultural transfer between the left-wing modernism of Weimar Germany and the culture of American protest music. Berman ends his essay recalling that Simone's performances are all the more important because they signify a moment when avant-garde aspiration and popular idiom briefly appear to coincide.

In his essay, "Roll Over Beethoven! Chuck Berry! Mick Jagger! 1960s Rock, the Myth of Progress, and the Burden of National Identity in West Germany," Richard Langston deconstructs two dominant modes of popular music in West Germany in the 1960s: rock-and-roll, imported from the United States and Britain, and *Schlager*, the home-grown domestic variant. This distinction between "them" and "us" produced a community that initially participated in rock-and-roll as an acoustical border-crossing beyond the reaches of official German culture. Though some radical intellectuals were immediately suspicious of the revolutionary potential of rock-and-roll, others argued that politically engaged rock redeemed itself because it reflected the realities of the antiauthoritarian struggle. Whereas rock was progressive, pop music *(Schlager)* and its commodified cultures were seen as delivering transitory, private pleasures that failed to signify anything beyond the immediate instant of gratification. However, Langston argues that this utopian potential was short-lived; stripped of its revolutionary politics in the following decade, rock soon joined pop music as a clichéd form of spectacular entertainment. Langston specifically hones in on how Rolf Dieter Brinkmann used rock to fashion and refashion his notion of a dissident identity politics before and after the failure of the student movement. Langston concludes that although its initial energy may have dissipated, rock never surrendered its claims to reflect or invigorate the authenticity of the everyday, a stance that would be challenged with the advent of other musical imports into Germany such as punk, the new wave, hip-hop, and techno.

In the final essay of this section, "The Music That Lola Ran To," Caryl Flinn focuses on Tom Tykwer's enormous hit *Lola rennt* to examine how techno music shapes and is shaped by the film's interwoven contradictions—freedom and containment; hipness and conservatism; spontaneity and calculation; the denial and assertion of Germanness. Through a detailed analysis of techno's origins and recent permutations, Flinn argues that the soundtrack of *Lola rennt* works to ensure that a number of traditional "contracts" are maintained, along with the film's thematic and diegetic obsession with contracts, deadlines, and faith. The postwar phenomenon of promoting films through a tie-in soundtrack, whose early manifestations Baer addressed in her essay, becomes paramount in the late

1990s. In addition to producing commercially lucrative products, film music defines, establishes, and sometimes transforms social, cultural, and geographical spaces. As Flinn demonstrates, techno has a strong relationship to place and location, despite its own complicated history and status as a hybrid product. Due to the fact that it is composed of sampling, modulating, remixing, and looping, it also poses a challenge to the models of authenticity and romantic expressivity established by rock-and-roll. Flinn constructs a parallel between the way in which Berlin functions as the city or locale for Lola and the manner in which techno is grounded to a region through local rave cultures and clubs, and shows that both film and music escape or evacuate geographical specificity. She concludes that like the film, which is at once German and non-German, techno operates as a form of Esperanto, poised for the global market just as surely as the character Lola is positioned to run out of her domestic environs at the beginning of each version of the story. Yet that very internationalism obliges a contemporary and hip musical genre to perform a traditional function—that of working as an "international language" not so far removed from the harmonizing strains of Mahler, Beethoven, and Wagner.

The final part of the anthology, "Memory, Music, and the Postmodern," comprises of two contributions that struggle specifically with the legacy of modernism. Continued from earlier in the volume is the importance of mixing genres and the blurring of national and cultural specificity. David Barnett's essay, ""Heiner Müller vertonen": Heiner Goebbels and the Music of Postmodern Memory," examines how the avant-garde composer Heiner Goebbels has engaged with the texts of Heiner Müller. Goebbels's experiments in sound form the basis for Barnett's exploration of how one might create space for Müller's textual landscapes in the realm of sound. Barnett contends that Goebbels continues the tradition of Brechtian composition, outlined in Alter's and Berman's essays, by working through strategies that open up the text to enable the listener to become an active participant in the creation of meaning. Goebbels looks abroad for sources for his musical scores and compositions, as well as for "found voices," in a methodology that may structurally bear some similarities to mixing and sampling found in contemporary rap, hip-hop, and techno music. According to Barnett, Goebbels thus realizes Müller's texts as landscapes occupied by the complex reworking of found voices and echoes of music. Landscapes of history, memory, and geography confront the listener with no detectable set of rules that dictate how they should be addressed or processed.

Finally, Larson Powell's essay, "The Technological Subject: Music, Media, and Memory in Stockhausen's *Hymnen*," takes as its point of departure the relative amnesia surrounding the figure of Karlheinz Stockhausen. In particular, Powell discusses the importance of the musical quotation of the "Horst-Wessel-Lied" in Stockhausen's highly influential *Hymnen* (1966 –67). *Hymnen*, Powell argues, is a musical anticipation of the New German Cinema's work of mourning, a reworking of the raw material of memory, even at it most corrupt, kitschy, and colonized. He shows how Stockhausen, like Goebbels, experiments with diverse musical traditions and seeks to bring his international materials into an internal relation with each other via the compositional technique of post-Webernist serialism. Powell concludes that Stockhausen's piece performs Adorno's hermeneutic aporia between abstract form and arbitrary quotation as it is technically mediated within the form of music.

Notes

1. Rick Altman, ed. *Sound Theory: Sound Practice* (New York: Routledge, 1992); Douglas Kahn and Gregory Whitehead, eds., *Wireless Imagination: Sound, Radio, and the Avant-Garde* (Cambridge, MA: MIT Press, 1992).
2. See, for example, Royal S. Brown, *Overtones and Undertones: Reading Film Music* (Berkeley: University of California Press, 1994); James Buhler et al., eds., *Music and Cinema* (Hanover: Wesleyan University Press, 2000); Michel Chion, *Audio-Vision: Sound on Screen* (New York: Columbia University Press, 1994) and *The Voice in Cinema* (New York: Columbia University Press, 1999); Scott Eyman, *The Speed of Sound: Hollywood and the Talkie Revolution: 1926–1930* (New York: Simon and Schuster, 1997); Caryl Flinn, *Strains of Utopia: Gender, Nostalgia, and Hollywood Film Music* (Princeton: Princeton University Press, 1992); Sarah Kozloff, *Overhearing Film Dialogue* (Berkeley: University of California Press, 2000); James P. Kraft, *Stage to Studio: Musicians and the Sound Revolution 1890–1950* (Baltimore: Johns Hopkins University Press, 1996); James Lastra, *Sound Technology and the American Cinema* (New York: Columbia University Press, 2000); Jonathan Romney and Adrian Wootton, eds., *Celluloid Jukebox: Popular Music and the Movies since the 50s* (London: British Film Institute, 1995); David Schwarz, *Listening Subjects: Music, Psychoanalysis, Culture* (Durham: Duke University Press, 1997); and Jeff Smith, *The Sounds of Commerce* (New York: Columbia University Press, 1998).
3. In opera studies, see, for example, Felicia Miller Frank, *The Mechanical Song: Women, Voice, and the Artificial in Nineteenth-Century French Narrative* (Stanford: Stanford University Press, 1995); Linda Hutcheon and Michael Hutcheon, *Bodily Charm: Living Opera* (Lincoln: University of Nebraska Press, 2000); David J. Levin, *Opera Through Other Eyes* (Stanford: Stanford University Press, 1994); and Herbert Lindenberger, *Opera in History: From Monteverdi to Cage* (Stanford: Stanford University Press, 1998). In contemporary music studies, see Georgina Born and David Hesmondhalgh, eds., *Western Music and Its Others: Difference, Representation, and Appropriation in Music* (Berkeley: University of California Press, 2000); Georgina Born, *IRCAM, BOULEZ and the Institutionalization of the Musical Avant-Garde* (Berkeley: University of California Press, 1995); E. Ann Kaplan, *Rocking Around the Clock: Music Television, Postmodernism, and Consumer Culture* (New York: Routledge, 1987). And in radio studies, see Daina Augaitis and Dan Lander, eds., *Radio Rethink: Art, Sound and Transmission* (Banff: Walter Phillips Gallery, 1994); and Neil Strauss, ed., *Radiotext(e)* (New York: Semiotext(e), 1993).
4. Kaplan, *Rocking Around the Clock.*
5. See Silvia Kolbowski, "an inadequate history of conceptual arts," *October* 92 (Spring 2000): 53–70.
6. Greil Marcus, *Lipstick Traces: A Secret History of the Twentieth Century* (Cambridge, MA: Harvard University Press, 1990); and Adrian Rifkin, *Street Noises: Parisian Pleasure 1900–40* (Manchester: Manchester University Press, 1993).

7. And here, radio may stand as an important and relevant exception, for it was developed during World War I, at least a decade before television.

8. Lance Sieveking, *The Stuff of Radio* (London: Cassel & Co., 1934), 15.

9. Even in the field of criticism there has been a recent abundance of volumes dedicated to the visual, starting with Hal Foster's collection *Vision and Visuality*, Martin Jay's *Downcast Eyes*, and any number of visual studies readers. See, for example, Teresa Brennan and Martin Jay, eds., *Vision in Context: Historical and Contemporary Perspectives on Sight* (New York: Routledge, 1996); Hal Foster, ed., *Vision and Visuality* (Seattle: Bay Press, 1988); Martin Jay, *Downcast Eyes: The Denigration of Vision in Twentieth-Century French Thought* (Berkeley: University of California Press, 1993); Chris Jenks, ed., *Visual Culture* (New York: Routledge, 1995); and Lucien Taylor, ed., *Visualizing Theory: Selected Essays From V.A.R. 1990–1994* (New York: Routledge, 1994).

10. And it is in this last meaning, i.e., the degree of loudness and noise, that the word shows how issues of class, gender, and race become encoded in social constructions of sound. For example to be "loud" is often a signifier of being lower class and of hysterical women. Another illustration may be with car stereo systems. The louder the system, the more "empowered" the person who produces it, because he/she fills space with his/her sound.

11. For recent work on this nexus, produced by Germanists in the United States, see, among many other, Lutz Köpnick, *Nothungs Modernität: Wagner's Ring und die Poesie der Macht im neunzehnten Jahrhundert* (Munich: Wilhelm Fink Verlag, 1994); David Levin, *Richard Wagner, Fritz Lang, and the Nibelungen: The Dramaturgy of Disavowal* (Princeton: Princeton University Press, 1998); and Marc A. Weiner, *Richard Wagner and the Anti-Semitic Imagination*, 2nd ed. (Lincoln: University of Nebraska Press, 1997).

12. Jacques Attali, *Noise: The Political Economy of Music*, trans. Brian Massumi (Minneapolis: University of Minnesota Press, 1985), 6.

13. Mel Gordon, "Songs from the Museum of the Future: Russian Sound Creation (1910–1930), in *Wireless Imagination*, ed. Kahn and Whitehead, 197.

14. Jürgen Habermas, "Modernity's Consciousness of Time and Its Need for Self-Reassurance," in *The Philosophical Discourse of Modernity*, trans. Frederick Lawrence (Cambridge, MA: MIT Press, 1987), 13.

15. Hans Christian Andersen, *Fairy Tales*, trans. Jean Hersholt (New York: The Heritage Press, 1942), 59.

16. Ibid., 72.

17. Jonathan Crary, *Suspension of Perception: Attention, Spectacle, and Modern Culture* (Cambridge, MA: MIT Press, 1999), 74.

18. Guy Debord, *Society of the Spectacle* (Detroit: Black and Red, 1983), 29.

19. Quoted in Felix Moeller, *Der Filmminister: Goebbels und der Film im Dritten Reich* (Berlin: Henschel, 1998), 60.

20. Béla Balázs, *Der Geist des Films* (Halle: Verlag Wilhelm Knapp, 1930), 155.

21. Michel de Certeau, *The Practice of Everyday Life*, trans. Steven Rendall (Berkeley: University of California Press, 1988), 117.

22. Roger Friedland and Deirdre Boden, "Introduction," in *NowHere: Space, Time and Modernity*, ed. Roger Friedland and Deirdre Boden (Berkeley: University of California Press, 1994), 3.

23. Anthony Giddens, *The Consequences of Modernity* (Stanford: Stanford University Press, 1990), 18.

24. Geoff Eley and Ronal Grigor Suny, "Introduction," in *Becoming National: A Reader*, ed. Geoff Eley and Ronal Grigor Suny (New York: Oxford University Press, 1996), 19.

25. Etienne Balibar, "The Nation Form: History and Ideology," *Becoming National*, ed. Eley and Suny, 140.

26. Craig Calhoun, *Nationalism* (Minneapolis: University of Minnesota Press, 1997), 10.

27. Wim Wenders, "Talking about Germany," *The Cinema of Wim Wenders: Image, Narrative, and the Postmodern Condition*, ed. Roger F. Cook and Gerd Gemünden (Detroit: Wayne State University Press, 1996), 59.

28. Jürgen Habermas, "Was ist ein Volk? Zum politischen Selbstverständnis der Geistes-wissenschaften im Vormärz," *Die postnationale Konstellation: Politische Essays* (Frankfurt am Main: Suhrkamp, 1998), 13–46.
29. Balibar, "The Nation Form," 147.
30. Richard Wagner, "What Is German?," in *Prose Works*, trans. William Ashton Ellis (New York: Broude Brothers, 1895) 4:160.
31. See, for instance, Celia Applegate, "How German Is It? Nationalism and the Idea of Serious Music in the Early Nineteenth Century," *19th-Century Music* 21 (1998): 274–96; David B. Dennis, *Beethoven in German Politics, 1870–1989* (New Haven: Yale University Press, 1996); Mary Sue Morrow, *German Music Criticism in the Late Eighteenth Century: Aesthetic Issues in Instrumental Music* (Cambridge: Cambridge University Press, 1997); and Pamela Potter, *Most German of the Arts: Musicology and Society from the Weimar Republic to the End of Hitler's Reich* (New Haven: Yale University Press, 1998).

Part I

SOUND NATION?

Chapter 1

HEGEMONY THROUGH HARMONY
German Identity, Music, and Enlightenment around 1800

Nicholas Vazsonyi

I'd like to teach the world to sing (in perfect harmony) …

— Coca Cola™ (1971)

I

In a speech entitled "Germany and the Germans," delivered in May 1945, Thomas Mann added a musical component to Helmut Plessner's assessment of Germany as a "delayed nation" *(verspätete Nation)*.[1] Linking German national identity and its fateful impact on twentieth-century history directly to the prominence of certain musical forms in modern Germany, Mann argued that the Germans "are late like music.… They are primarily musicians of the vertical, not the horizontal, greater masters of harmony … than melody, instrumentalists more than admirers of the human voice."[2] Theodor W. Adorno made this connection between Germany and music even more ominous when he wrote in 1942: "Hitler and the Ninth Symphony: Be encircled, all ye millions," a macabre twist on Schiller's "Seid umschlungen, Millionen" (Be embraced, all ye millions) and its use in the last movement of Beethoven's last symphony.[3]

What both Mann and Adorno, in their critique of German culture and nationalism, took for granted—the nexus of music and German identity—has come under rigorous scrutiny in recent scholarship. Landmark studies by Celia Applegate, Pamela Potter, and Mary Sue Morrow[4] have explored how German musicians, critics, and academics, prior to and during the Nazi period, sensed the sound of music to be the German nation's most common ground. Just as importantly, however, these scholars have also encouraged us to make Mann's and Adorno's genealogies more complex by probing the specific historical contexts in which German music became tied to issues of national identity in the first place.

Conventional wisdom holds that it was not until the early nineteenth century that instrumental, so-called absolute music assumed the significance it would hold for the remainder of that century. Accordingly, it was not until after 1800 that German composers enjoyed the same status as poets, painters, and sculptors, and it was only in the wake of Romantic authors such as Wackenroder, Tieck, and E. T. A. Hoffmann that music was praised as the only art form capable of plumbing the depths of the soul, of giving shape to the metaphysical, and of affording a glimpse of the transcendent. By extension, and consistent with the program of Romanticism, such instrumental music became an acoustical icon of German national identity.

Morrow's recent work persuasively questions this kind of periodization. Her research suggests that the transformation of instrumental music's cultural signification had already commenced in the 1760s, when German music critics began to challenge the dominant denigration of instrumental music as a nonmimetic, and therefore inferior, art form. Morrow's study shows that around 1760 German critics began to extol instrumental music for its intellectual, "serious," and thus truly "German" properties. They now declared it to be a "manly" idiom, while they disparaged Italian and French vocal music as effeminate, overly simplistic, and often monotonous.[5] Rejecting former aesthetic paradigms, critics after 1760 increasingly rated composers for their ability to write "interesting" (that is, original and complex) music, wherein complexity was generated by elaborate counterpoint and effective modulations. Paradoxically, the most intellectually complex and hence nationally significant form was the fugue, even though it had originally been developed in Baroque Italy. Presenting both composers and listeners with the ultimate musical challenge and emotional reward, the fugue thus became the quintessential marker for the expression of Germanness in music well into the nineteenth century, even if by then it was nothing more than a stylistic anachronism.

While Romantics after 1800 expanded on the significance of instrumental music, by the late eighteenth century, a superior "German" musical style had already been discursively established, and its heroes—C. P. E. Bach, Haydn, and Mozart—suitably recognized and acclaimed. As Morrow demonstrates, absolute music was seen as a distinct form of conceptual and cultural representation well before the rise of German Romanticism. Beyond communicating individual feelings and modes, it served as a semiotic code signifying national specificity and particularity during the decades commonly labeled as the era of late Enlightenment. In predating the advent of "German" music, Morrow's work thus echoes important recent shifts in the study of German identity formation in general.

Like musicologists, historians have traditionally considered 1806—the year of the formal end of the Holy Roman Empire and Napoleon's occupation of German lands—as the trigger that launched the "nationalist" movement, which would lead to the unification of 1871 and, arguably, to Hitler. While nineteenth- and, by extension, twentieth-century "nationalism" has been seen as aggressive, violent, territorial, politically extreme, and irrational, eighteenth-century "patriotism" has been viewed as emancipatory, cosmopolitan, humanist-universal, and antifeudal—in a word, "enlightened."[6] The recent work of Wolfgang Hardtwig and Hans Peter Herrmann has called this differentiation into question. Both scholars argue that the discursive construction of national identity in modern Germany had already begun several decades before 1806, the 1760s once again playing a highly catalytic role.[7] They suggest that the emancipatory-democratic ideals of the eighteenth century cannot be entirely separated from the violent-destructive tendencies of the nineteenth century, that discourses on national identity were tainted from their very inception with images of violence, hegemony, and patriarchal projections of domination.[8]

To point out this difference between 1806 and 1760 is significant precisely because it calls into question seasoned juxtapositions of the Enlightenment and Romanticism. Unlike Thomas Nipperdey, who has argued that German nationalism was directed "against the universalism of the Enlightenment,"[9] recent scholarship no longer hesitates to implicate the influence of eighteenth-century German "patriotic" discourse on nineteenth-century constructions of German nationalism. Hence, certain continuities between the rationalism of the Enlightenment and the putative irrationality of German Romanticism are stressed.

This essay explores the enlightened legacy of German nationalism in further detail. By revisiting both Mozart's *Die Zauberflöte* (The Magic Flute, 1791) and Beethoven's Ninth Symphony (1824), I want to demonstrate the extent to which, around 1800, the German enlightenment project (or the idealistic German project for universal enlightenment) became synonymous with the building of a German nation and vice versa. Even though the rhetorical posture of the German enlightenment was the "harmonious" transformation of the world by the peaceful introduction of reason and aesthetic education, the music of both Mozart and Beethoven evidences a darker and—to quote Max Horkheimer and Adorno—"totalitarian"[10] undercurrent of this project.

Following Horkheimer and Adorno's lead, these pages explore what it really meant to "teach the world to sing in perfect harmony" around 1800. To be sure, unlike Adorno, I do not seek to indict Beethoven ex post facto in the genesis of National Socialism. Nor do I intend to formulate a new kind of *Sonderweg* thesis that would render German music of the post-1789 era as a unique site of fantasies of world domination. Instead, I will examine a few isolated moments from two well-known German musical works to see whether Adorno's suggestion of hegemony through harmony—"Be encircled, all ye millions"—can be sustained in a historical perspective. My intention here is not to question the aesthetic achievements of Mozart's or Beethoven's work, let alone—like Thomas Mann's Adrian Leverkühn—to "take back" Beethoven's last symphony.[11] Rather, the primary point of this essay is to explore the extent to which musical pleas for universal harmony and reason around 1800 contain disquieting claims that involve German cultural superiority, claims that involve projections of violent homogenization and domination.

II

In a poem fragment of 1801, subsequently entitled "Deutsche Größe" (German Greatness), Friedrich Schiller made just such an attempt to synthesize the universal aspirations of the Enlightenment with the national mission of German culture. Even though Schiller emphasized that the "Germans' greatness does not entail conquering with the sword,"[12] his text clearly articulates imperial zeal, indicating the extent to which nationalist vocabularies normally associated with German Romanticism were firmly established well before 1806. Applying the familiar notion of the German *Kulturnation*, Schiller locates Germany's greatness "in the culture and in the character of the nation, which is independent from its political fate."[13] German national identity, for Schiller, is inseparable from the act of spreading the blessings of German culture and enlightened reason to the world: "He [the German] is destined for the highest, and just as he finds himself in the middle of Europe, so is he also the core of humanity.… He has been chosen by the world spirit to work on the eternal edifice of the development of humanity."[14] According to Schiller, the German language is the primary tool to carry out this project. Like German music, the German language is seen as a universal cipher that simultaneously reflects and expresses the German national character: "Language is the mirror of a nation, and when we look into this mirror, we see a magnificent image of ourselves."[15] Schiller views the German language as second to none in offering a new lingua franca to the world, for it alone "expresses everything, the most profound and the most trivial, the soul at its most meaningful,… the naïve Greek and … the modern ideal."[16]

In becoming a universal medium of reason and self-enlightenment, Schiller's German language produces a world of enlightened citizens who overcome conflict and national difference. Unlike other national languages and cultures, it is the German language and *Kulturnation* that can and should serve as a universal platform of understanding and self-transformation. As Schiller unabashedly formulates it, "Our language will rule the world."[17] The remainder of this essay, will show how both Mozart's *The Magic Flute* and Beethoven's Ninth Symphony reflect Schiller's formulas by using compelling musical structures. Both works promote German harmony and enlightenment as blueprints for universal transformations. They model global solutions on national particularities, and in doing so they envision a "supra-national humanity,"[18] populated no doubt by *Weltbürger deutscher Prägung* (world citizens of a German stamp).

The interpretive challenges of Mozart's *Magic Flute* are well known. However, rather than discuss the entire work here, I examine only one episode, which illustrates the way in which Mozart's opera pursues (universal) hegemony through (German) harmony. Toward the conclusion of the act 1 finale, Papageno and Pamina, attempting to flee Sarastro's realm, are intercepted by Monostatos and his minions. Out of desperation, Papageno plays the magic glockenspiel given to him by the Queen of the Night. Upon hearing the sound of music, Monostatos and his slaves begin to dance and sing. Mesmerized, robbed of independent thought, they are rendered speechless, as evidenced by the repeated and meaningless chant

Example 1

"la-ra-la, la la, la-ra-la" (example 1). According to the stage directions, "As they sing, Monostatos and the slaves go marching off."[19] Despite its comic effect, the moment is not meant to be taken lightly because it is rare in opera that music per se becomes the subject of contemplation, and because Papageno's and Pamina's evaluation of the moment's significance espouses the "enlightenment" objectives discussed above: "If every brave man/ Could find such bells!/His enemies would then/Disappear with ease./ And he would then live without them/In the best of harmony."[20]

I contend that far from simply asserting the telos of global harmony, as Papageno and Pamina rhetorically claim, the scene instead depicts a battle of competing wills—true to Antonio Gramsci's insight that hegemony is never a given but rather a matter of articulation and contestation, an unstable force field in constant need of sustenance and reproduction.[21] Papageno responds to Monostatos's threat, "I will teach you manners," with "let the bells sing, so their ears may ring!" Papageno prevails by invoking music and reducing Monostatos to a state of torpor that renders him unable to control his own mind or body.

This verbal contest of wills is also depicted within the musical structure. The battleground is G major, previously established as both Papageno's and Monostatos's tonality. In many respects, these two characters represent the musical inverse of each other. Papageno's signature—introduced in his opening aria—is a descending third within the tonic triad from mediant to tonic (b to g), and a memorable octave leap from d to d^1 (example 2). The first encounter with Monostatos, during his brief duet with Pamina, features a rising third from tonic to mediant (g^1 to b^1) and a falling octave from d^2 to d^1 (example 3). These characteristics are repeated in the attempted escape scene, when Monostatos once again sings a falling octave from d^2 to d^1 and Papageno sings both a descending third—this time from the dominant to the mediant—and the octave leap from d to d^1. The same melodic pattern is continued by the glockenspiel, which thus functions as an extension of Papageno's will, commencing

Example 2

Example 3

(...)

with a descending third from dominant to mediant and containing an interrupted octave leap from d^2 to d^3. Papageno's triumph becomes evident when the musical line sung by Monostatos and the slaves mimics the essence of the glockenspiel melody, beginning with the same descending third from dominant to mediant. Monostatos, the slaves, and usually the audience have literally been brainwashed into humming the "right" music[22] (example 4). The naive innocence that is conveyed by the glockenspiel and heightened by the beguiling softness of the pizzicato accompaniment from the string section articulates nothing less than hegemony through music. Evidently, sound matters.

The following duet between Papageno and Pamina trumpets the goal of "happiness on earth" achieved by "the best of harmony," but this seems possible only once the enemy has been eliminated: in other words, utopian harmony requires the effacing of difference. Their lines ("und er lebte ohne sie/in der besten Harmonie") are fetishized by repetition in the brief middle section of the duet, structured as a canon in accordance with the "German" rules of counterpoint. Recalling Morrow's study, the subtext suggests that German music containing appropriate counterpoint, voice leading, and harmonic resolution delivers a harmonious world void of discord. The "German" stake Mozart had in the opera is supported by the elaborate overture written in sonata form, the fugal first subject, and the astounding contrapuntal wealth throughout: a clear expression of "German" complexity, and innovation, with simultaneous profundity and childlike naiveté (to paraphrase Schiller).

Example 4

(Papageno plays on his bells.)

spiel,   laß   die Glöckchen klingen, klingen, daß   die   Ohren ih-nen   singen.   *(The slaves dance.)*
bell,   Let   your mel - o - dy be ringing. Save   us   by your magic   singing!

Monostatos and Slaves

Ten.
Bass   Das klinget   so   herrlich,   das klinget   so schön!   La la ra,   la la

This   jingles   so   soft-ly,   this jingles   so clear!   La la ra,   la la

Hegemony welds a "multiplicity of dispersed wills with heterogeneous aims" together with a single aim.[23] It articulates what is different, particular, or incommensurable into some kind of social-cultural unity, while radically excluding and denigrating as hostile everything that may not fit in the first place. At the conclusion of *The Magic Flute*, "wise" Sarastro asserts that whoever cannot rejoice at his teaching "does not deserve to be a human being."[24] Enlightenment harmony and reason, which according to Horkheimer and Adorno have "always aimed at liberating men from fear and establishing their sovereignty,"[25] here produce a fearful other—the irrational—in order to prove their own authority. And yet as Schiller's "Ode to Joy" (1785) manifests, this other haunts the new order of harmony like a specter, prompting the poet to command that he who has no joy should "steal weeping from our company."[26] The Enlightenment project of universal harmony at once needs and loathes the dissonant in order to define itself. The construction of hegemony through harmony cannot do without separating the world into friend and foe, self and other, a strategy in which Adorno detected a preview of fatal attractions: "[T]he passage from Schiller's 'Ode to Joy,' in which those who are not accorded all-embracing love are banished from it, involuntarily betrays the truth about the idea of humanity, which is at once totalitarian and particular."[27]

III

Set to the text of Schiller's "Ode to Joy," Beethoven's Ninth Symphony has come to represent the Enlightenment vision of universal harmony like perhaps no other work in the Western canon. The obligatory and mindless replaying of Beethoven's Ninth at every event intended to celebrate global unity, peace, and brotherhood bears testimony to this canonization. And yet like Mozart's *The Magic Flute*, Beethoven's Ninth Symphony has its darker side as well. The violent and dissonant chord that opens the last movement broadcasts the extent to which this symphony stages a battle and crusade for harmony not unlike the one we witnessed in Mozart's opera. In response to the cacophonous opening, the double basses play a searching recitative to which the orchestra answers (unsatisfactorily) by sounding the main themes from the preceding movements. Eventually, a new theme is found by the basses and is made "unforgettable" by constant repetition, as one by one the sections of the orchestra gradually join in to play what is now apparently the "correct" music. As if to explain what has transpired on the level of absolute music, Beethoven repeats the exposition, this time with text.

"O Friends, not these sounds!" implores the bass soloist in words Beethoven added to Schiller's poem. "Rather let us play more pleasing and joyful ones."[28] The "theme" is born again, and soloists and chorus again join in with the whole orchestra on the way to a satisfying climax. But this climax is jarringly undermined, and even the untrained listener feels suspended in a limbo caused by the standard preparation for a modulation from D major to A major but where Beethoven, in the last moment, inserts an F-natural into the bass—a note which in the context sounds as if it "doesn't belong." This causes a wrenching instability which makes sense only later after B-flat major is established: as if to say that the telos has not yet been reached, or more insidiously that there is no room for foreign sounds.

The theme reemerges now, transformed into a delightful, celestial march: delightful because of the triangle, and celestial because of the piccolo. Could this be a peace march? Although the martial bass drum and cymbal are also involved, they are in the background and should barely be audible at first, because the drum is covered by the contrabassoon and the cymbals play pianissimo with half the frequency of the triangle (example 5). "Run your course, Brothers, joyful like a hero to victory [wie ein Held zum Siegen]," sings the tenor soloist. The human voice disturbs the march's angelic purity with words that invoke imagery of a military campaign. The march turns even darker as the pianissimo gradually yields to a fortissimo, the cherubic purity of the triangle and piccolo is drowned out by the bombastic timpani and crashing cymbals, and the male chorus repeatedly chants "wie ein Held zum Siegen." This reveals that beneath the rhetoric of peace lurks a party-political rally or perhaps a drunken sing-along at the

Example 5

local beer hall. Extreme though the "beer-hall" analogy may be, Adorno used the same image to describe Schiller's verbal demeanor, which "calls to mind the young man … who starts shouting to make himself heard…. German tirading and sententiousness are modeled on the French, but rehearsed in the beer-hall."[29]

The following orchestral episode connects the call to victory with the triumphal tutti itself—the most famous section. This passage of "absolute" music depicts struggle no longer in the verbal domain but rather in what I will call the realm of "pure reason." Not surprisingly, the musical device Beethoven uses is the fugue. Ironically, the heterogeneous fugue culminates in nothing less than its musical opposite: the orchestra playing F-sharp in unison, as if the mask behind which the fugue feigns heterogeneity has been pulled off to reveal the homogenized world at its core. In other words, counterpoint paradoxically results in sonic homogeneity, thus rendering even the concept of harmony (temporarily) obsolete. With everyone playing the same note in octaves, we arrive at both unbreachable limit and tabula rasa (example 6). The now "purified" world of unison carries us to the long-anticipated utopia: all the world singing together in perfect harmony, with the strings providing (German?) counterpoint. Paraphrasing Schiller: "Our music will rule the world." But

Example 6

what kind of a world is this, where the very next sequence offers an insidious chorus of basses again in unison with somber double basses, and
trombones, singing the words: "Seid umschlungen, Millionen! Diesen
Kuß der ganzen Welt!" (Be embraced, all ye millions! This kiss to the
whole world!) Behold another sonic paradox of a "kiss" delivered by
brute male force (example 7).

Note the grotesque and, for Beethoven, uncharacteristic ninth leap (that
is, one tone greater than an octave) between "umschlungen" (embraced)
and "Millionen" (millions), which conveys powerfully the full and quite
violent scope of this embrace. The last movement of the Ninth Symphony
thus presents us with something unusual for the otherwise serene and
inwardly expansive late Beethoven: a world of reason haunted by sounds
of the irrational and violent, a paradox unresolved by the frenzy that
accompanies the closing moments of the work. It is as if Beethoven wants
Papageno's and Pamina's dream to come alive, as if he wants us to march
off and sing mindlessly like Monostatos and his slaves. And yet he is
unable (or unwilling) to fully hide the costs of this celebration, to forget
the repression it takes in order to achieve universal harmony and become
an enlightened *Weltbürger deutscher Prägung*.

Example 7

IV

Musical works such as Mozart's *The Magic Flute* and Beethoven's Ninth Symphony are the most audible representation of the broader late-eighteenth-century glorification of "harmony" that pervaded German thought, evident in notions of tolerance (Lessing), and universal peace (Kant), and in Schiller's idea that "freedom" of the individual is achieved "where duty and inclination are in *harmony*" (emphasis added).[30] Harmony played a central role in the tonal musical system of that time, whereby a move away from the "home" tonic, modulation to a new tonality and, in extreme cases, dissonance or sonic discord signaled tension, unrest, even pain and suffering, thus creating a sense of yearning for the reestablishment of equilibrium represented by harmonious tonal resolution. This movement from harmony to tension and back to harmony gave tonal art music its distinctive shape. However, while it was necessary that the simultaneous sounding of notes (the "vertical") be harmonious, much of a composer's skill rested on the ability to effect the appearance of "freedom" and independence on the part of each individual musical line (the "horizontal"), even though such lines were subservient to the harmonic imperative.

Morrow has shown that this skill, known as the art of counterpoint, was adopted by German music critics in the late eighteenth century as constitutive and representative of the "German" musical style. But this seductive style involved a diabolical paradox: the appearance of freedom, yet the necessity of harmony. In Adorno's view, these paradoxes of tonality evidenced both the totalitarian and the repressive sides of modern society. They indicated the extent to which, in a broader perspective, reason and enlightenment, while emancipatory in intent, could yield totalitarian effects. Like the Enlightenment itself, the formal rationalism of tonal music and its harmonic imperative exerted a despotism that one must "escape." Within the context of the music, nonidentical particulars were homogenized and differences erased in such a way that—to modify the famous opening of *Dialectic of Enlightenment*—the fully harmonized earth radiated "disaster triumphant."[31]

William Wordsworth wrote in 1800 that "a multitude of causes, unknown to former times, are now acting with a combined force to blunt the discriminating powers of the mind, and, unfitting it for all voluntary exertion, to reduce it to a state of almost savage torpor."[32] In spite of all of their aesthetic achievements and emancipatory commitments, both Mozart's *The Magic Flute* and Beethoven's Ninth Symphony play their part in generating this torpor. Both works hail the power of what contemporary discourses considered manly German music in their efforts to establish universal harmony. Both works engage the formal rationality of the tonal system in order to unify minds and mollify (or prohibit) unruly emotions and thoughts. To be sure, neither Mozart nor Beethoven anticipate Hitler in the way that Adorno's polemical remark suggests. Yet as contemporary listeners, we cannot but ask ourselves how to respond to the hegemonic technique and provocative agenda of Mozart's and Beethoven's signature works. Shall we, like Odysseus's crew, plug our ears in order to escape the Sirens' song?[33] Or shall we, like Odysseus, invent arrangements by which we as a "subject need not be subjected" to their song, for example, by having ourselves bound to a mast while still listening to their voices?[34] Or do both strategies, thanks to their inherent cunning and strategic reasoning, simply reproduce the very logic that was at the core of Mozart's and Beethoven's project itself, the ambition of producing universal hegemony through rationalistic "German" harmony?

Notes

1. Helmut Plessner, *Die verspätete Nation: Über die politische Verführbarkeit bürgerlichen Geistes* (Stuttgart: Kohlhammer, 1959), a reworking of *Das Schicksal deutschen Geistes im Ausgang seiner bürgerlichen Epoche* (1935).
2. Thomas Mann, "Deutschland und die Deutschen," in *Ausgewählte Essays in drei Bänden*, vol. 2, ed. Hermann Kurzke (Frankfurt am Main: Fischer, 1986), 281–98, here 292 and 285. The speech was given on 29 May 1945.
3. Theodor W. Adorno, *Beethoven: The Philosophy of Music. Fragments and Texts*, ed. Rolf Tiedemann, trans. Edmund Jephcott (Stanford: Stanford University Press, 1998), 77. Originally, "Hitler und die IX. Symphonie: Seid umzingelt, Millionen," in *Beethoven: Philosophie der Musik* (Frankfurt am Main: Suhrkamp, 1993), 120.
4. Celia Applegate, "How German Is It? Nationalism and the Idea of Serious Music in the Early Nineteenth Century," *19th-Century Music* 21 (1998): 274–96; Pamela Potter, *Most German of the Arts: Musicology and Society from the Weimar Republic to the End of Hitler's Reich* (New Haven: Yale University Press, 1998); Mary Sue Morrow, *German Music Criticism in the Late Eighteenth Century: Aesthetic Issues in Instrumental Music* (Cambridge: Cambridge University Press, 1997).
5. See also Mary Sue Morrow, "Building a German Identity through Music," in *Searching for Common Ground: Diskurse zur deutschen Identität 1750–1871*, ed. Nicholas Vazsonyi (Cologne: Böhlau, 2000), 255–68.
6. For a traditional reading of the distinction between eighteenth-century "patriotism" and nineteenth-century "nationalism," see Peter Alter, *Nationalism* (London: Edward Arnold, 1989), 6.
7. See also Nicholas Vazsonyi, "Montesquieu, Friedrich Carl von Moser and the 'National Spirit Debate' in Germany 1765–1767," *German Studies Review* 2, no. 2 (1999): 225–46.
8. Wolfgang Hardtwig, *Nationalismus und Bürgerkultur in Deutschland 1500–1914. Ausgewählte Aufsätze* (Göttingen: Vandenhoeck & Ruprecht, 1994), esp. 12; Hans Peter Herrmann et al., *Machtphantasie Deutschland: Nationalismus, Männlichkeit und Fremdenhaß im Vaterlandsdiskurs deutscher Schriftsteller des 18. Jahrhunderts* (Frankfurt am Main: Suhrkamp, 1996); and Hans-Martin Blitz, *Aus Liebe zum Vaterland. Die deutsche Nation im 18. Jahrhundert* (Hamburg: Hamburger Edition, 2000).
9. Thomas Nipperdey, "Auf der Suche nach der Identität: Romantischer Nationalismus," *Nachdenken über die deutsche Geschichte. Essays* (Munich: Beck, 1986), 117. See also Geoff Eley and Ronald Gregor Suny, "Introduction," in *Becoming National: A Reader* (New York: Oxford University Press, 1996), 23.
10. Max Horkheimer and Theodor W. Adorno, *Dialectic of Enlightenment*, trans. John Cumming (London: Allen Lane, 1973), 6, 24. On the point of "modernization" as a "totalitarian system," see also Saree Makdisi, *Romantic Imperialism: Universal Empire and the Culture of Modernity* (Cambridge: Cambridge University Press, 1998), 14.
11. Thomas Mann, *Doctor Faustus: The Life of the German Composer Adrian Leverkühn, as Told by a Friend*, trans. H. T. Lowe-Porter (New York: Vintage, 1992), 478.
12. Friedrich Schiller, "[Deutsche Größe]," in *Nationalausgabe*, vol. 2.1 (Weimar: H. Böhlaus Nachfolger, 1983), 431–36. For debate on when the poem was drafted and why Schiller never completed it, see Joachim Müller, "Schillers Gedichtentwurf 'Deutsche Größe': Zum Problem der Kulturnation in der deutschen Klassik," *Wissenschaftliche Zeitschrift der Friedrich-Schiller-Universität* 2, no. 3 (1952–53): 97–109, and the apparatus of the *Nationalausgabe*.
13. The term *Kulturnation* was coined by Friedrich Meinecke, *Weltbürgertum und Nationalstaat. Werke*, vol. 5, 1st ed. 1907 (Munich: Oldenbourg, 1962), 9–26. Meinecke also discusses Schiller's poem, see 54–57 and 251.
14. Schiller, "Deutsche Größe," 433. Germans were not alone in formulating a world-historical mission. For a contemporaneous Anglocentric account, see Makdisi, *Romantic Imperialism*, 171; and Nipperdey, "Romantischer Nationalismus," 121–22.

15. Schiller, "Deutsche Größe," 432.
16. Ibid.
17. Ibid. "Unsre Sprache wird die Welt beherrschen."
18. Meinecke, *Weltbürgertum*, 24. Nipperdey also asserts that "romantic nationalism was rooted in universalist, cosmopolitan and humanitarian ideas" ("Romantischer Nationalismus," 121).
19. Wolfgang Amadeus Mozart, *Die Zauberflöte*, libretto by Emanuel Schikaneder (Stuttgart: Reclam, 1991), I.18.
20. Mozart, *Die Zauberflöte*, I.18.
21. Ernesto Laclau and Chantal Mouffe, *Hegemony and Socialist Strategy: Towards a Radical Democratic Politics* (London: Verso, 1985), 85.
22. Brainwashing reappears in *The Magic Flute* when Sarastro orders the initiation of the two newcomers who must first be "purified" (Sie müssen erst gereinigt sein) (I.19). He later presumes to speak in the name of humanity (II.1).
23. Laclau and Mouffe, *Hegemony and Socialist Strategy*, 67–68.
24. Mozart, *Die Zauberflöte*, II.12.
25. Horkheimer and Adorno, *Dialectic of Enlightenment*, 3.
26. Friedrich Schiller, "An die Freude," *Nationalausgabe*, 185–87, here 185: "stehle/Weinend sich aus diesem Bund." The rhetoric of *Brüderlichkeit* found in "An die Freude" served both the cosmopolitan and nationalistic agendas with equal force. See also Eley and Suny, *Becoming National*: "In Europe's Enlightenment traditions, we are now better able to see, certain constructions of value, agency, and interest were centered at the expense of others" (27).
27. Theodor W. Adorno, *Kulturkritik und Gesellschaft II. Gesammelte Schriften*, vol. 10.2 (Frankfurt am Main: Suhrkamp, 1977), 620. See also Adorno, *Beethoven: The Philosophy of Music*, 32–33 and 212.
28. Ludwig van Beethoven, *Symphony No. 9 in D minor, Opus 125* (New York: Dover, 1989). Even a partial bibliography of analyses and critiques pertaining to Beethoven's last symphony would exceed the scope of this study. However, for a recent and rather comprehensive discussion of both the work and its history of appropriation – political, ideological, and cultural – since 1824, see Esteban Buch, *Beethoven's Ninth: A Political History*, trans. Richard Miller (Chicago: University of Chicago Press, 2003).
29. Theodor Adorno, *Minima Moralia: Reflections from a Damaged Life*, trans. E. Jephcott (London: Verso, 1994), 88 [#53].
30. Friedrich Schiller, "Über Anmut und Würde," in *Werke und Briefe*, vol. 8, ed. Otto Dann and Axel Gellhaus et al. (Frankfurt am Main: Deutscher Klassiker Verlag, 1992), 330–94, here 371: "wo ... Pflicht und Neigung harmonieren."
31. Horkheimer and Adorno, *Dialectic of Enlightenment* 3. Adorno's combined critique of Western tonality and rationality—the harmonic imperative of the Enlightenment—has found resonance in unexpected places. Jean Baudrillard, for instance, avails himself of musical allusions in his psychosociological discussion of the "liberal bourgeois *tonality*" (emphasis added) of modernity, which trumpets the autonomy of the individual subject but increasingly "seeks global simultaneity" and "imposes itself on the world as a homogeneous unity" ("Modernity," trans. D. J. Miller, *Canadian Journal of Political and Social Theory* 11, no. 3 [1987]: 63–72, here 70, 65, 68 and 63). A recent study adds contour to Baudrillard by asserting that modernity is "not a blanket homogeneous culture, but rather a hegemonic project that is always in the process of reinvention ... always with the potential of some apocalyptic purification into the homogeneous, the abstract" (Makdisi, *Romantic Imperialism*, 181–82). Gilles Deleuze and Felix Guattari have argued, too, that modernity tends toward global homogenization and orchestrated harmony (*A Thousand Plateaus: Capitalism and Schizophrenia*, trans. Brian Massumi [Minneapolis: University of Minnesota Press, 1987], 436); while for Michel Foucault, harmony through homogeneity represents one of the four constitutive elements of the Enlightenment ("What is Enlightenment?" *The Foucault Reader*, ed. Paul Rabinow [New York: Pantheon, 1984], 48).

32. William Wordsworth, "Preface (1800) to the *Lyrical Ballads*," in *Selected Prose* (London: Penguin, 1988), 278–307, here 284.

33. The final image of Hans Jürgen Syberberg's seven-hour epic *Hitler: Ein Film aus Deutschland* (1977) is of a little girl—who functions as a leitmotiv in the film—covering her ears with her hands while the last movement from Beethoven's Ninth Symphony plays in the background.

34. Horkheimer and Adorno, *Dialectic of Enlightenment*, 59.

Chapter 2

MAHLER CONTRA WAGNER
The Third Symphony and the Political Legacy of Romanticism

Carl Niekerk

I

In recent years, scholars working in the field of German cultural studies have produced a substantial literature on Richard Wagner and the cultural-political dimensions of his work. Gustav Mahler, on the contrary, has received little attention from these authors, even though his orchestral works are at least as popular and as frequently performed as Wagner's. This curious lack of interest, I suggest, reflects a certain scholarly bias against the literary sources on which Mahler based his compositions. Unlike Mahler, Wagner employed mythological texts that had considerable canonical status in the German cultural tradition.[1] In addition, Wagner published a panoply of theoretical essays that presented his compositions as mouthpieces of larger political and aesthetic transformations. Mahler, on the other hand, drew on cultural traditions that—as ironic as it may seem—questioned the sanctity of tradition and actively contested unified meaning. True to this legacy, Mahler also abstained from public exercises of self-explanation, commenting on his work instead primarily in the form of fragmentary remarks.

It is the intention of this essay not only to think through these disjunctures between Wagner and Mahler, but also to show how Mahler's Third Symphony took issue with Wagner's agendas. By incorporating certain strains of German Romanticism and Friedrich Nietzsche's critique of Bayreuth, Mahler's Third, I submit, turns Wagner upside down. It inverts Wagner's nationalist visions of community and thereby contests the kind of hegemonic traditions that German cultural studies, in its efforts to trace the cultural production of nationhood, all too often seems to take for granted.

It is useful to recall at the outset that Wagner's operas did not articulate a political agenda directly, but rather translated political interests into the search for a "new mythology," or a new collective symbolism. The function of this new mythology was to create community, more specifically, a German national community. Whether consciously or not, Wagner thus revived well-established traditions in German thought and culture. Facing political disappointments such as the debacle of the French Revolution, German poets and intellectuals around 1800 actively sought to compensate for the defeat of their political ideas by creating in art a forum that would allow them to remain active in the public domain while avoiding the pitfalls of everyday politics. Art, for these intellectuals, constituted a sort of compensation for the lack of direct political engagement. They established the aesthetic in general, and music in particular, as an alternate route for pursuing political ends, as a means of generating community and defining particularity.

The popularity of Wagner's music since the mid-nineteenth century doubtless has something to do with the hidden but nevertheless omnipresent national agenda that Wagner pursued in practice as well as in theory. Wagner's aesthetic-political agenda climaxed in his last work, *Parsifal*, the opera Nietzsche hated most (and which Mahler quotes at the end of his Third Symphony).[2] More than any other work by Wagner, it contained the call for a new, purified community. *Parsifal* actively attempted to create a collective of chosen ones, those allowed to take part in a ritual of initiation in a sacred place, and it is for this reason that the Wagner family decided that for thirty years *Parsifal* could be performed only at Bayreuth.[3]

It has become a commonplace among Wagner scholars to point out that the cultural and political project of Wagner's operas, including *Parsifal*, relied on highly problematic stereotypes of gender and race. Wagner's texts are built around exemplary, heroic men. The plots of several works center on the possession of certain phallic symbols. *The Ring of the Nibelungen*, for instance, is not as much about a ring as it is about the possession of a sword, and the plot has a strong oedipal component as well. The positive masculine ideal in Wagner's work is created simultaneously with and in contrast to what George Mosse calls an effeminate and racially degenerate "countertype."[4] This "countertype" has a strong anti-Semitic dimension in Wagner's work, both in his theoretical writings and in his compositions.[5]

Mahler, whose work was widely indebted to Wagner's musical language, was well aware of the anti-Semitic subtext of Wagner's work. Natalie Bauer-Lechner's memoirs include an interesting reference to a Vienna performance of Wagner's *Siegfried* that Mahler conducted:

> In "Siegfried" Spielmann is the new Mime. Although he was by no means insignificant, and as far as both his musical talent and his gift of acting are concerned is

full of character and ingenuity, he did too much of a good thing; "wanted to be," as Mahler said full of anger, "wittier than witty, and got because of that from characterization into parody, which means the end of his role and him— because I will fire him immediately. He is too much ruined by the theater routine. What is worst about him is his *mauscheln*. Although I am convinced that this figure is the embodied persiflage of a Jew, as intended by Wagner (with all the traits which he gave him: his petty cleverness, greed and all the complete musically and textually excellent jargon), in God's name that should not be exaggerated and dished up so thickly here, as Spielmann did this—especially in Vienna, at the 'k.k. Court Opera,' it is clearly laughable and a welcome scandal for the Viennese! I know only *one* Mime (we all looked at him anxiously) and that is *me*! You will be surprised to see what lies in the part and what I could make of it!"[6]

Himself born a Jew, Mahler had no illusions about the anti-Semitic stereotypes personified by Mime in Wagner's *Ring of the Nibelungen*; in fact, he had no problem admitting that Mime could represent *him*. But the ease with which Mahler, armed with that knowledge, turns Wagner's anti-Semitism against one of the singers, Spielmann, is astonishing. It is Mahler who chides Spielmann for his *mauscheln*, thereby using one of the dominant stereotypes about Jews against his own subordinate.[7]

The quotation from Bauer-Lechner's memoirs indicates the extent to which Mahler did not wish to deal with the anti-Semitic agenda underlying Wagner's art. Exposing Wagner's agenda in all of its details would be counterproductive, and when Spielmann attempts to do just this, the result is professional suicide. Nevertheless, it would be incorrect to say that Mahler the composer completely ignored Wagner's racist stances as well as the rampant anti-Semitism of his time.[8] On the contrary, it is the aim of this essay to show not only that Mahler participated in the same cultural-political discourses that structured Wagner's work, but also that Mahler did so far more critically and came to very different conclusions than Wagner. Mahler's work, in other words, energized social discourses similar to those that were circulated by the works of Wagner, even though Mahler—unlike Wagner—did not develop a broad essayistic framework explaining and promoting the philosophical-political dimension of his own music.[9]

II

Both Mahler and Wagner are often considered late Romantics. Yet it is in their different interpretations of German Romanticism, and their respective appropriations of the Romantic quest for a "new mythology," that some of the most fundamental differences between Wagner's and Mahler's aspirations become the clearest. German Romantics around 1800 embraced art as a new mythology that not only had its origins among the

(German) people,[10] but also was written and composed for the (German) people. The new mythology of the Romantics was supposed to provide a new collective symbolism that would found a unique sense of community.[11] Some kind of return to nature was meant to be the basis for this new collective symbolism.[12] For the early Romantics, the concept of a new mythology thus had a normative function, legitimizing certain ways of living and the concomitant social institutions.[13]

Wagner's dedication to the idea of a new mythology is featured prominently in a famous passage of the essay "Religion and Art" (1880–81): "One could say that when religion becomes artistic, it is up to art to save religion's core by conceiving of mythical symbols (which want religion to be understood as actually true) in their metaphorical sense; and by showing via their ideal presentation, their hidden, deep truth."[14] For Wagner, a decisive difference between religion and art is that the latter does not conceive of mythical symbols as straightforward references to a literal truth. Instead, art understands these symbols as expressions of a deeper, hidden meaning. While religion attempts to de-emphasize the symbolic character of myth, art illuminates myth's mediating quality and the fact that the truth of myth is irreducibly connected to the symbols that represent it.

Nietzsche was one of the first to discuss the Romantic legacy—the figuration of art as myth, the translation of religion into art—in Wagner. In his first lengthy and still celebratory text about Wagner—the essay "Richard Wagner in Bayreuth," section 4 of the *Unfashionable Observations* (1874)—Nietzsche applauds Wagner's work as an attempt to conceive of a new form of art that entails a return to an older and a more original way of creating art.[15] It is significant that nature plays a central role in the creation of this higher form of art. Wagner's music, in Nietzsche's perspective, articulates a return to nature that breaks down all traces of alienation. It restores understanding and reciprocity to the human race. Wagner's art is intended for the people in general, not for the intellectual; it appeals to collective emotions rather than dissecting minds. The mythic undertones of Wagner's music do not simply articulate specific ideas or a utopian order of things. Rather, Wagner sees myth as a form of thinking itself, an idea Wagner shares with the Romantic program and its insights into the subjective nature of all knowledge.

Nietzsche's later turn away from Wagner can be seen as the result of a fundamental reevaluation of Romantic subjectivity and the project of modernity in Nietzsche's overall work. While the young Nietzsche saw Wagner as a forerunner of a specifically modern aesthetics, the later Nietzsche considered him the enemy of such a conceptualization of modern art. According to Nietzsche's revised image of Wagner in *The Case of Wagner* (1888), the master of Bayreuth now represents everything that is wrong with modern German culture, including its nationalistic and anti-Semitic elements.[16] After the death of God, it is Wagner who pretends that God still lives and therefore fails to appreciate the ultimate consequences of living in a postmetaphysical world. There are many reasons to be at least somewhat skeptical about Nietzsche's critical turnaround. What it illustrates, though, is that even in its own historical context, Wagner's work could mean many things at once, and that the relation of Wagner to the project of modernity was already seen by Wagner's contemporaries as highly ambiguous. As I will show in the following pages, it is precisely this ambiguity of Wagner's modernism that Mahler—learning from Nietzsche—will explore in further detail. Mahler's Third Symphony tries to wrest the legacy of German Romanticism away from Wagner. It stresses the skeptical, ironic, and critical side of Romanticism while rejecting the dogmatic, reactionary, and nationalistic aspects that, according to Nietzsche, increasingly dominated Wagner's later work.

III

It is no exaggeration to say that Nietzsche was a key figure in Gustav Mahler's intellectual development.[17] As a student, Mahler was a member of what was informally known as the Nietzsche Society of Vienna. This same group supplied Mahler (who was not financially well off in his student days) with a piano that enabled him to work on his compositions, but on which he also had to accompany the society's frequent performances of nationalistic songs.[18] This gift was clearly a mixed blessing, but one should not dismiss Mahler's participation in this very nationalistic student group as a purely opportunistic move. He may very well have been attracted to the society's Nietzschean cultural criticism,[19] which at times may have superseded its nationalistic tendencies.

Nietzsche's writings left many traces in Mahler's work. One of the most obvious influences was, for instance, Mahler's interest in Romantic songs, which resulted, among other things, in the orchestration of the Romantic collection, *Des Knaben Wunderhorn* (The Youth's Magic Horn, 1806–8). In *The Birth of Tragedy* (1872), Nietzsche celebrates the folk song as a modern example of the Dionysian art that he considered far superior to the Apollonian epic forms of literature. One point of contrast between Apollonian and Dionysian art concerns their relation to nature. Apollonian art, according to Nietzsche, has lost its bond to nature; it is subjugated to random, man-made, and therefore artificial, rules. Dionysian art, on the other hand, has not lost its ties with nature. It is unmediated in a double sense—as a direct expression of the nature surrounding us and also as a mirror of human nature. Folk songs exemplify this model because of the prevalence of melody over text and the richness of the images that the melody generates. In folk songs, language seeks to mimic music rather than the world of appearances or images. Language in folk songs is, in other words, a direct and unmediated expression of nature itself, rather than the result of an attempt to recapture a lost experience in words. Nietzsche calls this the only possible relation between poetry and music.

While composing the Third Symphony, Mahler seems to have read Nietzsche particularly intensively.[20] This is most obvious from the fact that Mahler originally considered naming his Third Symphony *The Gay Science*. Clearly, Mahler saw his symphony as a fulfillment of Nietzsche's philosophical program. It should therefore come as no surprise that Mahler first intended to reference natural imagery and folk songs in order to name individual movements of the Third Symphony just as he had done previously in his First Symphony, pursuing the generative principle to which Nietzsche had alluded in both *The Birth of Tragedy* and *The Gay Science*.[21] On a separate sheet together with a letter to Friedrich Löhr on 29 August 1895, Mahler outlined the following structure for the Third Symphony:

Symphony No. III.
"THE GAY SCIENCE"
A SUMMER MORNING'S DREAM

    I. Summer marches in.
   II. What the flowers in the meadow tell me.
  III. What the animals in the forest tell me.
  IV. What night tells me. (Alto solo).
   V. What the morning bells tell me.
     (Women's chorus with Alto solo).
  VI. What love tells me.
     Motto: "Father, look at my wounds!
     Let no creature be lost!"
     (From *The Youth's Magic Horn*)
 VII. The Heavenly life.
     (Soprano solo, humorous).[22]

Deeply steeped in and mimicking "the sound of nature,"[23] Mahler's Third Symphony sought to put Nietzsche's concepts of the Dionysian and the natural—Nietzsche's own new mythology—into practice. The movements create "a Nietzschean framework to convey an idea of community that is expanded to embrace not only all of humanity but all levels of being in the world of nature."[24] Unlike Wagner, however, Mahler's vision of community remains ambivalent and ironic. Learning from both Nietzsche and Romantics such as Friedrich Schlegel, Mahler's new mythology at once hails and questions the image of a new community; it at once celebrates and probes any redemptive union of being and nature.

Mahler's ambivalent view of community is best illustrated by the incorporation of Nietzsche's *Thus Spoke Zarathustra* (1883–86) into the fourth movement of the Third Symphony. As Manfred Frank has pointed out, Nietzsche's *Zarathustra* presents a complex and highly symbolic language, whose purpose was to envision new modes of collective integration that could supersede what Nietzsche understood as the alienating logic of modern society. Appropriately, much of *Zarathustra* takes the form of a sermon. But *Thus Spoke Zarathustra* is also, in a sense, a document of desperation, a text in which Zarathustra/Nietzsche acknowledges his feelings of existential isolation and solitude. What first looks like a sermon in the process of the text turns into a reclusive monologue. A primary example of this second and darker side of *Thus Spoke Zarathustra* is "Zarathustras Mitternachtslied" (Zarathustra's Midnight Song), which Mahler chose for the fourth movement of his Third Symphony.

O man! Watch out!
Zarathustra's Midnight Song

CONTRALTO
O man! Watch out!
What does the deep midnight say?
I slept!
I have awakened from a deep dream!
The world is deep!
And deeper than the day conceived!
Deep is its woe!
Joy deeper still than heartache!
Woe says: Be lost!
But all desire wants eternity,
Wants deep, deep eternity.[25]

Mahler set "Midnight Song" to music that illustrates a specific, and somber, frame of mind, whereas the fifth movement, based on a text from *The Youth's Magic Horn*, becomes astonishingly lighthearted. This juxtaposition of musical moods remains a subject of controversy among Mahler's critics. Alphons Diepenbrock, a Dutch composer and conductor, who in later years was Mahler's friend, initially responded quite critically to the idea of combining a text by Nietzsche with lyrics from *The Youth's Magic Horn*.[26] Peter Franklin supports this observation when he summarizes the differences between the fourth and the fifth movements as follows: "The elaborate artifice of the previous [i.e., fourth] movement's song of individuated inwardness is now replaced by a public celebration—a musical party to which everyone has been invited, from the local church choir to the village band."[27] Both Diepenbrock and Franklin point to the discontinuous and fragmentary character of Mahler's symphony. Rather than striving for organic integration and totality, Mahler's combination of lyrics and music produces a highly diverse, broken, and fundamentally open work. Celebrating the spontaneous and immediate, Mahler refuses Wagnerian closure and instead stresses the discontinuous work of mediation—the assembly of individual fragments—that it takes to create a new mythology.

While it is questionable whether Mahler had Romantic aesthetic theory in mind when composing these movements, it is nevertheless very interesting to see that Mahler's Third Symphony makes use of a typically Romantic aesthetic form that represents a skeptical trend within modernity. For the Romantics, the fragment was not merely an important literary form but the key element in their way of viewing the world. For early Romantics such as Schlegel and Novalis, a fragmentary way of thinking and writing was the only appropriate response to the metaphysical and political crises of their time, crises that materialized in the philosophical idealism of Kant and Fichte and the French Revolution. In the perspective of early Romanticism, the fragment was the embodiment of modernity.[28]

It is Mahler's emphasis on mediation and the fragmentary that marks the fundamental difference between his work and Wagner's, between their respective visions of community and modernity. Wagner was much less interested in the aesthetic program of early Romanticism than in the later Romantics' turn toward nationalism and dogmatic religiosity. Beyond that, Wagner specifically considered the fragmentary and nonorganic as a Jewish trait in the music of his time. In "Judaism in Music" (1850), Wagner characterized Mendelssohn as the prototype of the assimilated Jew, cut off from his native culture. Paul Lawrence Rose summarizes Wagner's argument as follows:

> In his new environment, the Jew can only mimic; but fortunately for him the degeneration of German art into mere technique has made it easy for the mimicking, formalistic Jewish artist to succeed. Thus Judaized, German art has been severed from its cultural roots and become 'entirely loveless', a perfect reflection of Jewishness itself. Worse, even the 'cultivated' or converted Jew who has abandoned Judaism is still, *faute de mieux*, forced back, for inspiration, on to this horrible tradition of synagogue music. The result is that his music has emerged as a confusion of styles, as chaotic formalism—cold indifferent and sterile—without genuine feeling or passion.[29]

What Wagner termed "chaotic formalism" and "confusion of styles" are stereotypes that have long been used to dismiss Mahler's work.[30] But the fragmentary and diverse character of his texts and music is neither a sign of musical inferiority nor of an inability to compose a stylistically unified piece of music. Mahler embraced the fragmentary in a conscious effort to find a musical language that could stress the indisputable fissures of the modern experience. Displacement and discontinuity were integral to Mahler's vision of community: he deliberately engaged those very characteristics that Wagner deemed Jewish as elements of his aesthetic modernism.

IV

Rather than simply refuting Wagner, Mahler turned Wagner's agendas, including his anti-Semitism, inside out. He embraced early Romanticism and Nietzsche so as to deliver a contrasting vision of modern life and community. This cunning strategy of inversion can be observed in regard to Mahler's use of the female voice as well. As Marc Weiner has discussed extensively, Wagner deploys voice as an "acoustical icon of race and nation."[31] Men in his compositions who sound or sing like women—such as Mime in *The Ring of the Nibelungen*—represent the degenerate opposites of the pieces' Germanic heroes. To secure his heroes' masculinity relative to the higher, "degenerate" voices, Wagner even created "a new kind of singer, never before heard on the operatic stage, the *Heldentenor*,"[32] that is, a tenor whose voice has a striking dramatic quality well suited for heroic roles.

Mahler's Third Symphony, by contrast, offers little space for heroic male voices of any kind. In fact, both the part of Zarathustra in the fourth movement and the part of Saint Peter in the fifth movement are to be performed by women, for they are written for the low female voice, contralto, rather than for a man's voice. Just as importantly, by incorporating a text from *The Youth's Magic Horn*,[33] "Armer Kinder Bettler-Lied" (Poor Children's Begging-Song), into the fifth movement, Mahler offered the listener sounds of vocal youth and lightness unheard of in the entirety of Wagner's work:

Poor Children's Begging-Song

BOYS' CHORUS
Bimm bamm, bimm bamm …

WOMEN'S CHORUS
Three angels sang a sweet song,
that resounded with joy in heaven.
They also shouted with joy,
that Peter was free from sin.

And when Jesus the Lord sat at the table,
and ate with his twelve disciples his evening meal,
Jesus the Lord said: Why are you standing here?
When I look at you, you make me cry.

CONTRALTO
And should I not weep, my good Lord …

WOMEN'S CHORUS
You should not weep!

CONTRALTO
I have broken the Ten Commandments;
I go and weep bitterly,
oh come and have mercy with me.

WOMEN'S CHORUS
If you have broken the Ten Commandments,
fall on your knees and pray to God!
Love always God alone,
and you shall receive heavenly joy!

Heavenly joy, the blessed city;
Heavenly joy, which has no end anymore.
Heavenly joy was granted to Peter
by Jesus and to all for eternal bliss.

At first the fifth movement seems to articulate a straightforward religious message. He who has strayed from God, he who has sinned against the Ten Commandments, will always be welcomed back into the collective (represented by the women's choir), if he so desires. The text thus articulates a desire for a new community similar to the desire underlying the Romantic idea of a new mythology. But why is the song entitled "Poor Children's Begging-Song"? And why is the discussion between the contralto (Saint Peter) and the women's choir accompanied by the "bimm bamm" sounds of a boys' choir? Is the text meant to be a dialogue between three parties? Does the third party as represented by the boys' choir somehow supersede the other two? Or do the other two act as figures in the imagination of the third?

It is by reading the "Poor Children's Begging-Song" through the lens of the fourth movement of Mahler's Fourth Symphony, I suggest, that we may answer these questions most persuasively. Similar to the Third Symphony, Mahler's Fourth will once again borrow from *The Youth's Magic Horn*. In fact, the Fourth's fourth movement, which includes the song "Das himmlische Leben" (The Heavenly Life), was originally intended as the seventh and final part of the Third Symphony (as is clear from the initial sketch for the Third that accompanies Mahler's letter to Friedrich Löhr). Like "Poor Children's Begging-Song," the lyrics of "The Heavenly Life" extend a utopian vision of joy, pleasure, and redemption. It culminates in a celebration of angelic music, an idiom unavailable in ordinary life:

No music exists on earth,
which can be compared to ours,
eleven thousand virgins
dare to dance,

Saint Ursula even laughs at that,
Cecilia and her relatives
are excellent court musicians,
the angelic voices
stimulate the senses,
so that everything wakes up for joy!

Mahler scholars have proposed the term "irony" to describe the utopian attitude behind the last movement of the Fourth Symphony.[34] To comprehend Mahler's intentions here, it helps to recall the specifically Romantic notion of "irony." "To say something ironically," according to early Romantic philosophy, "means to take it back by the manner *in which* it is said."[35] The final movement of the Fourth lives up to this formula. The song was written for a female voice, but seen in its context, it was clearly meant to articulate the vision of a child—a child's fantasy.[36] In a congenial move in his last recording of the Fourth, Leonard Bernstein, in fact, replaced the woman's voice with that of a child. Mahler himself apparently recommended that the soprano soloist sing the part as if it were performed by a child.[37] The use of a child's voice raises the question of whether the utopian moment is intended seriously, whether it should be perceived consciously by those listening as a (child's) fantasy, or both at once. Mahler's ironic attitude here first articulates a lighthearted, redemptive vision of community and then takes it back, drawing our attention to Nietzsche's point that in the modern world any return to religion, to the old mythologies, must be illusory. Only children can hold such a belief, and the rest of us will have to accept that we live in a postmetaphysical age.

Bernstein's highly original reading of the score of the Fourth Symphony suggests that Mahler radically questions Wagner's turn to religion by evoking a rupture between sound and text. Unlike Wagner's, Mahler's modernist composition technique does not aim for a unity of text and music, but instead emphasizes the conflict between them. The same principle is at work at other points in the song, for instance, in the second half of the second stanza of "The Heavenly Life":

Saint Luke slaughters the ox
without giving it a thought,
the wine costs not a penny
in the heavenly cellar,
and the angels bake the bread.

This passage is a clear example of two diametrically opposed but equally valid feelings, which is another stylistic marker of early Romantic irony.[38] While the text makes us forget the slaughter of the ox quickly and moves on to more pleasant topics—there is plenty of wine, bread is being baked—the music tells us something else. French horns at the back of the orchestra mimic the sound of the ox being slaughtered, while the text focuses on the everyday pleasures of life in heaven. Text and sound lead us to contrasting, if not contradictory, readings of Mahler's art.

In the end, Mahler decided not to use "The Heavenly Life" for his Third Symphony. Bernstein's interpretation of the final movement of the Fourth, however, enables us to read the fifth movement of the Third in a new light. The "bimm bamm" of the boys' choir accompanying the "Poor Children's Begging-Song" is neither a simple ornament nor meant to evoke a certain atmosphere but is used instead to articulate a fundamental ambivalence toward what initially seems to be the song's central message. Here, too, sound prevails over text. "Voice" is the preferred medium in which Mahler expresses the ambiguities that undergird his art. Due to its indeterminate status between sound and text, "voice" is for Mahler the ultimate place of competing visions and ideologies. Rather than securing a specific ideology, as Wagner intended to do with his heldentenor, Mahler uses women's and children's voices to destabilize belief systems. The Third doubtless contains a critique of Wagner's completely unambiguous use of religious imagery in *Parsifal* (which Mahler, as mentioned before, quotes in his final movement). Furthermore, the ironic interpretation proposed here would also place Mahler's conversion to Catholicism not long after he finished the Third in a somewhat different light.

V

At the beginning of this essay, I noted that Wagner has received much attention from scholars working in German cultural studies, while the philosophical and political aspects of Mahler's work have remained largely unexplored. But what explains the fascination of cultural studies scholars with Wagner? Our contrastive reading of Mahler in the context of Wagner's cultural and political agenda may help to answer that question.

By examining the reception of literary and philosophical Romanticism in the work of these two composers, this essay has demonstrated that the German cultural tradition is a place of competing visions and political interests. But does German cultural studies see it similarly? I contend that in spite of its critical ambitions, contemporary German cultural studies often tends to reproduce hierarchies inherent to the traditions it dissects, specifically, those hierarchies that reflect the cultural interests of the German middle class in the late 1800s and early 1900s—interests that decidedly included Wagner but not Mahler (not to mention Alban Berg, Arnold Schoenberg, Hugo Wolf, and Alexander Zemlinsky, among other composers working within the same literary, political, and cultural traditions). The relationship of German cultural studies to these traditions is marked by a double bind. On the one hand, the dominating attitude is, in general, very critical toward Wagner and the type of audience that supported him. On the other hand, Wagner remains the focus of intense scholarly interest.

German cultural studies, in other words, seems unable to move beyond the canon of previous stages of German culture. Although it is interested in the power dynamics underlying Wagner's work and will reconstruct that work's political agenda in detail, it is remarkably indifferent to (and perhaps even ignorant of) positions of resistance or attempts from outside the canon to subvert the power hierarchies inherent therein.

Interestingly, within the development of the German cultural tradition, Wagner has come to be identified with new, "modern" forms of experiencing art. Informed by Theodor W. Adorno's work, Andreas Huyssen, for instance, sees powerful parallels between Wagner's music dramas and the emerging culture industry.[39] Such insights are certainly helpful for explaining how Wagner, through his work, attempts "to beat his audience into submission."[40] However, one should consider that Wagner's was, in essence, a very elitist conception of art that tried to block the progress made by new technical media for the reproduction and dissemination of cultural products. I have already made reference to the thirty-year ban on performances of *Parsifal* outside of Bayreuth. This ban made attending performances possible only for the elite, who could afford the trip, and resulted in the Wagner family's attempt to prevent the publisher of Wagner's music, Schott, from distributing the scores of *Parsifal* to orchestras outside of Bayreuth.[41] If we want to understand Wagner's work as making possible new forms of aesthetic experience, we also should be aware of the contradictory dynamics underlying its history. (Huyssen's evaluation of Wagner otherwise concurs with Adorno's and is clearly aware of the ambiguities inherent in Wagner's work.)

I do not wish the above remarks to be read as arguments against the German cultural studies movement. I also do not intend to suggest that contemporary scholars should stop tracing the effects of Wagner's aesthetic-political agenda, including its gendered and racist aspects, on his art or on German cultural history in general. But it is equally important to realize that Wagner's agenda is part of a larger dialogue. Mahler's music and texts are, in an exemplary way, part of the discourse concerning the legacy of German Romanticism as well, and their study can, as I hope to have shown, lead to more complex and challenging readings of the musical politics of modern German culture.

Notes

1. David Levin, *Richard Wagner, Fritz Lang, and the Nibelungen: The Dramaturgy of Disavowal* (Princeton: Princeton University Press, 1998), 98, points to the interesting paradox that the Nibelung saga was both extremely popular and at the same time considered to be part of high culture (in the program book to his film *Nibelungen*, Fritz Lang problematized its elitist status in German culture).

2. William J. McGrath, *Dionysian Art and Populist Politics in Austria* (New Haven: Yale University Press, 1974), 159.

3. Nike Wagner, *Wagner Theater* (Frankfurt am Main: Insel, 1998), 12–13, 195.

4. George L. Mosse, *The Image of Man: The Creation of Modern Masculinity* (New York: Oxford University Press, 1996), 56ff.

5. See Paul Lawrence Rose, *Wagner: Race and Revolution* (New Haven: Yale University Press, 1992); Marc A. Weiner, *Richard Wagner and the Anti-Semitic Imagination*, 2nd ed. (Lincoln: University of Nebraska Press, 1997).

6. Natalie Bauer-Lechner, *Gustav Mahler in den Erinnerungen von Natalie Bauer-Lechner*, rev. ed. (Hamburg: Verlag der Musikalienhandlung Karl Dieter Wagner, 1984), 122.

7. Sander L. Gilman, *Jewish Self-Hatred: Anti-Semitism and the Hidden Language of the Jews* (Baltimore: Johns Hopkins University Press, 1990), 139: "[*Mauscheln*] is the use of altered syntax and bits of Hebrew vocabulary and a specific pattern of gestures to represent the spoken language of the Jews. What is stressed is the specifically 'Jewish' intonation, the mode of articulation as well as the semantic context." Mahler's remarks also confirm Gilman's insight that "*Mauscheln* was a quality of language and discourse that Jews perceived as a major problem in their true and total acceptance within the German community" (141).

8. See Henry-Louis de la Grange, *Gustav Mahler. Volume 2. Vienna: The Years of Challenge (1897–1904)* and *Volume 3. Vienna: Triumph and Disillusion (1904–1907)* (Oxford: Oxford University Press, 1995 and 1999), for a detailed reconstruction of the many anti-Semitic incidents surrounding Mahler's tenure at the Vienna Staatsoper 1897 to 1907.

9. In addition, Mahler's fascination with Wagner very well may have had musicological grounds. In comparison to the music of the more traditionally oriented Brahms, Wagner's music was truly progressive, even if it represented a conservative ideological agenda. See Henry-Louis de la Grange, *Mahler*, vol. 1 (Garden City: Doubleday, 1973), 43ff., for an overview of the musicological debates in Mahler's student days and Mahler's position vis-à-vis Wagner in the context of these debates.

10. Manfred Frank, *Der kommende Gott. Vorlesungen über die Neue Mythologie* (Frankfurt am Main: Suhrkamp, 1982), 218.

11. Ibid., 198.

12. Ibid., 201.

13. Manfred Frank, *Gott im Exil. Vorlesungen über die Neue Mythologie*, vol. 2 (Frankfurt am Main: Suhrkamp, 1988), 16; see also Frank, *Der kommende Gott*, 207.

14. Wagner, "Religion and Art," opening sentence. Richard Wagner, *Gesammelte Schriften und Dichtungen*, 3rd ed., vol. 10 (Leipzig: T.F.W. Musikalienhandlung R. Linnemann, 1913), 211; see also Frank, *Der kommende Gott*, 226.

15. It is clear that Wagner's work here serves as an illustration of what Nietzsche had called Dionysian art in *The Birth of Tragedy*, the text Nietzsche published immediately before his *Unfashionable Observations*. Frank has pointed out many parallels between the Romantic concept of a new mythology and Nietzsche's ideas in this text; in fact, *The Birth of Tragedy* ends with Nietzsche's programmatic call for a rebirth of German myth, which he sees realized in Wagner. See Friedrich Nietzsche, *Sämtliche Werke. Kritische Studienausgabe in 15 Bänden*, ed. Giorgio Colli and Mazzino Montinari (Munich: DTV/ de Gruyter, 1980) 1:147; see also Frank, *Gott im Exil*, 49.

16. This is especially clear in Nietzsche's summary of *The Case of Wagner* in *Ecce Homo* (Nietzsche, *Werke* 4:357–64). It is interesting to note that recent Nietzsche scholarship has

distanced itself sharply from the anti-Semitic image of Nietzsche that dominated reception of his work during the Third Reich. Some scholars argue that Nietzsche's attitude to Jews is in essence a positive one; see Jacob Golomb, ed., *Nietzsche and Jewish Culture* (London and New York: Routledge, 1997), and especially the contribution of Weaver Santaniello, "Nietzsche and the Jews: Christianism and Nazism," 21–54. Others point out that Nietzsche's thinking uses racial categories, but that Nietzsche himself takes the position of an anti-anti-Semite—that is, of someone who opposes anti-Semitism because of the political use certain nationalist groups make of it for their own benefit; see Sander Gilman, "Heine, Nietzsche, and the Idea of the Jew," 79, in Golomb, *Nietzsche and Jewish Culture*, 76–100. Gilman's observation concerning Nietzsche's anti-anti-Semitism can be supported by looking at Nietzsche's writings on Wagner. In *Nietzsche contra Wagner*, for instance, Nietzsche concisely summarizes the causes of his break with Wagner (see esp. Nietzsche, *Werke* 4:431f.). All elements identified above—Wagner's return to Christianity, his identification with German nationalism, and his anti-Semitism—are mentioned there.

17. An extensive analysis of Nietzsche's importance for Mahler, emphasizing especially the thematic affinities between both, can be found in Eveline Nikkels, *"O Mensch! Gib Acht!" Friedrich Nietzsches Bedeutung für Gustav Mahler* (Amsterdam: Rodopi, 1989).

18. William J. McGrath, "Mahler and the Vienna Nietzsche Society," *Nietzsche and Jewish Culture*, ed. Golomb, 226.

19. McGrath, "Mahler," 55

20. McGrath, *Dionysian Art*, 121.

21. Additional elements connect the Third Symphony with Mahler's student membership in the Nietzsche Society. A melody Mahler inserted into the first movement at the last moment seems borrowed from a student song used to protest the decision of the Austrian government to dissolve the German Students' Reading Society of Vienna, informally known as the Nietzsche Society. See McGrath "Mahler," 229–30; and Peter Franklin, *Mahler: Symphony No. 3* (Cambridge: Cambridge University Press, 1991), 81. After finishing work on the project, Mahler visited Lipiner, his old acquaintance from student days and one of the leading figures in Vienna's Nietzsche Society.

22. Gustav Mahler, *Briefe*, ed. Herta Blaukopf, 2nd rev. ed. (Vienna: Paul Zsolnay Verlag, 1996), 151; see also Franklin, *Mahler*, 48. Later Mahler questions the relevance of these titles, and remarks that they did more to confuse his listeners than to clarify his music (see Mahler, *Briefe*, 297).

23. Mahler, *Briefe*, 203.

24. McGrath, "Mahler," 218.

25. Nietzsche, *Werke* 4:404.

26. Grange, *Mahler*, 642; Franklin, *Mahler*, 28.

27. Franklin, *Mahler*, 70.

28. Philippe Lacoue-Labarthe and Jean-Luc Nancy, *The Literary Absolute: The Theory of Literature in German Romanticism* (Albany: State University of New York Press, 1988), 40.

29. Rose, *Wagner*, 82.

30. Jens Malte Fischer, "Gustav Mahler und das 'Judentum in der Musik,'" *Merkur* 51 (1997): 665–80.

31. Weiner, *Richard Wagner and the Anti-Semitic Imagination*, 105.

32. Ibid., 164.

33. L. A. Arnim and Clemens Brentano, *Des Knaben Wunderhorn. Alte deutsche Lieder* (Berlin: v. Arnim's Verlag, 1857), 3:77–78.

34. Adolf Nowak, "Zur Deutung der Dritten und Vierten Sinfonie Gustav Mahlers," in *Gustav Mahler*, ed. Hermann Danuser (Darmstadt: Wissenschaftliche Buchgesellschaft, 1992), 202; see also Grange, *Mahler*, 772.

35. Manfred Frank, *Einführung in die frühromantische Ästhetik. Vorlesungen* (Frankfurt am Main: Suhrkamp, 1989), 373.

36. When Mahler was still debating which text to choose for the seventh movement of the Third, he considered the title "What the child tells me" (Mahler, *Briefe*, 150).

37. Grange, *Mahler*, 771.

38. Frank, *Gott im Exil*, 389.

39. See Andreas Huyssen, *The Great Divide: Modernism, Mass Culture, Postmodernism* (Bloomington: Indiana University Press, 1986), 36ff.

40. Ibid., 36.

41. Concerning the controversy surrounding the 1902 performance of *Parsifal* by the Concertgebouworkest in Amsterdam, see Frits Zwart, *Willem Mengelberg 1871–1951. Een biografie 1871–1920*, vol. 1 (Amsterdam: Prometheus, 1999), 104ff. Mahler, in contrast, experimented with the increased possibilities of technical reproduction in his time. In 1905 he "recorded" four of his compositions on piano rolls, which permitted exact, "authentic" mechanical reproductions of performances of his own works on the piano for an audience that could not experience such performances live (see Grange, *Mahler*, 265ff.).

Chapter 3

CONDUCTING MUSIC, CONDUCTING WAR
Nazi Germany as an Acoustic Experience

Frank Trommler

I

In his novel *Doctor Faustus,* Thomas Mann confronts the reader with haunting scenes of terror and despair as the demise of the incurably ill composer Adrian Leverkühn's is increasingly tied to Germany's demise in the self-inflicted catastrophe of World War II. These scenes—based on the quiet life of Leverkühn as he is composing at a remote farm in upper Bavaria, whose owner has the ominous name Schweigestill (total silence)—conjure a soundscape in which music and destruction intermingle in a momentous way. "The terror of the almost daily air raids on our nicely encircled Fortress Europe increases to dimensions beyond conceiving," Serenus Zeitblom, the narrator, laments.

> What good does it do that many of these monsters, raining destruction with ever growing explosive power, fall victim to our heroic defenses? Thousands of them darken the skies of this brashly united continent, and more and more of our cities collapse in ruin. Leipzig, which plays such a significant role in Leverkühn's evolution, in the tragedy of his life, has recently borne the full impact: Its famous publishing district is, I sadly hear, only a heap of rubble ...[1]

Delineating Germany as this shrinking territory over which thousands of bombers release their explosives day after day, Zeitblom interjects extensive chapters about Leverkühn's premier compositions that become a direct reflection of Germany's catastrophe, even though they had been created many years before the war. These chapters culminate in the description of *Apocalypsis cum figuris* and *Dr. Fausti Weheklag* as pieces of music in the 12-tone mode in which the combination of aestheticism and barbarism

---

Notes for this chapter begin on page 75.

that characterizes Germany's descent finds its unforgettable expression. Unforgettable? After all, the power of apocalyptic sounds is evoked only with words. And yet Mann, with the help of Theodor W. Adorno, leads the reader into an experience of aesthetic abhorrence whose symbolic layers make the evocation of cacophony into a fascinating chart of *Untergangs-bewußtsein* (consciousness of doom). Being locked into the position of a listener, the reader develops a sense of acoustic understanding that reaches beyond Zeitblom's faint-hearted voice as chronicler and grasps the terror of the ongoing destruction as both aesthetic and material, defined by the musical structure as well as the inhuman conduct of war. In a precarious transfer into acoustic space, war reveals both its conditioned, almost pre-determined nature and the terrifying manipulation on the part of its creators. As the narrator conjures the never-ending, circulatory formation of dissonance in *Apocalypsis*, Hitler's war, which cannot be comprehended in its myriad of horrid details, becomes accessible as an event. In one of the more unnerving passages, Zeitblom speaks of Leverkühn's

> extraordinarily frequent use of the sliding tone, at least in this work, in the *Apocalypse*, whose images of terror certainly supply the most enticing and, at the same, legitimate reasons for employing this wild device. In the passage where the four voices from the altar order the four avenging angels to be let loose to slay horses and riders, emperor and pope, and a third part of mankind, trombone glissandi represent the theme—and the devastating slide across the instrument's seven positions is used to terrifying effect! The howl as a theme—how ghastly! And what acoustic panic flows from the repeated instrumentation for timpani glissandi, a musical or sound effect achieved here by adjusting the pedal mechanism of the timpani to various pitches even as the hands are performing the drum roll. The effect is extremely eerie. But the most bone-chilling sound is the application of the glissando to the human voice (which as the first object of tonal ordering had, after all, been liberated from its primal howl across a range of pitches), the return, that is, to a primal stage, as it is horrifyingly reproduced by the chorus of the *Apocalypse* when it assumes the role of screaming humanity upon the opening of the seventh seal, when the sun grows black, the moon is turned to blood, and all ships founder.[2]

Unfolding the nasty glissando as an acoustic web of destruction is a powerful device indeed, and Mann gives the reader every reason to believe that when the war is over and Zeitblom indicates for the last time that Germany is now to pay for its pact with the devil, peace means, above all, silence. Obviously, silence does not mean the end of suffering. Yet Germany's self-inflicted fall from grace, reflected in the lamentation of Dr. Fausti Weheklag, whose emotions are stirred by the untimely death of Leverkühn's nephew, is sealed by the denouement of meaningful sound. The analogy between Leverkühn's and Germany's pact with the devil for the sake of a heroic breakthrough hits the ground of reality, and this ground is devoid of music.

Much has been said critically about the validity of this analogy, but it is, to use the obvious pun, sound in its acoustic aspects. The notion that music represents, most poignantly, Germany's fateful course between aesthetic abstraction and barbarism, laid out by Mann in his lecture "Deutschland und die Deutschen" a few weeks after the end of the European war in 1945, is confirmed by the acoustic scenario that makes *Doctor Faustus* an astonishingly apt reflection of the enormous role that the Nazis attributed to music. What counts in this analogy is not the type of music—Leverkühn's 12-tone compositions would undoubtedly have been labeled degenerate *(entartete Musik)* and banned—but rather the symbolic weight of music, of producing and reproducing music as part of the national self-understanding.

The fact that *Doctor Faustus*, Mann's last major novel, written between 1943 and 1947, can be read as both an introduction into the pernicious force of German "musicality of soul" and its ultimate conclusion. Mann, never shy in confessing his own allegiance to the musicality of soul that became, according to his speeches and writings, part of the German predicament, at least since Richard Wagner, went to great lengths in documenting the validity of this notion in all phases of his life. His confession at the end of the war that there were not two Germanys, a bad and a good one, but rather one Germany, whose best traits turned into its worst ones due to the devil's cunning *(Teufelslist)*,[3] was meant to include himself as a representative of this ominous national character. Projecting no closure to this entanglement, he distances himself in *Doctor Faustus*, however, by making it discernible in Leverkühn's provocative sound inventions. In this way, what seems to be an outgrowth of Germany's descent into barbarism becomes, at the same time, a means to overcome it. Listening to Leverkühn, so to speak, entails in its alienating aspects a realization of what the symbol of the pact with the devil means. It also documents the pernicious flaws in music when it seeks sublimity, transcendence, disengagement from the ordinary world—when the aesthetic triumphs over the merely human.

II

A look at the extensive organization of musical life under National Socialism in its bureaucratic rigor, political pettiness, and plain exploitation of opportunism seems to lead far away from any manifestation of the purported German musicality of soul. Recent studies have left no official document unturned in order to present a clear overview of the regime's immense effort in the years after 1933 to place the production and reception of music under its control, to which the exclusion of Jews added a terrifying chapter.[4] Although the state had always played a prominent role as a patron of music, the Nazi regime lost no time establishing administrative institutions—the Reichskulturkammer, the Reichsmusikkammer, and thousands of local organizations—which were designed to integrate German music and musicians into its national mission. Indeed, sound carried this mission further than any other mode of expression. While the efforts to inculcate the visual sphere with print media, newspapers, paintings, theatrical events, and film were substantial, musical activities enjoyed a measurably high rate of participation, from singing in the Hitler Youth and music education classes in schools, to performing in parades and attending innumerable musical events, and, above all, to listening to the radio. Due to the high unemployment rate among musicians during the economic depression of the early 1930s, the state had little problem enrolling almost everyone in its activities, unless musicians were excluded on racial grounds. It also found that most of the famous musicians, singers, and composers were prepared to collaborate—as detailed in the particularly long and disconcerting chapters in Prieberg's and Kater's well-documented studies.

When Joseph Goebbels reviewed the Third Reich's organizational achievements in a speech at the *Reichsmusiktage* in Düsseldorf in 1938— which also featured the exhibition "Entartete Musik" –he reveled in the complete success of *Gleichschaltung* (coordination) in the area of music.[5] Well-known composers eagerly submitted new pieces for performances: Richard Strauss composed and conducted a musical introduction to Goebbels's address, while Furtwängler stayed away and Bela Bartok protested the absence of his work from the "Entartete Musik" exhibit.[6] The investment in music, considered since the nineteenth century to be the most distinguished German contribution to world culture, was to yield respectability for the Nazis both inside Germany, where Hitler's close connection to the Wagner circle in Bayreuth allowed him to ingratiate himself into certain segments of the bourgeoisie, and in other countries, where admiration of the three "German Bs" (Bach, Beethoven, Brahms) and Wagner represented a crucial part of a higher cultural identity.

Beethoven and, even more abundantly, Wagner were made part of innumerable official events; their reinterpretation as creators of the acoustic *völkisch* community was, of course, anchored in arguments that Wagner himself had developed. It also inspired—and bored—those audiences that previously had little contact with classical music before 1933 and secured a respectable percentage of radio broadcasts. This music stirred emotions of the "heroic" and the "Faustian," which were needed for stylizing Hitler as the leader and the German *Volk* as the carrier's of a historic mission, a mission that seemed to need no explanation as long as the voluminous orchestral sound or imposing fanfares conveyed a feeling of self-importance. In addition to the "heroic" Third and Fifth Symphonies, Beethoven's *Weihe des Hauses,* and *Coriolan* and *Egmont* Overtures were in particularly heavy demand. Even *Fidelio*, the opera of faithfulness and liberation, was pressed into service with a festive performance in Vienna after the invasion of Austria. Whereas Beethoven was reserved for more celebratory and commemorative rituals,[7] Wagner, similarly segmented and edited, was more popular and reached broader audiences. His music accompanied newsreels and propaganda films, and his operas were performed at special occasions such as Nazi Party conventions. The funeral march *Götterdämmerung* was heard more and more often on the radio as the war progressed and as funerals of "heroes" were used to demonstrate the unshakable strength of the national community, the *Volksgemeinschaft*.[8]

This employment of classical music combined official representation with emotional guidance, not unlike the use of music in movies. The preponderance of Wagner was indeed not unrelated to his enormous influence on movie music. This use had been inspired by Wagner's arousal of feelings in narrative sequences, first, when orchestras accompanied silent films, then when the soundtrack was integrated into the movie. But this was only one part of the soundscape in Nazi Germany. The other originated in the extensive organization and collectivization of musical practice everywhere—at home and in the street, as well as at school and in the workplace. The ubiquity of marches, Hitler Youth songs, *Volkslieder* and *Volksmusik* (folk songs and music), and, above all, the "Horst-Wessel-Lied" has been documented. This song's psychological impact on the postwar generation illustrates the intensity of the experience.[9] Nowhere were the emotional aftereffects of the Third Reich easier to grasp—and more often evoked—than in the acoustic realm, either by singing songs or by associating certain musical pieces with war events. Some pieces, such as Franz Liszt's *Les Préludes*, during the war was followed by the announcement, "Das Oberkommando der Wehrmacht gibt bekannt ..." (The supreme command of the armed forces announces ...), were more or less banned from public performance after the war.

In his astounding novel about the soundscape of the Third Reich and its manipulation, *Flughunde* (The Karnau Tapes), the German author Marcel Beyer has re-created scenes of everyday life through their acoustic presence. For the title character Karnau, a technical savant who makes sure that the speeches at Nazi rallies will be intelligible even in large arenas, everything is encoded in sound—a fascinating reflection of the intensity with which the Nazi leadership tried to control the acoustic public sphere. In his sober pursuit of the everyday sounds of life during this period, Karnau is the complete opposite of Mann's eccentric composer of the German apocalypse. What Karnau records with his inner ear is devoid of artfulness but no less indicative of the weight of music in the life of Germans. Only the full description of a grim idyll of a summer evening in some German town conveys the echoes of what once was called Romantic but has now become part of National Socialist reality:

> The air is exceptionally warm tonight. The strains of a brass band are wafted from far away, so it seems, by a gentle breeze. The sound fluctuates, reverberating from distant streets. The music grows louder. With a sudden explosion of noise, the band merges from a side street followed by a detachment of Brownshirts

marching in step. They, in turn, are followed by a group in regional costume and some civilians who have joined the procession *en route*. Many windows are open, and the din invades the rooms behind the fluttering curtains. Across the way, curious residents are already leaning on their window sills and gazing down into the street. Many wave. The window of one darkened room is closed and the curtain drawn as if by some ghostly hand. The windowpane at my back begins to vibrate. The night air resounds to the blare of trumpets and the rattle of snare drums. They're passing the house now. The color bearer's flag, propelled by a headwind, slaps him in the face.

The marchers break into a folk song, and the local inhabitants, their cheeks soon hot and flushed, loudly join in the first verse. An entire family sings along, clustered together in a small kitchen window. Clearly visible in their open mouths are tongues, teeth, even threads of saliva. Down below them, noisy expulsions of breath mingle, elbows collide, men jostle one another and break step, their eyelids beaded with sweat in the torchlight. Now they're out of sight. The music fades, the spectators retire into their living rooms. No sound save the agitated twittering of a bird roused from sleep as it flies across the street. A last, smoldering cigarette butt glows in the night-dark roadway.[10]

This is indeed a National Socialist idyll, if there ever was one. Beyer plays skillfully with the romantic notion of serenading on a warm summer evening; interjects it with the disturbing marching, drumming, and collective singing, including the appalling close-up of the family's open mouths; and sends the reader off without further explanation—an apt description of a soundscape that is not yet fully dominated by the radio, as it would later become during the war years. As a result of enormous organizational efforts to cover every square kilometer with musical activity, many Germans in the first six years of the Third Reich gravitated to music as a means to express and experience the new communal mood. While the Nazi Party hardly succeeded in its efforts to create a new, *völkisch* music, the message of music's crucial role for national identity resonated everywhere. To be sure, Mann's insistence that German music sought sublimity, transcendence, and disengagement from the ordinary world did not exactly converge with the rather personal and uncouth, yet sensuous, pursuit of acoustic entertainment in those years. But his assertion that music was the quintessential experience in this culture was not far from reality. What the Nazis would build upon the established German music culture, however, would change with the war and with the irreversible use of radio as the main producer of the national soundscape.

III

For historians of everyday life during wartime, one of the most fascinating, yet still underexplored, differences between the two world wars lies in the fact that the latter was omnipresent in people's existence through its acoustic reproduction, while contemporaries of World War I experienced the war mainly through images, newsreels, and reports from those who returned from the front; by reading; and through the impoverishment of life at home. Beginning in 1939, radio broadcasts brought the front in direct contact with everyday pursuits, and the concept of "front," quite different from the mainly geographical one in the earlier war, took on a tangible quality, accessible with the turn of the radio switch. This front was not necessarily the one at which soldiers fought and died; it extended into a larger space whose limits were marked by the conditions of broadcasting and the strength of radio waves (which were themselves often embattled by means of enemy sabotage).

Speaking of the *reproduction* of the war has its legitimacy if one analyzes the work of the propaganda units in all areas of engagement with the enemy, something that was a perennial bone of contention between Goebbels's Propaganda Ministry and the Oberkommando der Wehrmacht.[11] The full extent of the acoustic manipulation, however, is encapsulated in a shorter version of the term: the acoustic *production* of the war. The six years of radio practice during which Goebbels consolidated his political power base were only a platform for an unprecedented musical, not just acoustic, staging of the war. In this transition, the symbolic dimension of music for national identity that the Nazis had expanded even beyond the use of Wagner was fully drafted into military service.

Specific musical pieces—mostly fanfares with orchestral accompaniment, but also marches, choral compositions, and edited excerpts of orchestral work—assumed a signaling function for the population and became *Erkennungsmusik*, like leitmotivs in a Wagner opera. Liszt's *Les Préludes*, already mentioned, identified the Russland-Feldzug with awesome and majestic brushes as a world historical event.[12] It was preceded, at least in the earlier phase of that campaign, by the "Russlandfanfare"[13] and became an acoustic signal for the daily report of the supreme command of the Wehrmacht. It was used in radio and newsreels as were other fanfare pieces, clearly indicating the advances of specific army, air force, and naval units. Major military campaigns were accompanied by varying *Erkennungsmusik*, "upon the assumption that a new marching song or new fanfare had been commissioned in time."[14] Fanfares were composed for special reports *(Sondermeldungen)*, among them an *Englandfanfare* and a *Frankreichfanfare*,[15] aside from songs that featured the new campaigns and consisted of simple texts and melodies. In the first days of the war against the Soviet Union, the song "Von Finnland bis zum Schwarzen Meer" (From Finland to the Black Sea) conjured the geographic expanse of the new operation.[16] One of the most frequently commissioned composers of fanfares was Herbert Windt, a close collaborator of Leni Riefenstahl who had composed the music for her films *Triumph of the Will* and *Olympia*. Windt's quintessential operatic presentation of the war's *Blitzkrieg* phase was produced by intermingling the high-flying, wildly galloping music of

Wagner's *Walkürenritt*, from *Die Walküre*, with the nerve-racking sounds of Stuka bombers attacking targets in Crete (in 1942) and other places. It was used in several newsreels to great effect. Indeed, it has become a classic of fascist media aesthetics, reenacted in 1979 by Francis Ford Coppola in his film epic about the Vietnam War, *Apocalypse Now*, when a swarm of American helicopters attack Vietnamese ground positions.

Yet while most newsreels have been preserved, little radio material has survived.[17] The full extent and impact of *Erkennungsmusik* is therefore hard to ascertain. Goebbels's manipulation of music as a crucial factor in staging the war for the German population is best documented through his direct interference in the production of the newsreels *(Deutsche Wochen-schau)* wherein he took great pains to enhance the impact of war images and commentary with emotionally gripping music.[18] In those instances when the film material was lacking drama or actuality, he compensated with infatuating music.

These kinds of multimedia productions *(Inszenierungen)* had their high point in the first phase of the war when German attacks were generally victorious. With most of the population having only grudgingly accepted the burden of fighting yet another war in 1939, the multimedia productions created an atmosphere of tension and expectation in which the voices of political and military leaders masked, not without success, the frivolity of this attack against humanity and the engagement with barbarism. Music was a crucial ingredient, but so was the *Inszenierung* of the acoustic technology itself. When Reich Marshall Hermann Göring delivered the official address at the Thanksgiving rally *(Erntedanktag)* in 1942, his speech was to be heard not only in Germany but everywhere in occupied Europe. Broadcast from a multitude of radio stations under German command, from Paris to the Ukraine, from Norway to Greece, the announcement evoked the experience of spatial extension—and the power of the new Reich—more than any of Göring's words.[19]

A truly popular acoustic event of a similar magnitude, which provided an experience of national community across the conquered space of Europe through music rather than politics, was the much celebrated *Wunschkon-zert*. Based on musical requests from and—at least in the beginning—for soldiers at the front, in combination with solicitations for the *Winterhilfs-werk* (Winter relief fund) the concert gave listeners a feeling for the enormous territory in which Germans were operating, projecting the image of the German family at home in close contact with their men in France, Crete, or Russia.[20] As a radio event, this concert exemplified the mode in which the staging of the war was to be complemented by the staging of the nation as a community of listeners or participants. Much thought was given to the ways in which the spontaneous participation of the listeners was demonstrated. It was all the more significant that the *Wunschkonzert* was discontinued after 1942. The fateful turn of the war into a gigantic *Rückzug* (retreat) did not encourage the composition of new fanfares. Still, the *Krimfanfare* of 1944, composed by Herms Niel as a *Durchhaltefanfare*, a fanfare of perseverance, for the German troops that had been surrounded on the Crimea peninsula by Soviet troops since the fall of 1943, documents the importance of music as an instrument of war politics for both the men on the front and the population at home.[21]

The technique of creating national cohesiveness through radio broadcasts was, of course, not unique to Germany.[22] As a comparison with the BBC in London shows, similar strategies for using music in conjunction with scripted programming were developed, whereby similar problems emerged, both in the allocation of popular and classical music and in the losing battle against American popular music.[23] Unique to Germany, however, was the amount of official attention paid to the promotion of the war's progress through music. Goebbels, Rosenberg, and Göring—and at times even Hitler—interfered intensively in the selection of the appropriate pieces. Goebbels, who was not particularly fond of classical music, increased the share of popular tunes substantially as the war became more and more problematic. As in earlier years, when Nazi zealots had tried to impose a completely revamped *völkisch* music on the population, Goebbels promoted flexibility. Concerned about overcharging weary people with the operatic *Inszenierung*, he made sure, as the leadership generally did in the first three years of the war, that the middle and working classes found enough entertainment. Light music had to distract the population and prepare listeners for moments of "serious" propaganda.[24] Plans envisioned a Beethoven station for classical music, a Johann Strauss station for popular music and entertainment, and a Goethe station for literature, political information, and propaganda, but Goebbels found the latter suggestion unacceptable. In 1941 three programs were instituted: a "Reichsprogramm," an entertainment program, and a "serious" (classical) music program, in which the Deutschlandsender was to broadcast orchestral, operatic, and chamber music in the evening.[25]

Looking at the program of the Grossdeutscher Rundfunk in honor of Hitler's birthday on 20 April, 1940, one would think that the spoken word had finally abdicated as official medium of celebration in favor of music. Of twenty-three program events, seventeen consisted of music, whereas only five were devoted to news and reports from the front. The music began at 5:30 A.M. by the SA Standarte Feldherrnhalle, awakened people at 6:00 A.M. with a chorus from Wagner's *Meistersinger*, and included festive Bach cantatas, children's choirs, the Musikkorps der *SS-Leibstandarte Adolf Hitler*, and a concert of the Berlin Philharmonic conducted by Wilhelm Furtwängler in the evening.[26]

Enough said about the centrality of music for the Nazi's conduct of war. Radio intensified the role of music as it amplified both its capacities for experiencing space and for slowing down or suppressing time, pulling its listeners away from the realization that the historical clock was ticking, especially against the Third Reich. Music aided in the manipulation of space and time. Whether or not this was based on the musicality of soul, as Mann suggested with regard to the Germans, could be the topic of another discussion. In any case, for Mann and his contemporaries, the Nazi's use of music seemed an outgrowth of the paramount national emphasis on music as a quintessential German creation. Nietzsche's later criticism that Wagner knew only how to exploit a fair talent for music in grandiose theatricality might contain a clue to answering the question about the fate of music in Nazi Germany.

Once the war turned against the Germans, Goebbels, Göring, and other leaders resorted to music that enhanced the feeling of *Schicksalhaftigkeit*, the awareness of being in a fateful encounter with history. Bruckner's symphonies and especially Beethoven's Third and Fifth symphonies were chosen, often in excerpts, to evoke the somber mood of greatness and loss without generating questions as to what had actually happened and why. But Beethoven was also used by those who did ask questions and began to mourn the terrible senselessness of the sacrifices made. Furtwängler's especially moving performances with the Berlin Philharmonic in the last years of the war were claimed by both sides as expressing support for their views.[27] When Stalingrad fell to the Russian troops in early 1943, Hitler, Goebbels, and Göring decided that this time the sacrifice had to be recognized and elevated as a heroic model.

> Goebbels did his utmost to give meaning to the great loss. His campaign reached an emotional intensity that exceeded even the victory celebrations of the summer and fall of 1941. The manner in which he relayed the news that Stalingrad had fallen was very effective. The radio broadcast of the Special Announcement opened with solemn marches, followed by drum rolls and three stanzas of one of the saddest German war songs, "Ich hatt' einen Kamera-den." Then came the announcement of the fall of Stalingrad, followed by the playing of the German, Italian, and Croat national anthems. Three minutes of silence were followed by Beethoven's Fifth Symphony, and a three-day period of mourning was ordered. The entire schedule of programs was changed for several days to fit the Stalingrad propaganda line.[28]

Hitler, aware that Stalingrad spelled disaster for Germans,[29] several months later forbade any public mention of Stalingrad. In doing so, he also destroyed the belief that official mourning of the dead was meant to be what it was. Music itself was drawn into the denouement of the Nazi conduct of war. Mann has Leverkühn retract the "Ode to Joy" from Beethoven's Ninth Symphony in his lamentation of *Dr. Fausti Weheklag*. "To the mystic horror of those who can hear it," Zeitblom reports, "what is realized there is a … gigantic *lamento* (lasting approximately an hour and a quarter) … properly speaking, undynamic, lacking development and without drama."[30] Leverkühn's cantata about Faustus does not end without a glimmer of hope for the future fate of art, yet the silence that Zeitblom conjures at the end of the novel does not carry much promise.[31]

Silence—the enormous weight of silence—had already been waiting in the cracks and niches of the acoustic mobilization of Germans under the Nazi regime.[32]

Scholars have shown that musical life in Germany after 1945 did not indicate much of a denouement. Other than Liszt and Wagner, denazification was cursory at best, nonexistent at worst.[33] Yet, fifty years later, the *New York Times* devoted broad space to the question of whether "serious" music ever recovered from the tremendous losses it suffered from the conduct on both sides of the war. "Music is still deeply haunted by World War II, a season of remembrance in Europe shows," Alex Ross wrote in a survey of the great composers, conductors, and musicians of this period. He added: "It will never be as it was."[34]

Notes

1. Thomas Mann, *Doctor Faustus: The Life of the German Composer Adrian Leverkühn As Told by a Friend*, trans. John E. Woods (New York: Vintage, 1997), 267.
2. Ibid., 393–94.
3. Thomas Mann, "Deutschland und die Deutschen," in Thomas Mann, *Essays*, vol. 5, ed. Hermann Kurzke and Stephan Stachorski (Frankfurt am Main: Fischer, 1996), 265.
4. See especially Joseph Wulf, *Presse und Funk im Dritten Reich: Eine Dokumentation* (Gütersloh: Mohn, 1964); Fred K. Prieberg, *Musik im NS-Staat* (Frankfurt am Main: Fischer Taschenbuch, 1982); Hanns-Werner Heister and Hans-Günter Klein, ed., *Musik und Musikpolitik im faschistischen Deutschland* (Frankfurt am Main: Fischer Taschenbuch, 1984); Michael Meyer, *The Politics of Music in the Third Reich* (New York: Lang, 1991); Michael H. Kater, *The Twisted Muse: Musicians and Their Music in the Third Reich* (New York: Oxford University Press, 1997); Pamela M. Potter, *Most German of the Arts: Musicology and Society from the Weimar Republic to the End of Hitler's Reich* (New Haven: Yale University Press, 1998).
5. Meyer, *The Politics of Music*, 123.
6. Ibid., 123–24, 305.
7. See David B. Dennis, *Beethoven in German Politics, 1870–1989* (New Haven: Yale University Press, 1996).
8. Hanns-Werner Heister and Jochem Wolff, "Macht und Schicksal: Klassik, Fanfaren, höhere Durchhaltemusik," in *Musik und Musikpolitik*, ed. Heister and Klein, 115–25, here 118.
9. Johannes Hodek, "'Sie wissen, wenn man Heroin nimmt ...' Von Sangeslust und Gewalt in Naziliedern," in *Musik und Musikpolitik*, ed. Heister and Klein, 19–36.
10. Marcel Beyer, *The Karnau Tapes*, trans. John Brownjohn (New York, San Diego, and London: Harcourt Brace, 1997), 67–68.
11. See the standard work by Ansgar Diller, *Rundfunkpolitik im Dritten Reich* (Munich: Deutscher Taschenbuch Verlag, 1980); Horst Bergmeier and Rainer Lotz, *Hitler's Airwaves: The Inside Story of Nazi Radio Broadcasting* (New Haven: Yale University Press, 1997).
12. Heister and Wolff, "Macht und Schicksal," 122–23.
13. Deutsches Rundfunkarchiv, Frankfurt am Main, tape no. 60 U 5.
14. Heister and Wolff, "Macht und Schicksal," 122.
15. Deutsches Rundfunkarchiv, Frankfurt am Main, tape no. 60 U 5.

16. An overview in Hans-Günter Martens, "Schau nur gradeaus! Schlager aus schlimmer Zeit." Part 1. Manuscript of the broadcast on Norddeutscher Rundfunk, 19 November 1980, in NDR archive, Hamburg.

17. See the scarce holdings of the Deutsches Rundfunkarchiv in Frankfurt am Main.

18. Felix Moeller, *Der Filmminister: Goebbels und der Film im Dritten Reich* (Berlin: Henschel, 1998), 377.

19. Diller, *Rundfunkpolitik*, 333.

20. Inge Marssolek and Adelheid von Saldern, eds., *Zuhören und Gehörtwerden I: Radio im Nationalsozialismus. Zwischen Lenkung und Ablenkung* (Tübingen: edition discord, 1998), 224–39.

21. Deutsches Rundfunkarchiv, tape no. 60 U 5.

22. For Britain, see David Cardiff and Paddy Scannell, "Broadcasting and National Unity," in *Impacts and Influences: Essays on Media Power in the Twentieth Century*, ed. James Curran, Anthony Smith, and Pauline Wingate (London and New York: Methuen, 1987), 157–73.

23. Konrad Dussel, "Kulturkonzepte im Konflikt: Britische, deutsche und schweizerische Hörfunkprogramme während des Zweiten Weltkrieges," *Vierteljahrshefte für Zeitgeschichte* 49 (2001): 441–63.

24. Helmut Heiber, *Joseph Goebbels* (Munich: Deutscher Taschenbuch Verlag, 1965), 162.

25. Willi A. Boelcke, ed., *Wollt Ihr den totalen Krieg? Die geheimen Goebbels-Konferenzen 1939–1943* (Munich: Deutscher Taschenbuch Verlag, 1969), 226.

26. Diller, *Rundfunkpolitik*, 347.

27. About Furtwängler's ambiguous position toward the Nazi leadership, see Fred K. Prieberg, *Kraftprobe: Wilhelm Furtwängler im Dritten Reich* (Wiesbaden: Brockhaus, 1986); and Kater, *The Twisted Muse*, 199–202 and passim.

28. Jay W. Baird, "The Myth of Stalingrad," *Journal of Contemporary History* 4 (1969): 187–204, here 198.

29. Ibid., 203.

30. Mann, *Doctor Faustus*, 511.

31. Susan von Rohr Scaff, "Unending Apocalypse: The Crisis of Musical Narrative in Mann's *Doctor Faustus*," *Germanic Review* 65 (1990): 30–39.

32. Claudia Schmölders, "Die Stimme des Bösen: Zur Klanggestalt des Dritten Reiches," *Merkur* 51 (1997): 681–93.

33. See Meyer, *The Politics of Music*; Potter, *Most German of the Arts*; and Kater, *The Twisted Muse*.

34. Alex Ross, "In Music, Though, There Were No Victories," *New York Times*, 20 August 1995, H 25, H 31.

Part II

DISSONANT VISIONS

Chapter 4

THE POLITICS AND SOUNDS OF
EVERYDAY LIFE IN *KUHLE WAMPE*

Nora M. Alter

A script has rarely been presented in Germany that did not show "people in the theatre," or socially colored figures who are living out their "fate," and instead one in which the filmic sequence is also a time sequence, a cross-section of daily life, one which becomes the existence of a Sunday, one which is formed from the celluloid and from the sound machine. Here we have a "dramalot"—"one unemployed person less"—which presents an unequaled "picture of life" both optically and acoustically. The everyday story of an entire class is constructed—a class who, despite its protection under constitution, and its natural human dignity, barely manages to exist in today's epoch.... A moment of solidarity comes through in this class, because the people, due to their shared existence, must rely on one another. [The moment] is visually and aurally perceptible via the chorus of the solidarity in sports, which gives this "weekend" film plentitude and pith.[1]

Started in 1931 and finally released in May 1932 after extensive censorship battles,[2] Bertolt Brecht and Slatan Dudow's *Kuhle Wampe oder wem gehört die Welt?* followed closely on the heels of G. W. Pabst's commercially successful *The Threepenny Opera* (1931). The latter, with the removal of the playwright Brecht from the production process and the infamous lawsuit that followed, represented for Brecht many of the problems and perils inherent in filmmaking. By contrast, *Kuhle Wampe* was, from the first, conceived and executed as a fully collaborative anticapitalistic project—one that sought to demonstrate the continued revolutionary potential of the filmic medium in the wake of Soviet socialist realism.[3] Its production received considerable coverage in the press before its completion and release, due not only to Brecht's status generally, but also to the controversy surrounding Pabst's unauthorized rendition of *The Threepenny Opera*. Indeed, as the above

---

Notes for this chapter begin on page 87.

quotation from a 1931 newspaper article reporting on *Kuhle Wampe* already indicates, the production process was carefully followed in the press, creating an atmosphere of anticipation and excitement around the new film. This suspense was only enhanced by the dramatic decision of the censor to hold back the film's release, and by the ensuing debate in the press. But just exactly what was it that was anticipated? And how was *Kuhle Wampe* supposed to be remarkable and different? The early reception of this film, together with an analysis of Brecht's ongoing exploration of the possibilities of the medium, casts light on some as yet undiscussed aspects of *Kuhle Wampe*, supporting my premise that it is inadequate to read Brecht's theory of film solely through the lens of his theatrical practice. The aim of this essay will be to show how these aspects—especially the blurring of the boundaries between fiction and nonfiction, the function of sound, and the problematization of identification—question the conventional reception of Brecht within film circles in the late twentieth century, and how they prompt a reevaluation of the spectator's engagement with the documentary film genre.

Kuhle Wampe, as much as Brecht's other work in film, has proven to be especially problematic for critics and theorists alike. The formal innovations Brecht experimented with in this medium have generally been dismissed as simplistic and ineffective. James Pettifer, for example, in a 1974 article published in *Screen*, writes that "in the great majority of the scenes in *Kuhle Wampe* the music has little or no distance from the text and in effect only attempts simple empathetic emotional effects."[4] Similarly, Martin Walsh notes, in his 1981 *The Brechtian Aspect of Radical Cinema*, that stylistically "the film appears to be fairly conventional, having none of the innovatory spirit that characterized the formal aspects of Brecht's stage work."[5] Even Fredric Jameson, in his recent monograph, *Brecht and Method*, sums up *Kuhle Wampe* in one sentence: "[S]plendid achievement as *Kuhle Wampe* may be, Brecht's Hollywood thoughts and projects do not particularly suggest an imagination receptive to the possibilities of film in quite the same way as with his later cinematographic would-be disciples (like Godard, for example)."[6] All of these comments are symptomatic of a type of Brecht film criticism that seeks to find a direct parallel between his theories of theatrical production and those of filmic production. Yet this interpretive strategy is not only inherently misguided, but also reveals a fundamental misunderstanding of Brecht who, all evidence seems to indicate, was keenly aware of the material (and historical) specificity of each medium. Here I agree with Jameson's observation that followers of Brecht have been so successful in adapting his theatrical theories to film that one judges Brecht's own cinematic production of the early 1930s through film of the 1960s. At the same time, however, theatre has not developed significantly since the 1930s, nor has there been a theorist of theatre anywhere near the caliber of Brecht from the second half of the twentieth century, to the present, which explains his continued primacy and relevance in this medium. The most trenchant critic of Brecht's film theory and practice remains Stephen Heath, who, ironically enough (given my claims about the wrong-headedness of reading Brecht's films through the theoretical lens of his theatrical productions), productively locates it in Brecht's writings on photography.[7] Heath, however, overlooks one fundamental difference between film and photographs: the sound track.

As already demonstrated, *Kuhle Wampe* was eagerly anticipated on several levels. The first and perhaps most obvious was its topic: the Berlin working class. Related to this was the expectation that the film was to be a collaborative production involving a number of acclaimed left-wing intellectuals and cultural workers: the writer Ernst Ottwalt, the musical composer Hanns Eisler, and the Bulgarian film director Dudow. Ottwalt had just published *Denn sie wissen, was sie tun* (For They Know What They Do), a novel that sharply critiqued capitalism, and Dudow had recently completed a documentary film, *Wie der Berliner Arbeiter wohnt* (How the Berlin Worker Lives), on the conditions of workers in Berlin. Ottwalt's novel, with its employment of an innovative antirealist technique that relied on a series of episodes incorporating much documentary material, and its repeated interruption of the narrative flow with an external commentary, is particularly relevant in the context of a discussion of *Kuhle Wampe*.[8] Brecht and Dudow's film also consists of independent parts with considerable documentary material. But rather than external commentary, it is music that interrupts the narrative flow of the film. Indeed, it is music, together with a number of documentary shots, that organizes the episodes of *Kuhle Wampe* and structures the viewer's relation of identification or distance.

Which brings me to another feature of *Kuhle Wampe*, one that most impressed contemporary critics: the documentary nature of the film—its montage of fact and fiction. Brecht and Dudow, making the film after the advent of Soviet socialist realism (which had discredited filmic productions relying entirely on montage), shot more than half of the film outside the studio. At the time, this was considered particularly remarkable. All previous attempts to represent the working class in feature films, such as Piel Jutzi's 1929 *Mother Krause's Journey to Happiness*, had been produced within the artificial confines of the studio world. Furthermore, not only did *Kuhle Wampe* feature actual footage of the workers' living quarters in Wedding, the wooded camping park of Kuhle Wampe, and the nearby Müggelsee lake, but also most of its actors were amateurs.[9] The participation of four thousand workers, in their capacity as members of sports clubs, was also unprecedented in film history. The final scene, which was shot in a fully operative Berlin streetcar, struck many early commentators as well, since it featured a spontaneity that no studio could ever hope to reproduce.[10] In short, the use of documentary material was seen to be one of the most novel features of *Kuhle Wampe*, especially to the extent that the material was thought to enable the audience to see their lives as they really were, with a minimum amount of distortion and artificial creation in the studios.[11] As yet another astute critic observed in reference to the censorship: "And herein lies the true motive behind the ban: Germany can only be photographed within the fences of New Babelsberg."[12]

Much of the initial appeal of *Kuhle Wampe* for its contemporary audiences was in that mixture of fact and fiction. But what purpose was served by such hybridity? And why did it not suffice to make either a fully documentary film or a purely fictional studio product? Not surprisingly, the reasons for this are complex. On the most obvious level, they probably have to do with Brecht's recent clashes with the studio system, which, as the *The Threepenny* lawsuit made bitterly clear, privileged the rights of the studio over those of the author. From this perspective, one can see why making a film outside of the studio system would be desirable. But there were also a number of theoretical motives underlying this hybridity. Brecht was very much aware of the different characteristics of theatre and film media, and was very careful not to confuse the two. *Kuhle Wampe* exemplifies this separation, for nothing could be further from a theatrical stage production than a film shot largely outside the studio. In sharp contrast to studio production, with its artificial sets and enclosures, the extensive shots of nature, architecture included in the cityscape, the four thousand athletes, and the rowing on the Müggelsee would all be virtually impossible to put on a stage. Brecht thus makes a very clear and sharp break with the medium of theatre. Indeed, he uses film precisely and specifically to do what theatre cannot, namely, to represent everyday life and, through shots of large crowds, a mobilized collectivity. Moreover, with *Kuhle Wampe* Brecht also sought to find a way of checking what he considered the most problematic features of film: its static nature and its too often characteristic lack of interaction between spectator and representation.[13] The challenge was to make a film that would produce an active spectator. This, he thought, could be accomplished through the *Verfremdungseffekt*, or alienation effect, that would break the audience's identification.[14] Yet for Brecht, the *Verfremdungseffekt* existed in tandem with identification.[15] As he once noted about Chinese theatre (which was to have a great influence on him): "The alienation effect intervenes not in the form of an absence of emotion, but in the form of emotions which need not correspond to those of the character portrayed."[16] Working in the medium of film, Brecht thus tried to strike a compromise between identification and distanciation. He found the possibility of such a balance, I argue, by combining documentary footage with fictional narrative, which is in direct contrast to the more common assumption that, rather than on documentary footage, identification is based primarily on the illusion of realism.

What is therefore at issue is the status of realism, and the fact that Brecht, among others, was at that time deeply engaged in a debate with Georg Lukacs. A believer in realism, Brecht, unlike Lukacs, felt that realistic representation could no longer be based on a nineteenth-century model because society and ways of looking at things had greatly evolved.[17] "We must not abstract the one and only realism from certain given works," he writes in the mid-1930, "but shall make a lively use of all means, old and new, tried and untried, deriving from art and deriving from other sources, in order to put living reality in the hands of living people in such a way that it can be mastered.... We will not stick to unduly detailed literary models or force the artist to follow over-precise rules for telling a story."[18] Thus, a new form of realism might be located within cinematic practice. Indeed, the use of documentary footage in *Kuhle Wampe* created this type of "realistic effect," encouraging the audience to identify with the film and fulfilling Brecht's dictum that "one need never be frightened of putting bold and unaccustomed things before the proletariat, so long as they have to do with reality."[19] The inherent realism of documentary footage functioned to reassure the audience, presenting it with a familiar image and thereby heightening the impact of the alienating effects, such as the unusual soundtrack and the anti-narrative, episodic, and disorienting visual composition of images produced in the editing process.[20]

Kuhle Wampe thus encourages a new form of interaction, one based not on a passive consumption of images but on an active participation and construction of meaning. Here, once again, are Brecht's thoughts on Chinese theatre: "The spectator's empathy is not entirely rejected. The audience identifies itself with the actor as being an observer, and accordingly develops his attitude of observing or looking on."[21] As with Chinese theatre, the film viewer's response would dialectically alternate between identification and distanciation, and the contradiction between the two responses would culminate in the "awakening" of the audience. The filmmaker, according to Brecht, like "our best painters ... should deliver more than mere reflections. The object before them splits into two parts, one that is present and one that is to be created, a visible one and one that is yet to be made visible; something is there and something is behind it."[22] One particularly powerful example of this is the shot of the Brandenburg Gate, a symbol of Berlin, that opens *Kuhle Wampe*. Serving at the most immediate level to establish the location of the film, the shot also reminds the spectator that revolutionaries of 1848 and 1918, though now invisible, once met at the Gate. As such, it also functions as a galvanizing force for future revolutionary groups to become visible there again.

To sum up thus far, I have proposed that not only the subject matter but also the way that documentary footage functions alongside fictive studio footage in *Kuhle Wampe,* were revolutionary in the early 1930s. I want to go further, however, and suggest that *Kuhle Wampe* was also heralded as the left's first sound film. Indeed, it was precisely in the arrangement of the soundtrack that the film was truly avant-garde. According to its producers, the division of the film into four episodes was determined by sound, which, from all accounts, functioned to arrange the image, and not vice versa.

Given that sound films were very expensive and that it was difficult to get financial backing, Brecht and Dudow's film was a remarkable achievement from a commercial point of view. In fact, Prometheus, which produced *Kuhle Wampe*, had experienced severe financial problems since the advent of sound in 1927, and had not produced a single major release. Technologically, sound had not yet been mastered, as it would be in the following few years under the Nazis, and it still represented quite a challenge. As such, *Kuhle Wampe* is limited to single channels without much synthesis. Yet as the following review, written immediately upon *Kuhle Wampe*'s release, makes clear, "From an artistic-technical standpoint, 'Kuhle Wampe' is a positive attempt because it undertakes, out of all of the features and possibilities of a sound film, to create a sound picture, and the effect reached is that it is the first German sound film that seriously and substantially breaks away from 'filmed theater' or from superficial artistic tricks."[23] What is particularly interesting here is that this reviewer links the introduction and use of sound to the fact that the film is not shot in a studio—it is not "filmed theatre," and does not contain artificiality. Thus, sound is interpreted as a feature of realism, an indicator of external reality.

In *Kuhle Wampe*, the soundtrack operates on three distinct recorded registers: the music (both diegetic and nondiegetic), the dialogue, and all of the other sounds synchronized with the film.[24] The music was composed primarily by the leftist composer and student of Schoenberg, Hanns Eisler, who emigrated to Hollywood in the 1930s. His coauthored (with Theodor W. Adorno) 1947 book, *Composing for the Films* (1947), retrospectively reflects on his experiences and theories of the 1930s. Following his exile in the United States, he returned to what was then East Germany, where he composed the soundtracks for numerous DEFA (Deutsche Film-Aktiongesellschaft) feature films. At the time of *Kuhle Wampe*, though, Eisler's film experience was limited. He had been involved with several Brechtian theatre productions, but *Kuhle Wampe* constituted his first foray into the world of sound film. Besides, since the film was a collaborative project and Brecht himself certainly had his own sophisticated theories on the use of music, it is difficult to distinguish Eisler's contribution from that of Brecht. Though Eisler was the actual composer, Brecht and Dudow were surely instrumental in how the music was employed.

What *is* certain is that Eisler, Brecht, and Dudow were at that time collaborating on a theory of dialectic music for film. As a starting point, their theory was heavily based on the film theory of Sergei Eisenstein and Vsevold Pudovkin, among others. The reception of *Kuhle Wampe* seems to indicate that Eisler was generally considered to be primarily in charge of the music and behind its revolutionary nature.[25] However, evidence available today indicates that it was indeed Brecht who developed *the theory* of music as a self-standing element, maintaining that the "separation of the elements of music and of action could bring about some new effects for the feature film as well."[26] Besides, despite Pettifer's conclusions that

Eisler's music only reinforced the montage cuts and came dangerously near to "being an abstract embodiment of fate that Brecht deplored in bourgeois dramas,"[27] this was not perceived to be the case at the time. The effect was quite the opposite—the audiences were struck by the music's jarring, and at times discordant, quality. As Lotte Eisner recollects, "[T]he miserable existence of the unemployed is portrayed with documentary restraint enhanced by the rhythm of the montage and the violence of the music.... Hanns Eisler's sublimely impetuous music burst onto the screen in a paroxysmal fortissimo of sound and image."[28] Eisler himself describes a sequence as "deteriorated houses on the edge of the city, slum district in all its misery and filth. The mood of the image is passive, depressing: it invites melancholy. Counterposed to that is fast-paced, sharp music, a polyphonic prelude, marcato style. The contrast of the music ... to the straightforward montage of image creates a shock that, according to the intention, stimulates opposition more than sympathetic sentimentality."[29]

True to a dialectical theory of montage, the acoustic contradicts the visual.[30] However, this is somewhat misleading since both Eisler and Brecht believed in the potential of diegetic music. In scenes from *Kuhle Wampe*, such as those of street musicians, radio broadcasts, singing at the engagement party, and, of course, the "Solidarity Song," we see a connection to Brecht's earlier theory of the visible and the nonvisible. For, to quote Eisler, not only is certain music supposed to illustrate "the superficial meaning of the image but it should also be connected to its deeper meaning."[31] An example of this is when the young Bönike, returning home after a fruitless day of searching for work, passes by street musicians playing the polka "In Rixdorf ist Musike" and pauses for a few seconds to listen to them. One is struck by the irony of the music in juxtaposition to Bönike's plight—the music however *is* in Rixdorf. A similar irony occurs when, as the family moves to a tent community of Kuhle Wampe, the soundtrack features Prussian military marches, cynically evoking the glorious days of the Kaiser as a bygone era of full employment—even if much of that employment was on the battlefield. Later, during the engagement party, the first song played is "Einzug der Gladiatoren" (Entry of the Gladiators), a triumphant melody of conquest and celebration. Then, when Fritz announces that he doesn't want to marry Anni, the music shifts to "Schöner Gigolo, armer Gigolo" (Handsome Gigolo, Poor Gigolo). The interplay between Eisler's nondiegetic composition, on the one hand, and diegetic inserts, on the other, is particularly striking when Anni discovers that she is pregnant and contemplates an abortion. At first, sharp music plays over the images of children, advertisements, and Anni's agitated stride. Then comes a cut to the price of a funeral and to the scene of Anni's brother's death. At that point, the music becomes diegetic: the source is a loudspeaker, and the song playing is "Leben ohne Lieben" (Life without Love). Whether the song refers to the fate of Anni's brother or to her present condition is not specified.[32]

There is another type of tension that exists in *Kuhle Wampe* between popular music and Eisler's more obscure and inaccessible compositions. It is as if Brecht and Dudow employed the juxtaposition of popular and high art forms to erase the hierarchy and class boundary between the two types of music, making them *both* equally accessible.[33] The aim was to produce an integrated soundtrack that paralleled the coexistence of fiction and documentary material on the visual track,[34] and it seems to have met with a considerable degree of success. As a particularly astute critic writing in 1931 observes after commenting on Eisler's soundtrack: "Dudow makes an interesting attempt to use the sound film as a means by which to conquer reality. He does not film his actors in the studio, but takes them to factories, tent sites, a streetcar, and a sports meeting."[35] Again, then, the link is made between realism and the film's soundtrack, but it is the working class that is represented as acoustically more connected to external reality. Just as the nonstudio visual or documentary elements create a sense of realism, so does the soundtrack, which provides the noises of everyday life. The noise of work and labor in particular is stressed throughout the film, such as in the deafeningly loud auto shop where Fritz works, the sirens of the ambulance that takes Bönike's body away, the factory that employs Anni, and even the hammering of tent pins in Kuhle Wampe. In short, as sound is used to increase the effect of reality, labor becomes acoustically defined. Following Eisenstein, who as early as 1928 had praised Japanese Kabuki theatre because it caused the audience to "actually 'hear movement' and 'see sound,'" Brecht and Dudow strategically employ sound in such a way that the film audience "hears labor."[36] But rather than an aesthetic of reproduction, Brecht and Dudow's goal (again following Eisenstein) was an aesthetic of transformation. Sound was to function dialectically. This is nowhere clearer than in a scene from *Kuhle Wampe*, subsequently censored, that featured several residents of the suburb swimming nude in the Müggelsee with the sounds of church bells in the background. Significantly, what bothered the censors was less the naked bodies than their conjunction with the church bell sounds, a juxtaposition that they interpreted as a critique of Christian culture from the standpoint of a naked communist one.[37]

In typical Brechtian manner, the dialogue in *Kuhle Wampe* is read as if it were composed entirely of quotations or clichés. This produces a stark detachment, or distance, between the actors and what they actually say. A case in point is the fragmentary sentence indicating that Bönicke has fallen from the window: "aus dem Fenster gestürzt." This could mean that he was either pushed or went out on his own volition, leaving open the possibility of blaming the state.[38] There is also the scene in which the father stumbles through a newspaper article on Mata Hari while his wife tries to balance the daily budget, his stutter reinforcing the disjuncture between the sound and image tracks.[39] However, what has been overlooked all too often is just how much the soundtrack also produces identification in

Kuhle Wampe. Class, for instance, is prominently figured through accent and dialect. In the last scene of the film, shot on site in a Berlin streetcar, each person's class position can be clearly identified through the audial track. Thus, a worker says "Jib dem Ollen doch ne Appelsine und schick'n ins Waisenhaus!" while the bourgeois officer says "Bei Ihnen merkt man auch, dass Sie nicht mehr beim Kommiss gewesen sind!" Once again, then, the documentary aspects of the soundtrack combine with the visual track to suture the viewer into the film diegesis.

The addition of sound to the filmic product increased the likelihood of audience identification. Brecht and Dudow, like many others in the early years of sound film, realized its great potential. More than merely complementing the visual dimension, the employed sound of labor, accents, dialects, and manners of eating and drinking allowed the directors to represent the working class aurally. In contradiction to these strategies of identification, however, Brecht and Dudow mobilized the contrapuntal music of Eisler, the various "songs" featured in the film, the clichéd dialogue, and a number of highly exaggerated noises, such as the gestic scream of young Bönicke falling out of the window, to push the soundtrack beyond an aesthetic of identification to an aesthetic of transformation. As such, the same dialectical strategy is at work in the audial track as in the visual track's interplay between documentary and fiction, truth and artifice. *Kuhle Wampe* thus presents an oppositional, nonfusion of the elements at every level, and the result is a fully dialectical film that operates on the interstices between identification and distanciation.

Notes

1. "Selten wurde in Deutschland—nein, es wird wohl hier überhaupt zum erstenmal—ein Drehbuch vorgelegt, in dem *nicht* Theatermenschen oder sozial angemalte Figuren ihr 'Schicksal' erleben, sondern in dem der Filmablauf gleichzeitig ein Zeitablauf, ein Querschnitt durch den heutigen Lebenstage, das Dasein eines Sonntags selbst wird, der sich von der Leinwand, aus der Tonmaschine formen soll. Es gibt hier ein einleitendes 'Dramolet'—'*Ein Arbeitloser weniger*'—ein optisch und tonlich unvergleichlich entworfenes 'Lebensbild', es baut sich hierüber die Tagesgeschichte einer ganzen Klasse auf, die unter dem Schutz von Verfassung und Menschenwürde ihre Existenz der heutigen Zwischenepoche fristet, duldet, durchvegetiert.... In dieser Vegetation ... setzt sich der Gedanke der 'Solidarität' dieser durch gemeinsames Dasein aufeinander angewiesenen Klasse durch, sichtbar, hörbar geworden durch den Chorus der Sportlersolidarität, die diesem 'Weekend'—Film Fülle und Mark geben soll." E.J., *Film-Kurier*, 13 August 1931, 153–54.
2. *Kuhle Wampe* was first censored on 31 March 1932, then again on 9 April 1932. It was finally approved on 21 April 1932. The first screening was in Moscow sometime in mid-May 1932 and the Berlin premier was on 30 May 1932.
3. Brecht was involved with film from very early on, writing film scripts in the early 1920s such a "Drei im Turm," "Der Brilliantenfresser," "Das Mysterium der Jamaikabar," and

"Robinsonade auf Assuncion." He then continued to write screenplays throughout his career and participated with Fritz Lang in *Hangmen Also Die*.

4. James Pettifer, "Against the Stream—*Kuhle Wampe*," *Screen* 15, no. 2 (Summer 1974): 49–64, here 56.

5. Martin Walsh, *The Brechtian Aspect of Radical Cinema*, ed. Keith M. Griffiths (London: BFI, 1981), 10.

6. Fredric Jameson, *Brecht and Method* (London: Verso, 1998), 49.

7. "The photograph has provided so central an image for the conventional thinking of realism and because it has evident bearings for the question of the specific practice of film…. More than ever, the 'simple reproduction of reality' says nothing at all about that reality. A photograph of the Krupp or AEG factories … tells us practically nothing about those institution…. We need effectively to 'construct something artificial,' 'something posed.'… For Brecht, the photograph is the sublimation of reality into passive ideality…. A materialist practice of film must then in turn be inevitably involved in combat against the sublimation of film in the luminous reality-truth of the photograph." Stephen Heath, "From Brecht to Film: Theses, Problems," *Screen* 16, no. 4 (Winter 1975–76): 34–45, here 36.

8. "[E]ine episierende Erzähltechnik an, die dokumentarieche Material montierte und die Handlung mit Kommentaren durchbrach." Wolfgang Gersch, *Film bei Brecht: Bertolt Brechts praktische und theoretische Auseinandersetzung mit dem Film* (Munich: Carl Hanser Verlag, 1975), 105.

9. For instance, Martha Wolter, who plays Gerda, was a professional seamstress.

10. E.J., *Film-Kurier*, 13 August 1931, 154.

11. Another contemporary reviewer writes prior to the film's release: "The events are based on factual occurrences. Material has been collected from conversations and changed into words again which are spoken during actual incidents. But it has to be mentioned that there was a commitment not to give a blasé account in spite of everything. It is not a reportage, but a creation which strives for critique and commentary at the same time. The actors had nothing to play but themselves," and he concludes with a particularly intriguing comment that "the use of professional with unprofessional actors will reflect life as it really is." "Das Ziel: eine Handlung zu zeigen, die in der Arbeiterklasse spielt und durch diese Handlung selbst die Arbeiterklasse, ihre Lage, ihre Anschauungen aufzuzeigen. Auf Tatsachen basieren die Vorgänge. Man hat aus Gesprächen Material gesammelt, das zum Teil mit den Worten verwandt wurde, bei den wirklichen Vorgängen gesprochen sind. Doch ist, das wird betont, Wert darauf gelegt worden, bei alldem nicht einen blassen Bericht zu geben. Keine Reportage ist es, sondern eine Gestaltung, die Kritik und Stellungnahme zugleich erstrebt…. Sie (the actors) hatten nichts zu spielen als sich selbst…. Zusammen mit den Berufsschauspielern sollen sie ein Bild geben vom Leben, wie es wirklich ist." *Film-Kurier*, 9 March 1932, 160.

12. "Und hier liegt die wirkliche Ursache des Verbots. Deutschland darf nur innerhalb der Zäune von Neu-Babelsberg fotografiert werden." *Die literarische Welt*, 22 April 1932, 190.

13. "Above all I believe that the effect of an actor's performance on the spectator is not independent of the spectator's effect on the actor. In the theatre, the public regulates the representation. The cinema in this respect has enormous weaknesses which seem theoretically insurmountable." Cited from Brecht's journal of 27 March 1942. Walsh, *The Brechtian Aspect*, 60.

14. Of course, Brecht did not formally articulate the concept of *Verfremdungseffekt* until after 1935, but its inarticulated presence as a formal theoretical strategy can already be found in his work in the early 1930s.

15. "Second, insofar as Brecht's political art includes the presence of the familiar world and yet presents a more attractive world as well, Brechtian art is an art of identification. In examining Brecht's theories, critics have too often declared that the theories allow no place for identification. In fact, Brecht's theory of art embodies two identifications: one empathetic and unquestioning—the one connected to the reified vision of the world—and

one critical—a new perspective of knowledge from which the old way is scrutinized."
Dana B. Polan, "Daffy Duck and Bertolt Brecht: Towards a Politics of Self-Reflexive Cinema?" in *American Media and Mass Culture: Left Perspectives*, ed. Donald Lazere (Berkeley: University of California Press, 1987), 353.

16. Bertolt Brecht, "Alienation Effects in Chinese Acting," in *Brecht on Theatre: The Develop-
    ment of an Aesthetic*, ed. and trans. John Willet (New York: Hill and Wang, 1964), 94.
17. "Copying the methods of these realists [Balzac and Tolstoy], we should cease to be
    realists ourselves." Brecht, "The Popular and the Realistic," in *Brecht on Theatre*, ed. and
    trans. Willett, 110.
18. Ibid., 109.
19. Ibid., 111.
20. As Bruce Murray concludes, "*Kuhle Wampe* prevented spectators from interacting with
    it as they had grown accustomed to interacting with mainstream films." Bruce Murray,
    Film and the German Left in the Weimar Republic: From Caligari to Kuhle Wampe (Austin:
    University of Texas Press, 1990), 224.
21. Brecht, "Alienation Effects," 93.
22. Brecht, as cited by Roswitha Mueller, *Bertolt Brecht and the Theory of Media* (Lincoln: Uni-
    versity of Nebraska Press, 1989), 53.
23. "Vom künstlerisch-technischen Standpunkt gesehen ist 'Kuhle Wampe' ein durchaus
    positiver Versuch, denn er unternimmt es wirklich, von den besonderen Bedingungen
    und Möglichkeiten des Tonfilms, der Tonbildmontage aus, seine Wirkungen zu erzielen
    und ist so der erste deutsche Tonfilm überhaupt, der ernsthaft und konsequent vom
    'verfilmten Theater' und von äußerlichen artistischen Mätzchen abrückt." *Die Rote
    Fahne*, 3 April 1932, 188.
24. For a detailed discussion of Brecht's "separation of elements," see Colin MacCabe, "The
    Politics of Separation," *Screen* 16, no. 4 (Winter 1975–76): 46–61.
25. As one critic notes in April 1932: "The music has been written by Hanns Eisler. The
    music is presented as a self-standing element and not, as was the case in silent films, a
    mere illustrative accompaniment to the image track." "Die Musik schreibt Hanns Eisler.
    Das vom stummen Film her noch herrschende Prinzip der rein illustrierenden Film-
    musik soll durchbrochen werden: die Musik soll als selbständiges Element wirken."
    Licht Bild Bühne, October 1931, 158.
26. Mueller citing Brecht. Mueller, *Bertolt Brecht*, 92.
27. Pettifer, "Against the Stream," 56.
28. Lotte Eisner, *The Haunted Screen* (Berkeley: University of California Press, 1990), 334.
29. Murray citing Eisler. Murray, *Film and the German Left*, 223.
30. Indeed, much has been made of non-diegetic music in the film. See Gersch, MacCabe,
    Mueller, Pettifer and Murray, among others. Perhaps it was the elimination of all
    nondiegetic music in Pabst's rendering of *The Threepenny Opera* that particularly irri-
    tated Brecht. For a discussion on this see Ben Brewster, "Brecht and the Film Industry,"
    Screen 16, no. 4 (Winter 1975–76): 16–33, esp. 26.
31. "Eislers Musik verkommt nicht zur (noch immer gängigen) impressionistischen Illus-
    tration des Sichtbaren. Sie übernimmt, in klassischen Formen gesetzt, eine kommentie-
    rende Funktion und konzentriert sich dabei 'nicht eigentlich auf das, was die Bilder
    äußerlich aussagen sondern bezieht sich auf ihren tieferen Inhalt'. Sie trifft selbständige
    Aussagen, die den 'Vorgängen hinter den Vorgängen' gelten (Expositionsmontagen,
    Annis Visionen, Solidaritätslied usw.), und entlastet so die Vorgänge nicht nur, sondern
    gestattet auch einen verstärkten revolutionären Gestus, der musikalisch leichter durch
    die Zensur zu bringen war als optisch oder verbal." Eisler in Gersch, *Film bei Brecht*, 133.
32. But it is not just the oscillation between the diegetic and the nondiegetic that is of sig-
    nificance. This use of songs recalls the function of music in *The Threepenny Opera*, where,
    as Brecht explains in "On the Use of Music in Epic Theater," "music, just because it took
    up a purely emotional attitude and spurned none of the stock narcotic attractions,
    became an active collaborator in the stripping bare of the middle-class corpus of ideas.

[Music] became, so to speak, a muckraker, an informer, a nark." Brecht, "On the Use of Music in Epic Theatre," in *Brecht on Theatre*, ed. and trans. Willett, 85–86.

33. Indeed, as Brecht once argued: "So-called 'cheap' music, particularly that of the cabaret and the operetta, has for some time been a sort of gestic music. Serious music, however, still clings to lyricism, and cultivates expression for its own sake." Ibid., 87.

34. To be sure, Eisler himself was very aware of the potential of music to function at once as an extremely powerful anticapitalist weapon and as a type of opiate for the masses. If he believed that music still had traces of a prerational, preindustrial order that made it a more suitable medium to tap into inner collectivity, he also clearly saw that it was precisely this same unconscious and irrational quality that led music to be easily co-optable, and manipulable, by the culture industry: "Die Anpassung an die bürgerlich rationale und schließlich hoch industrielle Ordnung, wie sie vom Auge geleistet wurde, indem es die Realität vorweg als eine von Dingen, im Grunde als eine von Waren aufzufassen sich gewöhnte, ist vom Ohr nicht ebenso geleistet worden. Hören ist, verglichen mit dem Sehen, 'archaisch', mit der Technik nicht mitgekommen. Man könnte sagen, daß wesentlich mit dem selbst vergessenen Ohr, anstatt mit den flinken, abschätzenden Augen zu reagieren, in gewisser Weise dem spätindustriellen Zeitalter widerspricht. Darum wohnt der akustischen Wahrnehmung als solcher unvergleichlich mehr als der optischen ein Moment von Kollektivität inne.... Eben dies Element der Kollektivität aber leiht sich, als undefiniertes, auch dem Mißbrauch in der Klassengesellschaft.... Alle bürgerliche Musik hat Doppelcharakter. Ist sie auf der einen Seite in gewisser Weise vorkapitalistisch, 'unmittelbar', ahnungsvolles Bild von Verbundenheit, so hat sie andererseits zugleich am zivilisatorischen Fortschritt teilgenommen, sie hat sich verdinglicht, ist mittelbar, beherrschbar, schließlich manipulierbar geworden." Eisler in Gersch, *Film bei Brecht*, 106–7.

35. "Dudow macht einen interessanten Versuch, dem Tonfilm die Wirklichkeit zu erobern. Er läßt seine Darsteller nicht im Film-Atelier, er führt sie in Fabriken, Zeltstädte und nimmt sie auf im Eisenbahnwaggon und beim Sportmeeting." *Licht Bild Bühne*, 15 October 1931, 158.

36. Eisenstein, *Film Form*, trans. Jay Leyda (New York: Harvest, 1949), 22.

37. "Die Nacktbadeszene, in der Arbeitslose Ball spielen und baden, hatte 1932 das Missfallen der Zensoren erweckt, weil durch einen Kirchturm im Hintergrund und fernes Glockenläuten 'offenbar die kommunistische Nacktkultur in scharfen Gegensatz gestellt werden soll zur christlichen Kultur, auf der das deutsche Staatswesen beruhte.'" Hecht in Gersch, *Film bei Brecht*, 167. In his 1959 feature film for DEFA, *Verwirrung der Liebe*, Dudow again tried to include a naked bathing scene which was again censored, despite the fact that Dudow was quick to point out that one of the censors had participated as an actor in the much earlier *Kuhle Wampe* scene.

38. "Er hat sich aus dem Fenster gestürzt" or "sie haben ihn aus dem Fenster gestürzt."

39. See Mueller, *Bertolt Brecht* and MacCabe "The Politics of Separation."

Chapter 5

SOUND MONEY
Aural Strategies in Rolf Thiele's
The Girl Rosemarie

Hester Baer

I

In his book *The Sounds of Commerce*, Jeff Smith describes the 1950s as a decade in which moviegoers could experience a fundamental transformation of Hollywood scoring practice, in large measure due to what Smith identifies as the rise of the pop soundtrack. While the scores of classic Hollywood cinema were dominated by classical-romantic background music that remained nearly inaudible to spectators, pop scores elevated the status of musical sounds so that they became virtually equal to visual elements within the cinematic experience.[1] A similar transition in film music had already occurred in Germany almost ten years earlier. While Nazi cinema had strongly adhered to its own inflection of the classical-romantic film score, the collapse of the Nazi filmmaking apparatus after 1945 brought an end to the hegemonic romantic soundtrack. Eager to catch up with the rest of the world, German consumers articulated a demand for diverse styles of popular music that had been banned or restricted during the Third Reich.

Whereas visual representation was subject to intense public scrutiny after the iconophilia of fascism, a wide range of musical styles shaped the acoustic landscape of postwar Germany. In this environment, German filmmakers responded by integrating the performance of popular music into film narratives, thereby showcasing sound as an essential component of spectatorial appeal. In the early postwar *Trümmerfilme* (rubble films), performances of jazz, swing, and cabaret songs are common, and in the *Heimatfilme* (homeland films) of the early 1950s, diegetic performances by choral groups and wandering minstrels are almost de rigueur. Though the *Heimatfilm* scores were often vehicles for the display of German folk songs, they also typically included other types of popular music such as jazz and swing, contrasting the modernity of the latter's style with the traditionalism of the folk songs.

By the mid-1950s, the presence of folk songs and light orchestral compositions gave way to the musical model presented in Hollywood films such as Richard Brooks's *Blackboard Jungle* (1955), which used rock-and-roll and jazz music to attract young audiences and to authenticate its "gritty" visual realism.[2] This move to adapt American popular musical styles and Hollywood compositional strategies to German film in the late 1950s accompanied a larger transition in the film industry toward a new set of genres. The *Heimatfilm*, which had addressed the concerns of a transitional society coming to terms with new national and gender identities, was no longer germane to the affluent, stabilized Federal Republic of the latter half of the decade. It was replaced by related genres such as the "vacation film" and by entirely different genres, for example, the crime film and the urban comedy. In addition to staple jazz and swing numbers, these films frequently included compositions or standard hits by American musicians. At the same time, directors such as Georg Tressler gained critical acclaim with films that translated the youth-oriented social commentary of *Blackboard Jungle* and *Rebel Without a Cause* into *Die Halbstarken* (The Rebels, 1956) and *Endstation Liebe* (Last Stop Love, 1958). However, the most sustained attempt to apply the Hollywood model to the domestic film market came in the uniquely German genre of the *Schlagerfilm*, an adaptation of the mainstream Hollywood "teenager film." *Schlagerfilme* such as *Tutti Frutti* (1957) and *Wenn die Conny mit dem Peter ...* (When Conny and Peter ..., 1958) were built around performances of rock-and-roll and exhibited the latest dance crazes.

Like Hollywood films of the same era, West German films from the 1950s evidence a broad range of aural strategies that often stand in tension with their mainstream visual style. "Modern" music (from jazz to rock to early electronic music) shows up in many mainstream films, generally evoking that which is threatening, disruptive, or unconventional. In Veit Harlan's *Anders als du und ich* (Different from You and Me, 1957) and Alfons Stummer's *Der Förster vom Silberwald* (The Forester of the Silver Wood, 1954), electronic music and swing are clearly characterized as perverse while at the same time inciting visual and aural pleasure. In these films and many others, sonic strategies open up multiple and sometimes contradictory spaces of reception; they perforate otherwise circumscribed narratives. Though sound in the form of popular music often familiarizes the exotic and facilitates structures of identification, it also distorts habitual perceptions and suggests the uncanniness of familiar images to the spectator. It is the task of this essay to elaborate on these ambivalences of film sound in 1950s German cinema by discussing Rolf Thiele's *Das Mädchen*

Rosemarie (The Girl Rosemarie, 1958). One of the most popular and most critical films of the decade, *The Girl Rosemarie* shatters the conventional unity of image and sound in order to question the political and social consensus of the postwar era. Thiele employed film sound to tailor his product to the demands of the domestic market. Just as importantly, however, he also incorporated popular music to complicate the spectator's relation to the filmic product.

II

Based on a true story, *The Girl Rosemarie* tells the tale of the unsolved murder of a high-class Frankfurt prostitute, Rosemarie Nitribitt, who was found dead in her apartment in November 1957. During a search of the premises, police found pictures of Nitribitt's clientele as well as a "little black book" listing their names. Many of these clients were instantly recognizable: they were influential politicians and industry bosses who played a vital role in shaping the Federal Republic's "Economic Miracle." From the beginning, the press covered the murder extensively, and police soon called for a media blackout. Since the 1950s, commentators have continued to speculate about the case, generally assuming that the investigation was intentionally sabotaged to protect the identities of Nitribitt's clients and to cover up the industrial intrigue surrounding her murder.[3]

Spurred on by this escalating scandal, the filmmaking team of screenwriter Erich Kuby, producer Luggi Waldleitner, and director Thiele set about utilizing Nitribitt's story to create a social-critical film that would tackle the double moral standard of the Economic Miracle as national mythos and lived reality. During production, the film was already the subject of numerous protests and lawsuits, primarily from businesses and individuals who feared their reputations would be damaged by their portrayal in the final product.[4] After *The Girl Rosemarie* was completed, the controversy took on international proportions. The film was set to premiere at the Venice Film Festival as the official West German contribution to the competition. However, shortly before the festival, an assistant reviewer on the cultural board of the Federal Republic's Foreign Office completed an evaluation of *The Girl Rosemarie*, demanding that it be pulled from the festival because it would "damage the reputation of West Germany abroad."[5] As a result, the Venice organizers issued an official invitation to the filmmakers to show their film outside competition. When they accepted, the West German Foreign Office and the Export Union filed a protest with the festival, asking them not to show the film. This controversy generated great interest in *The Girl Rosemarie* in the Italian press, where it was praised for its self-critical depiction of Germany. German newspapers, in turn, reprinted the positive Italian reviews at great length, fueling interest in the film at home.[6] Before the film could be shown in

West Germany, however, it had to be evaluated and rated by the Voluntary Self-Censorship Commission of the Film Industry (Freiwillige Selbstkontrolle der Filmwirtschaft, or FSK). The Central Committee of the FSK decided to endorse the film's release for adult audiences, but only over the objections of the censorship board's Working Committee. Echoing the conclusions of the Foreign Office, the Working Committee of the FSK argued that the vicious portrayal of "the deplorable state of affairs" among an entire social class of German men would be perceived as fact by international audiences and would thus damage the political reputation of West Germany. Furthermore, the committee contended that the film constituted a "primer" in prostitution that endorsed women's pursuit of fortune by immoral and exploitative means "under the sign of the Economic Miracle."[7] Anxieties about gender roles, money, and the unstable political identity of the emergent West German nation were conflated in the objections articulated by these censorship documents.

While the FSK endorsed the film's release despite these objections, it demanded two changes to *The Girl Rosemarie*. The filmmakers were asked to add a new "preface" to the film, a disclaimer of its accurate depiction of events despite the fact that it was based on a true story. More significant for the purposes of my argument here, however, was the censorship of a montage sequence that accompanied one of the film's most critical songs. The lengthy censorship documents that were generated about the relationship between sound and image in this sequence suggest that contemporary spectators took notice of the film's aural strategies.

III

The Girl Rosemarie extrapolates from the few known facts of Rosemarie Nitribitt's life to posit an explicit connection between her murder and German rearmament—and, by extension, the escalating Cold War. The film begins as Rosemarie (Nadja Tiller) is still a small-time streetwalker, living with two street musicians (Mario Adorf and Jo Herbst) who double as her pimps. Rosemarie has high aspirations and makes frequent journeys to a Frankfurt luxury hotel, hoping to seduce rich men. One day she succeeds in capturing the attentions of an industry boss, Bruster (Gert Fröbe), who is a member of the mysterious Isoliermattenkartell (Insulation Matting Cartel), a cover for a top-secret armaments cooperative comprising numerous captains of industry. This encounter turns out to be Rosemarie's big break, and she eventually becomes the mistress of the cartel member Hartog (Carl Raddatz). Hartog gives Rosemarie her own apartment and a wardrobe of nice clothes, but she wants more: she seeks to transcend class boundaries and hopes to participate in Hartog's life, or at least his lifestyle.

When Hartog refuses to introduce Rosemarie to his colleagues and relatives or to include her in his social life, she turns to his French colleague

Fribert (Peter van Eyck), with whom she hopes to have an affair. Fribert, however, has something else in mind. As he tells her, "Here I am trying to explain to you the connection between your bed and the Economic Miracle, and you're trying to unbutton my jacket." He then proposes a plan to Rosemarie: he will school her in true elegance and glamour, clothe her "like a suburban Paris housewife," and help her to become "a great coquette." In return, she will spy on her clients for him. Fribert gives Rosemarie a tiny spy camera and a reel-to-reel tape recorder that she hides in her boudoir. One by one, the men from the arms cartel enter Rosemarie's bedchamber and confess to her—and the tape recorder—secrets about their shady business dealings. It is significant that although Rosemarie does photograph the contents of the men's calendars and address books with her spy camera, the film does not focus on the visual secrets that are thereby revealed. Instead, it is the aural revelations of the tapes that constitute Rosemarie's primary transgression.

Rosemarie prospers in her new role, but her ascent does not last long. When Fribert receives the first installment of information from Rosemarie, he leaks it to the French press, blowing her cover and exposing the secret activities of the German cartel. Realizing the source of the information, the cartel plots to get rid of Rosemarie. The men try to pay her off and send her out of the country, but she refuses, withholding the tapes and demanding that Hartog marry her. When he declines, Rosemarie's life spirals out of control. Returning home from a confrontation with her clients at a bar, Rosemarie is murdered by a dark figure lurking behind a curtain in her apartment. While neither the murder nor the murderer is shown, the film clearly implicates the cartel in the crime. By suggesting that West Germany's most prosperous business leaders were not only philanderers and shady arms dealers but murderers as well, the film highlights continuities between the Third Reich and the Federal Republic.

IV

Like other mainstream films from the period, *The Girl Rosemarie* evidences traits typical of the 1950s Hollywood pop soundtrack: it combines traditional musical components, popular songs built around hooks, diegetic musical performances, and modern stylistic elements taken from jazz and swing. The film's songs, which proved both catchy and controversial, were an essential tool in the marketing campaign for *The Girl Rosemarie*. Promotional stills showed Tiller together with the film's roving musicians Adorf and Herbst, posed with their musical instruments, and the press kit included a reprint of all of the song lyrics. In contrast to the contemporary trend toward the inclusion of American-style film music, Thiele and composer Norbert Schultze instead resuscitated two German traditions for the score: cabaret-style music, associated with both the Weimar era and early postwar "rubble films," and the folksy idiom of roving musicians, typical of the *Heimatfilm*.

Written by Herbst and Rolf Ulrich, the film's cabaret-style songs put a modern spin on the dissonant tonal compositions associated with Weimar-era musical and theatrical traditions. Like Kurt Weill's compositions for *The Threepenny Opera*, to which *The Girl Rosemarie* was often compared in reviews, Herbst's and Ulrich's songs incorporate various popular idioms taken from jazz, swing, ballads, military marches, dance hall music, and commercial folk songs. Compositionally diverse, the songs range from simple folk ballads for banjo, accordion, and trombone, to swing numbers performed by showgirls in the local "gentleman's club," to more complex compositions that present a pastiche of disparate musical styles. Several of Herbst's and Ulrich's songs recall nothing other than Friedrich Hollaender's compositions for *Der blaue Engel* (The Blue Angel, 1930), a film that *The Girl Rosemarie* clearly references both in individual scenes and in its larger narrative trajectory.[8]

Dressed in a bow tie and top hat like Marlene Dietrich's Lola Lola in *The Blue Angel*, the showgirl played by Karin Baal in *The Girl Rosemarie* performs a racy Dietrich impersonation that ends in a striptease. In contrast to Dietrich's sultry performance of "Falling in Love Again," however, Baal dances to a song called "Boredom," a slow swing number sung by the bar's proprietress whose musical style is sexy, but whose lyrics are far from seductive: "[Boredom] sits next to you in an evening dress/Mixes you a cocktail of uncertainty/Fills your glass with melancholy/Kisses you with lips so cold and pale …/Boredom has many eyes at night/But all the eyes are dead and blind!"[9] Like "Boredom," the lyrics to songs throughout *The Girl Rosemarie* typically enunciate a critique of the visual spectacle taking shape on screen: the spectatorial relationship to Baal's strip show, both within the diegetic space of the nightclub and for the audience in the cinema, is necessarily problematized by the song's accusation about "dead and blind" eyes. In the case of "Boredom," however, this critique stands in tension with the popular musical styles of the song. If "Boredom" articulates the perspective of a woman who is fed up with the sexual role she is compelled to play as the object of the voyeuristic gaze, this textual message is almost subsumed by the erotic associations suggested by the song's slow, rhythmic sound. Numbers such as this contributed strongly to the film's commercial viability and eventual success.

In addition to its accessible soundtrack, *The Girl Rosemarie* also uses a second aural strategy to underscore its criticism of the immorality of the Economic Miracle. Time and again, ominous, disorienting synthetic sounds accompany visual images that evoke wealth and power: a line of black Mercedes cars, the revolving doors of a luxury hotel, the elevator of Rosemarie's chic apartment complex. The diegetic noise made by each of these mechanisms is abstracted and musically embellished; rhythmic sets of processed sounds, produced with a tone generator or primitive synthesizer, replace the mechanical sounds of the car engines, revolving doors, and elevator.[10] The taped, filtered, and electronically processed noises are aurally decoupled from their sources but remain visually connected by the presence of the sources on-screen. Like the song texts, the warped soundtrack functions as a distanciation effect, signifying the artifice of the spectacle on the screen, and it evokes the Cold War climate of surveillance that is the subtext of the film. Sonic distortion in *The Girl Rosemarie* thus encodes a paradox: it suggests the impossibility of representing authentic sexuality and desire within the moral confines of the Federal Republic in the 1950s.

V

I would now like to turn to the opening sequence of *The Girl Rosemarie*, since it establishes a series of aural and visual links that will recur throughout the film. Rosemarie enters the lobby of the luxury hotel through the revolving doors, whose ominous whooshing implies that something is amiss. The diegetically motivated noise of the doors is a rhythmically modulated set of two electronically processed flat tones that resembles an inhalation and exhalation, or a decelerated, flanged radar blip. The first is a wheezy bass tone that steadily rises in pitch; it is followed by a muted blast of white noise, and then by a sliding, reverberating treble tone that falls in pitch. This set of tones is repeated in a rhythm that evokes the pneumatic turning of the doors, but the rhythm picks up and slows down independently of the doors' actual pace. The sound is clearly linked to the doors, but its abstraction of their noise verges on the musical. The aural space created by this distorted noise clashes with the naturalistic sound space that characterizes the rest of the film, an effect that immediately draws the spectator's attention to the soundtrack of *The Girl Rosemarie*. The intermittent moments of emphatically synthetic sound stand in tension with the realist visual style of the film, thereby denaturalizing the film's images.

The concierge is shocked that Rosemarie has dared to penetrate the hotel, and scuttles over to throw her out. As she walks out of the hotel, the camera pans down Rosemarie's body to close in on her legs and high heels, and the title of the film comes up on screen. As the credits continue, the soundtrack shifts to foreboding modern music, an atonal composition featuring haunting woodwinds. We see external shots of Frankfurt in the thrall of the Economic Miracle: the facades of brand new buildings, neon signs, the sparkle and glow of life in the late 1950s. The music's jazzy tempo matches the pace of the montage, but its sinister tones stand in tension with the upbeat images. Like the sound of the revolving doors, the music mediates the visual spectacle of the luxurious signifiers of reconstruction, underscoring their artifice. The soundtrack abruptly shifts to a popular, folksy instrumental arrangement featuring accordion and banjo, an aural cut away from modern music to a more traditional—and more typically German—sound. The camera focuses on a bombed-out building and slowly pans down its exterior, in a shot that parallels the previous pan down Rosemarie's body, thus establishing a link between the female figure and the rubble of the building. Neither has been reconstructed; neither reflects the glamorous sheen of the Economic Miracle.

Next, the camera tracks down from the bombed-out building to the music's diegetic source: the street musicians, whose song ends with the words "Yes, the blossoms of our Miracle shine brightly in neon light. And if you fail to pluck them, you'll always remain a poor might." The implication of the lyrics is clear as the film cuts away to a shot of Rosemarie, who hopes to profit from the Economic Miracle, a point that is reiterated by the soundtrack's return to jazzy modern music. Back in front of the hotel, a long line of black Mercedes whooshes by, producing a warped, synthetic sound like that of the revolving doors in the hotel lobby. Again, though the noise is diegetically motivated by the cars, what we hear is a processed and synthetic abstraction of engine noise. The soundtrack thus contrasts with the film's realist visual style throughout the entire opening sequence of *The Girl Rosemarie*. While the image track focuses on material signifiers of wealth and power, manifesting the scopophilia of a socioeconomic order obsessed with turning rubble to riches, the soundtrack—whether diegetic music or nondiegetic sound effects—signifies that things are not always as they appear. Fragmenting the conventional unity of image and sound, Thiele at once draws attention to the hollowness of the postwar spectacle and promotes a form of spectatorship that pushes the viewer to negotiate the full range of cinematic expression and experience.

VI

The Girl Rosemarie maps the rags-to-riches transformation of the Federal Republic in the 1950s onto the body of a prostitute. Like the women of the rubble films produced after 1945, Rosemarie wears a wrinkled trench coat at the outset of the film. As the narrative progresses, her image is slowly reconstructed; in one of the film's final sequences, we witness her wearing a remarkably expensive Christian Dior dress at a lavish party. If the trench coat linked her to the street and the crumbling façades of the rubble, the Dior dress marks her arrival in the upper echelons of the nouveau riche, her move from the street into the private sphere, and the transformation of her body into a luxury commodity. This party is the pinnacle of Rosemarie's success, but at the same time it marks her immanent decline. Of course, she has not really arrived; as a prostitute, she will never truly transcend class boundaries, and she is punished by death for her attempt to do so. In this sense, the Dior dress, with its layers of glistening and translucent fabric, serves as yet another marker for the false sheen of the Economic Miracle.

The film utilizes acoustic devices to narrate Rosemarie's transformation as well. In the opening sequence, Rosemarie sings with the street musicians, and is thereby linked to the traditional music they perform. The synthetic, distorted sounds that accompany her attempt to enter the luxury hotel in this sequence highlight her transgression of class boundaries. As she moves up in the world, Rosemarie rejects the street musicians and their music. She becomes rich and truly glamorous only through her use of a modern sound apparatus, the tape recorder. She seeks to consolidate her entry into the upper class by taking control of the tapes and refusing to turn them over to the cartel. However, like the transition from trench coat to Dior dress, the move from cabaret music to modern sound apparatus indicates the superficiality of Rosemarie's transformation.

The tape recorder was a relatively new commodity on the German market in 1958. Though it was based on magnetic recording technology invented by German engineers in the early 1940s, the tape recorder was developed for the home market by an American company, the Brush Development Corporation, which released its first models in the United States in 1946. In creating its small portable reel-to-reel recorders, Brush relied on technical information obtained by the American army from German industrial records after Germany's defeat.[11] As the market for durables opened up in West Germany in the mid-1950s, the tape recorder was sold next to televisions, radios, and stereo equipment. Like the television that Hartog gives Rosemarie to distract her from the boredom of living in isolation as his "kept woman," the tape recorder manufactures only illusions for Rosemarie. When she is lonely late at night, she plays back the voices of her patrons, editing out their diatribes about business and listening only to the compliments they pay her. As the film suggests, the modern technical apparatuses that surround Rosemarie propel her illusory belief that she will be able to transcend her past and "make it" in the Economic Miracle.

VII

Sound in *The Girl Rosemarie* suggests events and associations that the film's realist visual style cannot fully represent. In one of the film's most controversial sequences, visual images, sonic distortion, and cabaret music form a dense web of associations that encapsulate the film's critical message. Hartog has returned from his first night with Rosemarie to his sister Magda's hotel room. Magda pokes fun at Hartog for being "in love" and warns him about neglecting his professional responsibilities. One of Hartog's colleagues enters the room, wishing to discuss a business matter. The colleague tells him only that "it has to do with this French business." At this precise moment, Hartog's gaze crosses a reproduction of Manet's *Olympia* that hangs over the bed in the hotel room. The camera follows his gaze, zooming in on the nude prostitute in the picture in a fast, zigzagging motion that is particularly striking in a film that is otherwise visually conventional. Hartog's colleague tells him that the business is worth "50 million dollars" and mentions the name Fribert in connection with spying. When their conversation is interrupted by Magda, Hartog's gaze returns to the nude Olympia, and a reverberating, synthetically processed ringing sound on the aural track draws the viewer's attention to the significance of this conversation. This scene establishes for the first time in the film connections among money, sex, power, and rearmament that will subsequently shape the rest of the narrative. Nondiegetic noise here highlights the continuity between Hartog's illicit patronage of a prostitute and his role in illicit business practices. At the same time, it implicates Rosemarie herself in the process and project of spying.

A dissolve from the Manet reproduction reveals Rosemarie in her apartment, posed on a divan in the same manner as Olympia. The time is five weeks later, and the street musicians are visiting their old friend for a payoff. They threaten to blackmail her if she does not come through with more money. Throughout the film, the shady business dealings of legitimate captains of industry are echoed by the pimps' financial arrangements with Rosemarie, in an intersecting narrative that points to the economic opportunism across class divides during the Economic Miracle. Hartog drives up just as the two men are leaving Rosemarie's building. He offers them a tip to carry some things upstairs: a radio, a television, and a kitchen mixer. As they carry these emblematic consumer goods to Rosemarie's apartment, they sing the film's most viciously satirical song, "Kanal: voll!"[12] An indictment of excessive consumption during the Economic Miracle, the song protests the remilitarization of the Federal Republic and its role in strengthening the country's economic prosperity. The song begins when Jo Herbst turns on the radio he is carrying upstairs and tunes it to a station that is playing brass marching band music. Adorf and Herbst march upstairs in time to the music and sing the song, which begins:

> We haven't nearly—we haven't nearly—
> We haven't nearly had our fill!
> We've achieved prosperity overnight,
> We're playing in major and no longer in minor!
> A radio appliance, a mixing appliance,
> In every household a television appliance!
> Gem on the hand, Picasso on the wall,
> Too bad we burned *Mein Kampf.*
>
> We love pomp and high finance,
> Advertising, snobs and arrogance.
> And here a mink coat and there a mink coat,
> And the bells of freedom in our hearts!

Out of social feelings and a sense of community,
We quickly build an insurance agency.
And here a bank and there a bank,
And we manage ourselves till we're sick![13]

As they sing these lyrics, the musicians stop on the landing of the stairs and plug in the television. Images of banks and mink coats flash across the screen. The two men then continue marching in step up the stairs, delivering the goods to Rosemarie. The tune of the song now shifts to a military march built around a citation from the "Badenweiler Marsch"—one of the most prominent pieces of military music during the Nazi period—and at this moment the film cuts to documentary footage of marching boots. Another cut reveals the helmeted heads of soldiers who now march past Adorf and Herbst as they sing the rest of the song. This citation of the "Badenweiler Marsch" makes not only a clear aural reference to Nazism, but a visual one as well: the documentary images of uniformed men marching immediately recall the penultimate sequence from Leni Riefenstahl's *Triumph des Willens* (Triumph of the Will, 1935), the triumphal procession of Hitler, other prominent Nazi Party members, and the SS through the streets of Nuremberg toward the end of the Nazi Party rally.

The "Kanal: voll!" sequence of *The Girl Rosemarie*—through its montage of Nazi music and imagery as well as in its lyrics—foregrounds the extent to which the affluent society of the 1950s is predicated on the Nazi past. What is more, the critique articulated by this sequence suggests that excessive consumption and prosperity are ultimately as morally questionable as sex for sale. It should therefore come as no surprise that the FSK objected fiercely to "Kanal: voll!" Demanding a number of cuts, the FSK wrote: "The working committee of the FSK ... held the removal of this scene necessary because the Federal Armed Forces, as a constitutional state establishment of the Federal Republic of Germany, is degraded by the popular song sung by street musicians in the named scene, and because, through the inclusion of the Federal Armed Forces, a generalization of the circumstances criticized by the film is shown and therefore an effect is called forth that is detrimental to the reputation of Germany."[14] The tortured language of the document never explicitly names the "circumstances criticized by the film." Specifically, the censors mention neither the song's musical citation of the "Badenweiler Marsch" nor the mention of Hitler in the song's lyrics—"too bad we burned *Mein Kampf*"—both explicit references to the Nazi past that are unusual in films from the 1950s. The document suggests, however, that the censors objected primarily to the connection posited by the film between illicit sex, rearmament, and the Economic Miracle, a constellation that is made clear throughout the "Kanal: voll!" sequence.

VIII

Like many other popular films from the 1950s, *The Girl Rosemarie* utilized sound in order to express a critical message that accompanied a visually conventional narrative. Departing from the dominant sound practices of both Nazi cinema and the *Schlagerfilm* of the late 1950s, *The Girl Rosemarie* employed different sonic strategies to question the morality of the affluent society. As I have argued above, Thiele's film successfully used cabaret music and distorted diegetic sound to signify the artifice and spectacle of the Economic Miracle. While the film's popular score no doubt attracted audiences and promoted close listening, sonic distortion distanced spectators from the film's visual imagery. Thiele's noise indicated the impossibility of expressing authentic desire and suggested the lack of solidarity within the German body politic—the profound and devastating silence of the postwar spectacle.

Notes

1. This breakthrough, as Smith argues, was a response to "a number of industrial, historical and sociological factors in the 1950s and early 1960s, including the trend toward diversification and conglomeration in film distribution, the emergence of studio-owned record labels, the establishment of radio and records as important ancillary markets, and changes in popular music tastes and consumption patterns." Jeff Smith, *The Sounds of Commerce: Marketing Popular Film Music* (New York: Columbia University Press, 1998), 2. See also Russell Lack, *Twenty-Four Frames Under: A Buried History of Film Music* (London: Quartet Books, 1997).
2. *Blackboard Jungle* was both immensely popular and controversial in Germany, as Uta Poiger has documented. See Poiger, *Jazz, Rock, and Rebels: Cold War Politics and American Culture in a Divided Germany* (Berkeley: University of California Press, 2000), 85–91.
3. See Marli Feldvoß, "Wer hat Angst vor Rosemarie Nitribitt? Eine Chronik mit Mord, Sitte und Kunst aus den fünfziger Jahren," in *Zwischen Gestern und Morgen. Westdeutscher Nachkriegsfilm 1946–1962*, ed. Hilmar Hoffmann and Walter Schobert (Frankfurt am Main: Deutsches Filmmuseum, 1989), 164–82; and Erich Kuby, *Rosemarie – des deutschen Wunders liebstes Kind* (Stuttgart: Henry Goverts Verlag, 1958).
4. On the various lawsuits, protests, and scandals surrounding the film, see a series of articles in *Der Spiegel*: "Nitribitt. Des Wunders liebstes Kind," *Der Spiegel* 12, no. 18 (30 April 1958): 50–52; "Nitribitt. Glückauf," *Der Spiegel* 12, no. 33 (13 August 1958): 44–45; and "Nitribitt. Die notwendige Klarheit," *Der Spiegel* 12, no. 38 (17 September 1958): 58–59. Kuby presents his own account of the scandal in *Alles über Rosemarie: Vom AA in Bonn bis Zensur* (Munich: Neue Film-Verleih-GmbH, 1958). Manfred Barthel provides a historical overview of the scandal in *Als Opas Kino noch jung war: Der deutsche Nachkriegsfilm* (Frankfurt: Ullstein, 1991), 351–57. See also "*Das Mädchen Rosemarie* II. Teil: Ein Film, der nicht gedreht wurde," *Weltbild* 21 (1 October 1958).
5. According to Kuby, the reviewer from the Foreign Office, Dr. Rowas, "said that this bird Rosemarie—not the prototype, who was murdered in Frankfurt, you understand, but the film—fouls the German nest (*beschmutze das deutsche Nest*)." See Kuby, *Alles über*

Rosemarie, 3. Kuby actually dedicates his book to Rowas and the Foreign Office for giving the film so much free publicity.

6. See "Beifall für Mädchen Rosemarie," *Frankfurter Rundschau*, 27 August 1958; "Beifall für den Nitribitt-Film," *Ruhr-Nachrichten*, 27 August 1958; "Rolf Thiele will Selbstkritik üben," *Badisches Tageblatt*, 27 August 1958; "Rosemarie mit Berliner Ballade verglichen," *Der Kurier*, 27 August 1958; and "Rosemarie gefiel in Venedig," *Telegraf*, 27 August 1958.

7. Quoted in Kuby, *Alles über Rosemarie*, 8.

8. Like *The Blue Angel*, *The Girl Rosemarie* narrates the construction of a female persona that both conforms to and threatens dominant male fantasies. Both films address issues of female sexuality in the context of class mobility and transgression. However, while most critics agree that narrative authority and audience sympathy for the most part lie with Professor Rath, who dies at the end of *The Blue Angel*, *The Girl Rosemarie* is not structured around male narrative authority; audiences are clearly meant to identify and sympathize with the prostitute Rosemarie.

9. "Die Langeweile," in *Lieder und Songs aus dem Roxy/NF-Film* Das Mädchen Rosemarie (Munich: Zentralpresseabteilung der Neuen Film Verleih, 1958), 7.

10. According to Karlheinz Stockhausen, the first real synthesizer (he mentions one developed by RCA in the United States in the mid-1950s) had not yet been imported to West Germany by 1958. While electronic instruments such as the melochord and the Trautonium had been in use in Germany for decades, composers and sound engineers generally used equipment that had been designed for other purposes when experimenting with synthetic sound. Commonly used equipment included noise generators, sinewave generators, electroacoustical generators, electronic filters, and synchronic tape recorders. See Karlheinz Stockhausen, "Electronic and Instrumental Music [1958]," in *Postwar German Culture*, ed. Charles E. McClelland and Steven P. Scher, trans. Ruth Hein (New York: Dutton, 1974), 355–70. I was unable to locate any information on the equipment used in producing the soundtrack to *The Girl Rosemarie*.

11. For a history of sound recording technologies such as the tape recorder in the United States, see David Morton, *Off the Record: The Technology and Culture of Sound Recording in America* (New Brunswick: Rutgers University Press, 2000).

12. Literally translated "Canal: full!" the phrase usually refers to the excessive consumption of alcohol, but it can be extrapolated to mean excessive consumption in general.

13. *Lieder und Songs aus dem Roxy/NF-Film* Das Mädchen Rosemarie, 4–5.

14. Dr. A. K. Gobert, "Prüfverfahren betr.: Spielfilm *Das Mädchen Rosemarie*, Prüf-Nummer: 17673," in file 3944 on *Das Mädchen Rosemarie*, Schriftgutarchiv, Deutsches Filmmuseum—Stiftung Deutsche Kinemathek, 3.

Chapter 6

THE CASTRATO'S VOICES

Word and Flesh in Fassbinder's
In a Year of Thirteen Moons

Brigitte Peucker

Resembling Roland Barthes's well-known description of the realist text as a "weaving of voices," an "obliterated network … a vast 'dissolve,' which permits both overlapping and loss of messages,"[1] Rainer Werner Fassbinder's film *In a Year of Thirteen Moons* (1978) presents its spectator—and auditor—with a multilayered and sometimes opaque textuality. Barthes's "voices" or codes, as we recall, structure the multivalent text, creating a "stereographic" space of writing that refers to a chain of prior textualities. In this system, "reality is what has been written" and its origin is lost in the chain of signification.[2] Famously based on an analysis of Honoré de Balzac's *Sarrasine*, Barthes's reading focuses on the realist text's discontinuous meanings, or its pluralities, smoothed over by the "natural movement" of its sentences.[3] In the case of *Sarrasine*, this "natural" style notably covers a "shocking" rupture in the chain of signification, since the body that anchors its symbolic field is that of a castrato and, as Barthes would have it, "castration jams all metonymy."[4] In contrast, Fassbinder's postmodern film— the story of a transsexual in whose significatory chain *S/Z* itself is surely a link—lacks Balzac's "natural" or *naturalizing* style: it lacks a "skin" to contain its heterogeneous parts. Its textual body is flayed and exposed.

Indeed, *In a Year of Thirteen Moons* has left one of Fassbinder's most astute critics suggesting that it is illegible, "a movie … about textualities that lose their ability to naturalize and balance the materials of signification with a sense of meaning," leaving us with a "dense overabundance of materialized markers."[5] In response, this chapter reads the film's "voices," or codes, through several specific instances of the human voice and delineates the material and symbolic aspects of exchange in the film through the multiple relations of sound and image, word and flesh, self and other that it establishes. The film's strategy, it is argued here, is to collapse the binary oppositions that structure these relations, transforming the "either/or" of binarism into a "both/and" of mutuality or simultaneity. As word and flesh, self and other are collapsed, the film embraces the condition Julia Kristeva terms "abjection."[6] But the question of whether the text is "realist," allegorical, or "oscillating between different referentialities,"[7] I will argue, remains suspended as the eroding distinction between self and other takes on the ideological task of imaging German-Jewish relations. What light, this essay will ask, can *Thirteen Moons* shed on the controversy over Fassbinder's alleged anti-Semitism?

I

Let us begin at the film's beginning, with the (failed) sexual encounter between Erwin/Elvire and the male prostitute, a scene whose indistinct, even veiled, images are accompanied by a nondiegetic five-minute excerpt from the Adagietto of Gustav Mahler's Fifth Symphony, an obvious homage to Luchino Visconti's *Death in Venice* (1971). Here is a link, to use Barthes's term, in the "code of Art." Art, the (gay male) body, and death are simultaneously evoked, of course, in the multiple references that the music generates: Visconti's film leads us directly to Thomas Mann's novella, leads through the novella's dichotomies of Apollonian (sculpture) and Dionysian (dance) to Nietzsche's *Birth of Tragedy* and back to Johann Joachim Winckelmann's eighteenth-century aesthetic. Nondiegetic music—incorporeal and unlinked to the ambient sound of the scene—conjures up a clichéd chain of textualities. These are, for the German spectator, at least, signifiers of a German tradition of high-cultural sublimation, in which the erotic, disease, and death are re-covered in the realm of the aesthetic. Exploiting the affective impact of its poignant strains, the film uses Mahler's music as one strand of the aural texture of this scene, while diegetic sound—angry words in Czech and the dull thud of blows—serves as its counterpoint. Here the human voice in "acoustic close-up" features "the breath, the gutturals, the fleshiness of the lips" in a way that introduces the material body into speech.[8] Simultaneously, the image track reveals and yet does not reveal the missing body part upon which signification and symbolization depend. Violence to the body puts an end to the haunting strains of Mahler; the scene terminates in a chilling moment of desublimation, a material blow to the aesthetic.

On to the next scene: Erwin/Elvire, rather badly beaten up, enters the apartment, whereupon s/he speaks a series of quotations, or we can rather say that Fassbinder's speaking subject "is spoken" by German culture. Again, the quotations are clichéd: one of Marlene Dietrich's theme songs from *The Blue Angel* ("Von Kopf bis Fuß") is followed first by a passage from *Rumpelstiltskin*, then by an expansionist military folk song that links the *Vaterland* with the banks of the Volga, and lastly by the famous opening lines of a Schiller poem ("The Ring of Polykrates"), familiar to German schoolchildren. Sentimental, ominous, and even mock-heroic, these quotations, torn as such from their context, seem to serve Erwin/ Elvire as assurances of a culturally generated subjectivity. Punctuated with sobs and cries of pain, the performance of these quotations is also marked by the "grain" of Erwin/Elvire's voice, by "the materiality of the body speaking its mother tongue."[9] When the next sound, the flushing of a toilet, announces the physicality of another body, the aural suggestion is made that the detritus of German culture has also been evacuated. This postmodern gesture, an "emptying out" of significance, gives priority to the material body while retaining the possibility of an allegorical function for sound. The oppositional relation, then, of nondiegetic music to closely miked (if not indexical) dialogue and sounds of pain in the opening scene[10] is repeated in another key: a series of quotations is undermined by the grain of the voice and ambient sound. Although the drives and affects, indeed the body itself, create ruptures in the symbolic order, these very ruptures (the flushing of the toilet) may be recuperated for signification.

But it is in our third example, the abattoir scene, that the layering of sound and image and the juxtaposition of the symbolic and the material take their most shocking form. Here a long, characteristic tracking shot reveals a row of slaughtered and dismembered animals: this steaming, bloody meat is the real itself. The violence of this sequence is not performed; it is recorded. And yet it, too, is under the sign of Art, for the carcasses are on display, at least for the moving camera and for the spectator. Suspended from hooks, they constitute a literal still life, a "cinematic *nature morte*"[11] of opened and flayed beasts, announcing a subject in painting of which Rembrandt's versions of the *Slaughtered Ox* (1643–55) constitute only the best-known examples.

Fassbinder's film eerily silences the cattle's cries of pain and the sound of blows or gushing blood. Instead, the soundtrack substitutes a voice-over, taken from Erwin/Elvire's taped interview with a journalist, which relates the story of her relationship with her erstwhile lover, Christoph, an actor. But it is not the occasionally glimpsed image of Erwin/Elvire in this scene that supports her voice, nor is the voice strictly acousmatic.[12] Rather, as Kaja Silverman has argued, "the corporeality which supports that voice is provided by the waiting and dying animals."[13] In this scene, too, the voice registers pain, rising to a hysterical pitch as Erwin/Elvire reaches the high point of her story, a recitation of Tasso's famous speech in Goethe's play, *Torquato Tasso*. But the voice speaks words at several removes, as Erwin/Elvire performs Christoph rehearsing his lines as Tasso. And since Tasso's speech in this play is said to have held autobiographical significance for Goethe, this chain leads to Goethe as poet and, by extension, to Fassbinder himself, very much the auteur of this film.[14] In her excerpt from Tasso's speech, Erwin/Elvire's voice-over describes the poet through the metaphor of the sacrificial beast: the artist is a beast to be sacrificed on a (political) altar. What is consigned to the realm of metaphor by Goethe is played out in the real by Fassbinder.

Along with sacrifice, aesthetic sublimation is again a theme: "Und wenn der Mensch in seiner Qual verstummt,/Gab mir ein Gott zu sagen was ich leide"(And when man is silenced in his agony/A god enabled me to speak my pain). Invaded from within by the "code of Art," Erwin/ Elvire's narrative is the story of a culturally constituted subjectivity. However, once again, language itself is infiltrated by the real (of hysterical anguish) through the medium of the voice. Nondiegetic strains of a Handel organ concerto accompany Erwin/Elvire's recitation, creating a liturgical "aural bath" that effects, by way of contrast, a connection between the bleeding carcasses and Erwin/Elvire's harrowed voice.

There is a further, more ominous, link in this chain, one that again undermines signification with an evocation of the real: the slaughterhouse scene in Fassbinder's film recalls another, infamous abattoir sequence in cinema, a scene from the most vile anti-Semitic film in the Nazi arsenal, Fritz Hippler's *The Eternal Jew* (1941).[15] In the corresponding scene of this Nazi film, a male voice speaks horrifying anti-Semitic commentary over documentary images of kosher butchering, complete with sounds of pain emitted by the dying animals. In *The Eternal Jew*, the agonizing images and sounds of this sequence are preceded by a warning to "sensitive viewers" to avert their eyes, and they are followed by Hitler's speech to the Reichstag (30 January 1939), in which he foretells the annihilation of the Jews. Thus, Hippler's film obliquely establishes a connection between kosher butchering practices performed by Jews in accordance with dietary law and the slaughter of the Jews in the Holocaust, outrageously suggesting that the kosher butchers must themselves be butchered. By stretching cinema's affective possibilities to their outermost limits, *The Eternal Jew* attempts to transport its spectators out of the realm of reason into that of bodily response and emotion. The disgust and nausea experienced by its spectators are, paradoxically, intended to promote acquiescence to a far greater violence.

What, we must ask, is the significance of Fassbinder's allusion to this propaganda film? The controversy over anti-Semitism in Fassbinder's *Garbage, the City, and Death*,[16] a play to which *Thirteen Moons* has been compared,[17] must give us pause. Since the sensibility of Fassbinder's film clearly emerges on the side of both the suffering Erwin/Elvire and the slaughtered beasts, can we assume that this allusion carries philo-Semitic ideological weight? Fassbinder's film yokes German idealist culture, namely, the extended quotation from Goethe's *Tasso*, to the most vile anti-Semitic propaganda, in both instances by means of a voice-over spoken to accompanying images of the suffering animal body. The slaughterhouse sequence of *Thirteen Moons* thus suggests a cultural continuity between idealism and Nazism that it then radically critiques by stylistic means, by bridging the gap between word and flesh through the medium of the hysterical voice. We will return to the ideological implications of this strategy later.

II

Unlike Balzac's castrato, a singer on the eighteenth-century Italian stage, Erwin/Elvire does not sing. As in *Sarrasine*, however, the human voice has an erotic dimension in Fassbinder's film. The prepubescent voices of the Vienna Boys Choir, in some sense standing in for the castrato's voice, are the voices most obviously connected with desire for Erwin/Elvire, since they create the acoustic space of his sadomasochistic masturbatory fantasy. Yet the voices of these young boys do not have the simple function of evoking homoerotic desire in Erwin/Elvire (which would no longer be homoerotic after the sex-change operation, in any case) but seem, rather, to transport Erwin/Elvire back into an eroticized childhood space and time. It is "Lo How a Rose E'er Blooming" from the choir's Christmas album to which Erwin/Elvire repeatedly listens. With its message of the Virgin birth, this hymn's evocatory power is both erotic and masochistic; evoking an idealized childhood, the boys' voices double Erwin's own childhood voice while conjuring up the fantasy of the maternal voice as a lost object of desire.[18]

Although the effects that this hymn evokes in Erwin/Elvire may not be surprising in one who spent his childhood in a Catholic convent orphanage, where questions of origin might reasonably find a religious articulation, there is more at stake here. Interestingly, Fassbinder makes use of the iconography of the *hortus inclusus*, the enclosed garden in which the Virgin Mary is so often depicted in visual art, for the setting in which we first discover Sister Gudrun. It is Sister Gudrun, of course, who will narrate the story of his childhood to Erwin/Elvire who, having repressed its painful memories, is even now unable to come "to terms" with its events. Sister Gudrun's narration, one of Fassbinder's relentless embedded narratives not imaged by the camera, is paralleled by the camera's tracking movements that keep the speaking Gudrun in frame. But Erwin/Elvire escapes the double syntax of Gudrun's narrative and the tracking camera by moving out of frame, evading the camera as s/he escapes the wounding knowledge imparted by language. In what seems an almost Kleistian moment of parody, Erwin, like Heinrich von Kleist's Marquise von O., who likewise finds herself in settings and scenarios that recall the Virgin birth, falls unconscious during Sister Gudrun's narration. The body asserts itself to protect the suffering mind; the flesh triumphs over the word.

The setting of the enclosed garden notwithstanding, the fantasized mother is precisely what Gudrun is *not* during this scene. Gudrun's demystifying narrative, her linguistic cruelty, aligns her with the enunciatory function of the father over and against the "sonorous envelope" created by the maternal voice.[19] Instead, it is Zora's voice, while telling a fairy tale, that most closely resembles the maternal "sonorous envelope." The setting of Zora's tale, the dimly lit bedroom in which Erwin/Elvire lies half-asleep in a state of drugged semiconsciousness, contributes to the atmosphere of enclosure produced by Zora's soothing, uninflected tone, and the genre of her narrative, the fairy tale, the maternal narrative par excellence, underscores these connections. Its content—the story of a brother and sister who have been transformed into a snail and a mushroom, causing one to eat of the other in a moment of hunger—has all of the horrifying literalness of the fairy tale. A story of incorporation, it recalls the oral phase of infancy, in which the infant does not distinguish between its own body and that of the mother. Thus, a maternal voice serves as the vehicle for a regression to a prelinguistic state of plenitude during which the relation to the mother is structured by ingestion/incorporation.

One more permutation of the maternal voice needs to be mentioned here: these are the disembodied, ethereal human voices that we hear in moments when, according to one critic, the trauma of castration is suggested by the soundtrack.[20] Composed for the film by Peer Raben, the music is atonal; these voices do not sing words but rather tones, distorted to heighten their emotional impact. Yet their sounds evoke celestial voices, voices akin to the maternal voice that bathes the child in a "celestial melody"—as Silverman puts it, rephrasing Guy Rosolato—"whose closest terrestrial equivalent is opera."[21] Like Zora's, these voices also call up a nonlinguistic state. Whether pointing toward prelinguistic plenitude or a radical divestiture that symbolically excludes the subject from the symbolic (castration; abjection)—in either case an unrepresentable condition—these tones are appropriately nonverbal. Here, then, we find another turning away from the realm of language toward the radical materialism of abjection. As a means of return to the body of the mother, abjection is aligned with the flesh and its dissolution, with viscosity and bodily fluids—and with death.[22] As Kristeva points out, the corpse also escapes the symbolic order, since it has been rendered an object, a thing. The transsexual, also outside the symbolic order, is read similarly: for Christoph, her lover, Erwin/Elvire is a "'thing' that has no soul," with brains that are "nothing but jelly."

III

As Georges Bataille points out, the origin of the slaughterhouse is the temple, a location in which the preparation of meat both for food and for sacrifice goes forward: "The slaughterhouse emerges from religion insofar as the temples of times past … had a dual purpose, being used both for supplication and for slaughter."[23] Having worked as a butcher earlier in life, Erwin/Elvire is not distressed by the carnage s/he sees in the slaughterhouse. Reading the slaughter of the beasts as part of "life itself," s/he attempts to recast these bloody deaths as "giving meaning to" their lives. For her, the animals have a more general part to play in the cycle of life and death; transforming the real into the spiritual, s/he asserts that the beasts' "screams of pain" are actually "screams for salvation." While Fassbinder's film as a whole will not permit this salvation, we should note that Erwin/Elvire is identified both as butcher and as beast, and that the return to the scene of the slaughterhouse belongs to a stage in a Passion that has Christological overtones and will culminate in death.

Let us linger for a moment with the theme of food and ingestion, a theme that occurs in several guises in the textual fabric of Fassbinder's film. It is evident in the offering of food (bread, wine, and cheese) that Erwin/Elvire brings to Anton Saitz, the man for whose sake s/he became a transsexual. It is present in the iconography of the Last Supper that composes the garden scene in which Erwin/Elvire finds her daughter and wife consuming a meal that also includes bread and wine. As mentioned above, food and ingestion are also featured in Zora's fairy tale about the sister, a snail, who eats of her brother, the mushroom. And not only the abattoir scene effects a connection between the slaughtered beasts and Erwin/Elvire: during their argument, Christoph, her lover, calls her a "horrible, ugly piece of meat." If, for a moment, we read Christoph's angry words that Erwin/Elvire is a "piece of meat" with the images of the butchered animals in the slaughterhouse, then these words contain a suggestion of cannibalism.

This is not a literal cannibalism, to be sure. But the topos is also present, in barely disguised form, in Zora's fairy tale of the lost children mentioned above, in which the sister/snail eats of her brother/mushroom. The mushroom is doubly dangerous to eat, both because it may be poisonous and because it is the body of the brother. But the greatest danger lies in the boundary-crossing that this act signifies: the sister's act of consumption is wholly marked by the abject, for it collapses the boundary between self and other, inside and outside.[24] In cannibalism, as read by Kristeva, the symbolic is once more relinquished for abjection.

In the Christian sacrament, bread and wine are actually thought to *be* the body of Christ through the doctrine of transubstantiation; just as, for the Christian, God's word becomes flesh in the body of Christ, so do the sacramental bread and wine become "flesh." For the believer, their metaphorical character is temporarily overcome, only, of course, to be raised to a higher level of metaphoricity thereafter. In the case of Erwin/Elvire, however, the conversion of word into flesh goes no further, and, once again, incorporation is revealed to be the operative dynamic in Fassbinder's film. The masochistic "ecstasy" of excorporation, the "taking outside of" the self in heteropathic identification stressed by Silverman, might make "salvation" possible.[25] But the entrapment within the body suggested by the repeated metaphors of ingestion and incorporation, by multiple figurations of the return to the maternal body, imply that for Fassbinder the body, or the real, cannot be converted into the symbolic. Bataille's temple, once a space of sacred as well as profane slaughter, has become merely a slaughterhouse.

IV

Without the attendant redemption, Christ's Passion and crucifixion play a prominent role in the fantasmatic that structures a number of Fassbinder's films, generating erotic tableaux or situations in *Berlin: Alexanderplatz*, *Despair*, and *Querelle* as well as in *Thirteen Moons*. Indeed, the fantasmatic of these films, as Slavoj Žižek reads it, is structured on the Passion of Christ as the "fantasy-scenario which condenses all the libidinal economy of the Christian religion."[26] And the role played by abjection in *Thirteen Moons* is in accordance with Žižek's contention that Christianity embraces abjection in the figure of the saint. If the saint "occupies the place ... of pure object, of someone undergoing radical subjective destitution,"[27] then the resemblance of the saint's position to that of Erwin/Elvire is obvious. But these identifications seem to structure a purely personal fantasmatic. If the fantasmatic has a sociocultural dimension, absorbing "social and political alignments,"[28] how does this play itself out?

Thomas Elsaesser has alerted us to the manner in which the theme of Fassbinder's personal guilt over the death of his lover, Armin Meier, is radically expanded in *Thirteen Moons* to encompass German guilt and responsibility for the Holocaust. As Elsaesser suggests, Fassbinder's film allegorizes German-Jewish relations after Auschwitz, and does so as "a matter of love."[29] The fantasmatic of Fassbinder's film, as we have seen, is governed by materialism, by abjection, or, in Kristeva's parlance, by the realm of the mother. It is here that "subject and object push each other away, confront each other, collapse and start again—inseparable, contaminated, condemned, at the boundary of what is assimilable, thinkable: abject."[30] In this condition, self and other collapse; Erwin/Armin and Saitz/Fassbinder, lover and beloved, are also Erwin/Fassbinder and Saitz/Armin.[31] Erwin is both butcher and beast; within the logic of abjection, the two are inseparable, indistinguishable in mutual contamination. Through the topos of the Passion, Erwin is both Christian and Jew, just as he is both a German and the victim of his own Germanness.[32] But how can an ethics or a politics emerge from the negation of distinctions? Amidst the collapse of dichotomies that governs this scenario, the political would seem to be subsumed within the structure of the drives, which are insusceptible to ethics.

At this point we must look again at the presence of Hippler's *The Eternal Jew* within the chain of textualities that relates to *Thirteen Moons*, and again, it is "sacrifice" that is the operative term. As Žižek points out, it is the idea of sacrifice that most radically distinguishes Christianity from Jewish structures of belief. Although kosher butchering is not a religious practice but simply mandated by dietary law, the insidious propaganda of *The Eternal Jew* suggests that kosher butchering does not adequately sever the slaughter of animals for food from their slaughter for sacrificial purposes. Indeed, the images of lambs we see cavorting in the meadows carry another, albeit subliminal, message beyond that of impending cruelty to animals, calling to the minds of Christian spectators the crucifixion of the "Lamb of God." Not only does Hippler's film heighten spectatorial affect by acts of violence and cries of pain, but it also intensifies affect by attaching it to the domain of the sacred and to ideology.

We have already seen the manner in which Fassbinder's radical materialism makes use of the imagery of the Passion in order to disconnect death from sacrifice as well as from salvation. The "perverse, Wagnerian scenario," as Eric Santner puts it, sees the "final solution" to "the Jewish question" in the resolution of tensions by a Christ-like redeemer.[33] In *The Eternal Jew*, this role is obviously assumed by Hitler in his speech before the Reichstag, a speech that culminates in the fateful words "annihilation of the Jewish race in Europe." Hippler's film ends with words of exhortation delivered by its anonymous male narrator in voiceover, urging the German people to "keep the race pure" and to unify. Harnessing its constituent textualities, fascist film covers them over in a paternal voice that interprets the image, speaking in behalf of purity and organic wholeness.

Fassbinder's text, on the other hand, refuses to its very end to harness image and voice, choosing instead to lay its textualities bare. During the final minutes of *Thirteen Moons*, the multiple layers of its soundtrack are at their most prominent, and music never has the function of linking voice to body.[34] The sound of traffic and other noises, a pop song, the strains of the Vienna Boys Choir, the disembodied "celestial" voices, various diegetic conversations are all accompanied by Erwin/Elvire's emotionally charged taped interview—a monologue that, running in real time, lends the final minutes of Fassbinder's film a nearly unendurable sense of anguish. As the taped voice of Erwin/Elvire contemplates suicide, that voice's severance from its source in the body becomes hopelessly final as we come to realize that s/he is already dead. While the recorded voice, separable from the body, continues its search for significance, the body itself has become a corpse beyond significance, wholly consigned to abjection. When, at the end of the film, the Vienna Boys Choir's Christmas record skips, the words "leise rieselt" (quietly falling) are heard over and over again. Neither the skipping record that "voices" the jamming of all textualities nor the taped interview is anchored in a body. Instead, the body is rendered mute, and voice, its residue, sings on, embalmed in the mechanisms of technology.[35]

Deliberately tearing the skin that would make the textual body whole (and, therefore, consonant with the aesthetic ideology perverted by Nazism),

Fassbinder presents the spectator with a "flayed" text, a filmic body that bears the marks of self-flagellation. Thus, Fassbinder's film accomplishes at the level of style what it cannot do at the level of its structuring fantasy: it severs itself from the contaminated aesthetic and insupportable ideology of fascism. If the spectator is taken aback by the film's abrupt termination in a few unexposed black frames, it is because this end to all signification leaves us with mere material, with film stock. It is as if the film itself had died—or been tortured to death.

Notes

1. Roland Barthes, *S/Z*, trans. Richard Miller (New York: Hill and Wang, 1974), 20.
2. Ibid., 39.
3. Ibid., 200.
4. Ibid., 202.
5. Timothy Corrigan, *A Cinema Without Walls: Movies and Culture After Vietnam* (New Brunswick: Rutgers University Press, 1991), 69.
6. Julia Kristeva, "Approaching Abjection," in *Powers of Horror: An Essay on Abjection* (New York: Columbia University Press, 1982), 18.
7. Thomas Elsaesser, *Fassbinder's Germany: History Identity Subject* (Amsterdam: Amsterdam University Press, 1996), 191.
8. Roland Barthes, *The Pleasure of the Text*, trans. Richard Miller (New York: Hill and Wang, 1975), 67.
9. Roland Barthes, "The Grain of the Voice," in *Image, Music, Text*, trans. Stephen Heath (New York: Hill and Wang, 1977), 182.
10. As John Belton points out: "[S]ound recorded at the same time as the image is recorded locks the sound indexically into the profilmic event." John Belton, "Technology and Aesthetics of Film Sound," in *Film Sound: Theory and Practice*, ed. Elisabeth Weis and John Belton (New York: Columbia University Press, 1985), 70. Although Fassbinder's multilayered soundtrack is heterogeneous, the closely miked dialogue and ambient sound in the opening scene suggest that they were recorded during production.
11. Robert Burgoyne, "Narrative and Sexual Excess," *October* 21 (1982): 59.
12. Michel Chion, *The Voice in Cinema*, trans. Claudia Gorbman (New York: Columbia University Press, 1999), 18.
13. Kaja Silverman, *Male Subjectivity at the Margins* (New York: Routledge, 1992), 258.
14. Fassbinder credits himself with virtually all of the authorial functions in this film. For details about the autobiographical significance of this film for Fassbinder, see Elsaesser, *Fassbinder's Germany*, 197–98, and Silverman, *Male Subjectivity*, 214–15. In her suggestive chapter, Silverman discusses what she calls a "relay" from Erwin to Tasso and Fassbinder, reading this structure under the sign of sadomasochistic excorporation (257).
15. While the film was not shown in its entirety in Germany after the war, from the 1960s on the abattoir scene was often included in documentary film and television programs, and Fassbinder is very likely to have seen it. Stig Hornshøj-Møller and David Culbert, "*Der ewige Jude* (1940): Joseph Goebbels's Unequaled Monument to Anti-Semitism," *Historical Journal of Film, Radio, and Television* 12, no. 1 (1992): 50.
16. See Andrei Markovits, Seyla Benhabib, and Moishe Postone, "Rainer Werner Fassbinder's *Garbage, the City, and Death*." *New German Critique* 38 (1986): 1–28.
17. Elsaesser, *Fassbinder's Germany*, 191, 207.

18. Kaja Silverman, *The Acoustic Mirror: The Female Voice in Psychoanalysis and Cinema* (Bloomington: Indiana University Press, 1988), 85.
19. Mary Ann Doane, "The Voice in the Cinema: The Articulation of Body and Space," *Yale French Studies* 60 (1980): 44. See also Silverman, *The Acoustic Mirror*, 80ff.
20. Norbert Jürgen Schneider, *Handbuch Filmmusik: Musikdramaturgie im Neuen Deutschen Film* (Munich: Verlag Ölschläger, 1986), 109.
21. Silverman, *Acoustic Mirror*, 85.
22. Kristeva, "Approaching Abjection," 3. For another reading of abjection in Fassbinder, see Steven Shaviro, "Masculinity, Spectacle, and the Body of *Querelle*," in *The Cinematic Body* (Minneapolis: University of Minnesota Press, 1993), 159–97.
23. Quoted in Neil Leach, ed., *Re-Thinking Architecture: A Reader in Cultural Theory* (London: Routledge, 1997), 22.
24. Kristeva, "Approaching Abjection," 7.
25. Silverman, *Male Subjectivity*, 264.
26. Slavoj Žižek, *The Sublime Object of Ideology* (London: Verso, 1989), 116.
27. Ibid., 6.
28. Ibid., 116. See also Shaviro, "Masculinity, Spectacle, and the Body of *Querelle*."
29. Silverman, *The Acoustic Mirror*, 218.
30. Elsaesser, *Fassbinder's Germany*, 210.
31. Kristeva, "Approaching Abjection," 18.
32. Interesting here is that Armin Meier may have been a *Lebensborn* child, the product of Nazi eugenics experiments. See Al LaValley, "The Gay Liberation of Rainer Werner Fassbinder: Male Subjectivity, Male Bodies, Male Lovers," *New German Critique* 63 (1994): 123.
33. My reading thus differs from the one put forward by Gertrud Koch, who points out that Fassbinder's suffering characters never include his Jewish characters among them. See Gertrud Koch, "Torments of the Flesh, Coldness of the Spirit: Jewish Figures in the Films of Rainer Werner Fassbinder," *New German Critique* 38 (1986): 28–38.
34. Eric Santner, "Postmodernism's Jewish Question: Slavoj Žižek and the Monotheistic Perverse," *Visual Display: Culture Beyond Appearances*, ed. Lynne Cooke and Peter Wollen (Seattle: Bay Press, 1995), 253.
35. Hanns Eisler, *Composing for the Films* (New York: Oxford University Press, 1947), 77.
36. See Michel Chion's work for a different discussion of recorded or "on-the-air" sound. Michel Chion, *Audio-Vision: Sound on Screen*, trans. Claudia Gorbman (New York: Columbia University Press, 1994), 76ff.

Part III

SOUNDS OF SILENCE

Chapter 7

BENJAMIN'S SILENCE

Lutz Koepnick

There is a curious silence at the center of both Walter Benjamin's seminal theory of film and the academic reception of his 1936 essay on art in the age of mechanical reproduction.[1] Benjamin, though writing almost a decade after the introduction of sound film, completely evaded any discussion of how in 1929 the advent of synchronized sound in Germany had changed film exhibition, style, and consumption. In the eyes of the film industry, sound improved the possibilities of producing mass-cultural audiences because it streamlined what in silent cinema had been notoriously variable and unpredictable. In the view of many industrialists, sound film not only allowed for a refocusing of the act of reception—as much as the amassing of box office returns—on mostly the film itself, but also promised a technology that could overturn the growing hegemony of Hollywood in Europe. Numerous film ideologues of the time valorized synchronized sound as a chance to rearticulate nineteenth-century notions of German national identity that had defined national belonging in terms of linguistic properties and domestic musical traditions. Given Benjamin's acute interest in the politics of the popular, it is therefore more than puzzling that sound did not fit into the picture of his analyses. Why did Benjamin remain silent on sound and thus ignore the role of sound cinema in the shaping of new modes of spectatorship and in redefining the location of film as a public horizon of experience? What are the costs of Benjamin's omission? And what would happen if we broke Benjamin's silence and tried to write sound back into his theory of film?

Benjamin's artwork essay intended to expose how fascism uses modern modalities of representation in order to sanctify political leadership as an auratic presence. Fascism co-opts mechanical reproduction so as to channel cultural expressions into what Benjamin calls the aestheticization of politics. Drawing on avant-garde concepts and practices of the 1920s, Benjamin presents montage cinema as an antidote to the fascist spectacle. Montage, he argues, disrupts the seductive force of images and their appeal to merely emotive registers of reception. Instead of casting a mythic spell over the masses, avant-garde cinema for Benjamin galvanizes the modern experience of shock, distraction, and self-alienation into a politically productive force. The formal means of cutting and editing in montage cinema destroy mind-numbing illusionism and elicit moments of profane illumination. They make the cult value of bourgeois art recede into the background, put "the public in the position of the critic" (Ill, 240), and in so doing pave the audience's way to communication and solidarity.

There is clearly no conceptual reason why Benjamin, when writing about the politics of film in the mid-1930s, could not have extended his valorization of montage to the use of film sound. As early as 1928, for instance, Sergei Eisenstein, Vsevolod Pudovkin, and Grigori Alexandrov had endorsed diegetic and nondiegetic sound as a welcome element in montage constructions. Film sound, they argued, introduces "new means of enormous power to the expression and solution of the most complicated tasks that now oppress us with the impossibility of overcoming them by means of an imperfect method, working only with visual images."[2] That Benjamin did not follow the luminaries of Soviet montage cinema and instead continued to define film well into the 1930s as an essentially visual media raises fundamental questions about Benjamin's general familiarity with contemporary developments. However, I argue that Benjamin's exclusion of sound is neither accidental nor a random oversight. Rather, his adherence to silent film must be seen as a symptom of repression consequent to salient anxieties about the role of the acoustical in the modern world. As we will see, Benjamin clearly articulated his unease about modern sound production in various texts written immediately preceding the advent of synchronized film sound and prior to the artwork essay: his 1936 silence on sound has a relatively unambiguous prehistory. Furthermore, it is precisely the shunning of sound that allowed Benjamin to conceal critical disjunctions between his political and aesthetic agendas. While his politics urged him to embrace cinema as a sphere of proletarian emancipation and counter-hegemonic struggle, his aesthetic preferences caused him to rely on bourgeois concepts of film as text and script, as a homogeneous and self-contained art form. Whereas the first perspective should have encouraged Benjamin at least to investigate in further detail how sound rerouted the ways in which films entered their spectators' minds, the second perspective prompted him to understand contemporary spectatorship mostly in terms of esteemed literary reading practices. Trying to incorporate diverse theories into one revolutionary formula, Benjamin got halfway stuck between competing conceptions of cinema as a public trading ground of meaning and experience. As I show, it is only by sacrificing sound that he was able to uphold the most radical assumption of his essay, namely the interdependence of artistic innovation and political reform, the identity of aesthetics and politics in the age of mechanical reproduction.

I

In his celebrated studies of nineteenth-century Paris, Benjamin conceptualized the breakthrough of modernity in terms of an unprecedented explosion of the visual. Modern society, in Benjamin's view, is preoccupied with looking and spectacle. It overwhelms the individual with a multitude of discontinuous optical stimuli, decenters contemplative modes of seeing, and incorporates the subject into an ever-more accelerated dialectic of visual distraction and attention. Benjamin, on the other hand, takes little notice of the fact that nineteenth-century urbanization and industrialization also resulted in an equally diverting and disruptive cacophony of sounds. The concept of noise, after all, was a product of the same process that, in Benjamin's view, replaced tradition with fashion, visual contemplation with distracted looking, storytellers with image-makers. In the metropolitan centers of nineteenth-century life, "there was a constant din of construction and pounding, of the shrieking of metal sheets being cut and the endless thump of press machinery, of ear-splitting blasts from huge steam whistles, sirens, and electric bells that beckoned and dismissed shifts of first-generation urbanized laborers from their unending and repetitive days."[3] Whereas the sounds of rural life, whether natural or man-made, were all more or less recognizable, the layering of novel sonic stimuli in industrial environments at first clearly exceeded the individual's capacity to isolate acoustical sources and directions. Industrial noise assaulted the subject from all sides; it restructured the social organization of attention, ruptured meditative silences, and undercut absorbed forms of listening. Similar to the human eye in Benjamin's analysis, then, the ear, too, needed to be retrained in order to ward off the trials of modern streets and factory halls. Due to physiological limitations, this modernization of acoustical perception turned out to be much more challenging than the remaking of seeing in modernity. Unable to shut down hearing entirely or to actively screen out unwanted acoustical stimulations, the urbanized ear seemed ill prepared to afford what, in Benjamin's eyes, rendered modern vision a catalyst of new aesthetic experiences: introspective reverie and aestheticizing flânerie.

A few years prior to the introduction of synchronized sound to cinema, Paris surrealism expressed perhaps most clearly why a modernist such as Benjamin would favor the sights of the metropolis over its unruly sounds. Dedicated to the exploration of the unconscious and the uncensored, surrealism denigrated the soundscapes of urban life in the hope of giving form to internal sounds alone, that is, to sonic impressions that could be heard best only in silence.[4] While surrealists embraced the urban imaginary as a conduit to experiences of trance and intoxication, they disparaged the acoustical, including music, because external sounds restrained spontaneity and free imagination. Giorgio de Chirico argued in 1913 that good paintings contained more music than music itself, and that the acoustical was therefore quite inferior to the visual in granting aesthetic inspiration.[5] George Ribemont-Dessaignes, in a famous statement, suggested in 1919 the ban of music for the purpose of political morale and the hanging of all musicians.[6] And, most importantly, André Breton, in one of his many attempts to codify the surrealists' project around 1924, pledged to emancipate the human ear from all sounds other than those of the unconscious in order to enable unbridled voyages into the unknown and nonintentional: "Silence, so that I may pass where no one has ever passed!"[7] According to surrealists such as Breton, the cacophonies of modern life obstructed the possibility of profane illumination. In all of its different manifestations, modern noise distracted from the effort of winning—in Benjamin's own words—"the energies of intoxication for the revolution."[8] Whereas the eye, in the surrealists' perspective, was able to convert discontinuous impressions into subversive visions, the ear could merely reaffirm the paucity of the real. Surrealism's praise of shock as a trigger of aesthetic experience and innovation thus remained ambivalent. Most surrealists might have endorsed the visual jolts of industrial culture, but they were as eager to silence the sonic blows and incommensurable sound bites that accompanied modernity.

Benjamin's thought circa 1930 was deeply influenced by French surrealism.[9] While synchronized sound swiftly invaded German movie theaters—by 1932, 60 percent of all German theaters had already been wired for sound projection and German film studios had entirely ceased the production of silent features—Benjamin in his writing closely followed Breton's disquiet about the acoustics of industrial life. Nowhere does Benjamin's own valorization of silence and internal sound as sites of aesthetic illumination become clearer than in his autobiographical sketches of the early 1930s, published later under the titles *Berlin Chronicle* and *Berlin Childhood around 1900*. In a famous vignette, "The Telephone," printed in the *Frankfurter Zeitung* in February 1933, Benjamin recalled the impact of early telecommunication on his childhood existence. This text describes Benjamin's first encounter with the telephone as something uncanny and violent, not simply because the electrification of speech severed voices from bodies but also because it intermingled what Wilhelminian society was eager to keep at a distance: public from private realms, fantasy from the real. To be sure, the young boy instantly welcomes the telephone as a new twin brother. Yet like every *doppelgänger*, the machine harbors elements of unexpected danger as much as fascination. It duplicates and displaces reality and hence destabilizes any proper sense of place and belonging. On the one hand, when used to call someone else, the telephone helped transcend the stuffy inwardness of *Gründerzeit* life. It offered escape from the repressive aspects of the bourgeois interior, its historicist abundance, its phantasmagoria of containing self-enclosed universes, its deadly silence. On the other hand, however, the arbitrary nature by which the outside world could now intrude on private life led to new anxieties. The bell, in particular when ringing during rest periods, turned into a terrifying alarm that "disturbed not only my parents' afternoon nap but the world-historical epoch in whose middle they dwelled."[10] Ruthlessly invading the sanctuary of the home and of the boy's imagination, the telephone's sudden ring melted all that appeared to be solid into the air. It disrupted contemplative attitudes and summoned unmediated responses. What made telephones, in Benjamin's recollection, into particular sources of dismay was that they knew no mercy. Their sounds produced a frightful sense of contingency that subjected the boy to new forms of discipline. Petrified by the phone's assault on interiority, young Benjamin quickly learned to agree to every "first suggestion that was issued to me" (GS, 4:243).

Whether man-made or created by modern machines, the acoustical in Benjamin's autobiographical writings is mostly recalled as something that disturbed the boy's imagination; it distracted the inner voice of fantasy and enslaved the child to the instrumental and incommensurable imperatives of the real. Similar to the way in which the Biblical fall from grace, in Benjamin's speculative philosophy, left humanity with an impoverished notion of language as a mere tool of communication, so the advent of modern industrial society reduces sound to a vehicle of identity and functional adaptation. Instead of nourishing spontaneous and noncoercive relations to the world, the random noises of modern life rationalize perception and deplete humanity's mimetic faculty. They quell "the gift for producing similarities" (SW, 2:720) and bar any playful and reciprocal interaction between subject and object. Like the surrealists, young Benjamin therefore thrives whenever he can keep his ears wide shut and explore the murmur of the imagination. When poring over the library's tomes, he holds his hands over his ears: silence enables the boy best to absorb distant times and spaces and transcend the burdens and boundaries of reality (GS, 4:275).

In some sense, Benjamin's covering of the ears is, of course, nothing other than a holding action; it briefly shuts out the inevitable without ever mastering it. The child therefore develops other modes of listening that do not escape from the noises of industrial life but rather seem to flee into them. Yet what this imaginative and, as it were, mimetic form of hearing requires is a curious discontinuity between sight and sound, interior and exterior apperception. Urban noise, for the child, becomes manageable when its actual origin does not impose itself directly onto the eyes, encouraging the listener to imagine surprising correspondences between source and effect: "What do I hear? I do not hear the noise of battle guns or of Offenbach's ball music, nor the howling of factory sirens or the screaming that pierces the stock market at noon, not even the horses' clip-clop on the pavement or the marching music during the guards' parade. No, what I hear, is the brief rattle of the anthracite as it falls down from a metal container into the iron oven, it is the muffled bang that sets the gas lamp's flame to light, and the clinking of the lampshade on the brass ring when a carriage drives by on the street" (GS, 4:262). Instead of over-whelming the boy's sense perception, the noises of the city here inspire him to imagine what he cannot see or to establish nonsensuous similari-ties between sights, sounds, and sources. Unable to shut his ears or dwell in silence, the boy masters the noises of industrial life by closing his eyes, by associating isolated sonic events with mental representations and visu-alizing an acoustical scenery before his inner eye. Sound in this way becomes image and thus loses its cutting edge; it remains at a distance however close its source may be. What Benjamin heard when he listened to the city echoed the whisper we might hear whenever we hold up a seashell to our ear—and listen deeply into ourselves.

Benjamin's disquiet about the noises of his urban childhood extends in many respects to the realms of the musical as well. Similar to the factory sirens and the brokers' shouts, public music is mostly perceived as inva-sive and unsettling. Instead of carrying the imagination into uncharted territories, musical sounds cause young Benjamin to raise protective shields and fend off possible encroachments. Nothing was more "dehu-manizing" and "shameless" (GS, 4:273), Benjamin recalls, than the mili-tary music that entertained the passersby near the zoo on Lästerallee. It beat individuals into mindless attitudes, pushing the zoo's innocent visi-tor into a ferocious stream of pleasure-seeking ramblers. Roaring brass music emerged as quite agreeable, though, at the Neuen See, where it inspired ice skaters to draw intricate figures across the frozen surface of the lake. Sound here became manageable because it could be mediated into visual perceptions. Unlike the faceless stream on Lästerallee, Ben-jamin's skaters fascinated the eye and captured the imagination. They transposed rhythm into ornate lines and inscribed melodies as labyrinthine traces. Once etched onto the ice as image and text, music at the Neuen See thus allowed Benjamin to practice that most difficult of all modern arts, namely, the art of getting lost in the midst of the metropolis.

Born three years before the first show of projected moving images at the Berlin Winterpalast on 1 November 1895, Benjamin recalls his child-hood around 1900 primarily as an early silent feature, as a fragmented series of visual astonishments that do not cohere yet into any kind of uni-fied narrative.[11] Authentic experience and memory, for Benjamin, draw mostly from the visual, not the acoustical. Unlike his intellectual associate Theodor W. Adorno, Benjamin, therefore, has little to say about music in his autobiographical writings. Musical sounds pass Benjamin's censors of perception only if they can trigger inner visions or enter the imagination as iconic signs. It is precisely because of this privileging of sight over sound that Benjamin also remembers with some fondness and nostalgia one of the most remarkable spectacles of Wilhelminian culture, the *Kaiserpanorama*. Introduced in 1883, the *Kaiserpanorama* was a large multiviewer version of Brewster's stereoscope of the 1850s. It was designed for twenty-five spectators who could simultaneously view different stereoscopic images at 120-second intervals. Rotated by an internal engine, the twenty-five slides of the *Kaiserpanorama* transported the viewer around the globe without really establishing any sense of temporal sequence or spatial continuity. The *Kaiserpanorama* thus became "one of the numerous sites on which we can credibly locate an 'industrialization' of visual consumption: it [was] a space in which the physical and temporal alignment of body and machine correspond[ed] to the rhythms of factory production and to the way in which novelty and interruptions were introduced into assembly-line labor in order to prevent attention from veering into trance and daydream."[12]

When recalling the *Kaiserpanorama* of the 1890s in the early 1930s, Benjamin is clearly aware of how this stereoscopic peep show contributed to the modern disciplining of attention. Benjamin in fact remembers as one of the contraption's most salient features the bell that rang whenever the images were about to change. This bell announced a brief hiatus in the sequence of slides aligning body and machine, attention and fantasy. And yet it was during this intermittent darkening of pictorial representation that the *Kaiserpanorama* was able to activate some of the most engrossing desires; it was the indeterminate space in between the images that set the boy's mind in motion and allowed his visual imagination to pass where no one else had passed before. Technologies of interruption, for young Benjamin, thus provided a powerful means to delve into reverie; and it was precisely the silence after the bell, the machine's stress on pure specularity, that in Benjamin's recollection allowed the user to transcend the industrial orders of the day and depart on unforeseen voyages to other spaces and times: "Music, which later was to make traveling with film tiresome because it corroded the image that nourished the imagination— there was no music in the *Kaiserpanorama*" (GS, 4:239).

It is easy to see that the *Kaiserpanorama*, in spite of its kitsch and its already antiquated status circa 1900, serves Benjamin as a preview of coming attractions. It allegorizes Benjamin's disjunctive mode of recollecting his own past as much as it foreshadows what in his understanding makes silent film art superior to sound cinema. Benjamin's discussion of the *Kaiserpanorama* suggests that under the conditions of modern life, genuine experience and memory come primarily into being in moments of rupture and silence. It is during the abrupt transition from one frame of representation to the next that the modern imagination works most productively. Sound and music, on the other hand, inhibit such moments of profane illumination. They might evoke images that can defeat the paucity of the factual, but they can just as equally well blind the mind's eye and numb perception. Like de Chirico and Breton, Benjamin believes that music never really adds anything to what we can experience through images— it will always remain inferior to the power of vision. The recollection of the *Kaiserpanorama* formulates, in this sense, a critical injunction against the coming of synchronized sound and music around 1930. By recalling his own childhood as a cinema of silent wonders and attractions, Benjamin wants us to believe that sound films have chained the viewer's imagination to the real and the reified. As we drift through the muted panorama of his past, we come to understand that for Benjamin sound represses nothing less than film's ability to muster the energies of intoxication for the revolution.

II

Given his ambivalent stance toward the acoustical, it might seem surprising that Benjamin enjoyed a brief career as a radio playwright between 1929 and 1932. The first regular radio transmission in Germany took place on 29 October 1923. Within only a few years of its inception, the new medium enjoyed great currency among Weimar artists and intellectuals across the entire political spectrum. In many different ways, pioneers such as Bertolt Brecht, Elisabeth Hauptmann, Ernst Schoen, and Kurt Schwitters explored radio as a means of bringing art and theater to the masses or, even more so, of reassessing the entire function of art in modern society. Just when synchronized sound started to permeate German movie theaters, Benjamin aspired to join the efforts of these pioneers. Building on Brecht's participatory theory of radio,[13] Benjamin wrote a number of radio plays—"Listening Models"—in which dialogue and sound effects were not simply meant to compensate for the missing visual dimension but to gain a status in their own right and take over new didactic functions. Benjamin foresaw radio as playing a critical role in replacing the bourgeois culture of knowledge and entertainment with a culture of training critical judgment: "Radio, which has a particular duty to take up older cultural products, will best do this by means of adaptations that not only do justice to modern technology, but also satisfy the expectations of an audience that is contemporary with this technology. Only in this way will the apparatus be freed from the nimbus of a 'gigantic machine for mass education' (as Schoen has described it) and reduced to a format that is worthy of human beings" (SW, 2:585).

Benjamin's notion of adaptation aspired to go beyond mainstream uses of radio as a theater of the blind. Radio plays, in Benjamin's perspective, should not simply translate existing theater productions into audible versions. Instead, they should exploit the absence of visual representation as an aesthetic and a political opportunity. Plays such as *Salary Raise? What Are You Thinking Of?* (GS, 4:629–40) and *What Germans Read While Their*

Classical Authors Were Writing (GS, 4:641–70), for instance, confronted their listeners with a virtual war of words. They assessed different rhetorical strategies of mastering mundane situations: how to convince your employer to pay you a higher salary, and how to make a good case for what kind of reading materials might be of greater or lesser importance. In juxtaposing examples with counterexamples and dialogue with commentary, Benjamin's "Listening Models" imported Brecht's didactic aesthetics of interruption and disidentification into the world of radio. Pragmatic lectures on everyday life, these plays embraced the media's stress on speech and dialogue as an instrument of rational persuasion and instruction: the absence of visual distractions was meant to focus the listener's attention on positions not persons, on arguments not emotions. More Brechtian, in fact, than Brecht's own radio work, *The Lindbergh Flight* (1929), which had woven different modalities of sound into an imaginative radio cantata, Benjamin's radio pieces hoped to turn disembodied speech into a medium of self-empowerment and emancipation. They were designed for focused listeners who were eager not only to improve their verbal skills but also to employ language for the sake of changing the naturalized orders of ordinary life.

Some of Benjamin's other radio plays, particularly, *Trouble with Kasperl* (GS, 4:674–95) and *Lichtenberg* (GS, 4:696–720), surpass this educational emphasis on discourse and rhetoric. The burlesque drama *Trouble with Kasperl*, for example, incorporates the medium of radio itself into the play. It presents the German Punch figure, who mocks Germany's new media authorities yet in the end becomes a viable broadcast commodity himself. A rich cast of sound effects plays an important role in this drama in setting scenes that cannot be seen. Noises from slamming doors, breaking glass, ringing telephones, honking cars, tooting ship sirens, whistling steam engines, and spinning carousels create a kind of visceral excitement, deepen dramatic space and action, and offer additional layers of signification. Similarly, in *Lichtenberg*, Benjamin imagines futuristic machines that can capture distant sounds, and whose malfunction—that is, silence—causes comical shifts in the action. The play recalls the life of the famous German intellectual of the eighteenth century as observed through the eyes and ears of a moon committee on earth research. The moon's inhabitants, we are told in the opening, sustain themselves on nothing other than the "silence of their fellow citizens, which they consequently do not wish to see interrupted" (GS, 4:697). Moon researchers have developed all kinds of instruments in order to investigate life on earth, not least of all, a so-called parlamonium, which allows lunar scientists to translate the sounds of human speech into more comforting celestial music. Even though Benjamin's listener will hear little of this music, the issue of sound production and reception thus structures the play's content as much as its form. It ties distant times and spaces together, enables effective transitions between humorous and more serious segments of the drama, and offers a convenient mechanism to turn the visual lack of radio into an incentive to use one's imagination. In both *Trouble with Kasperl* and *Lichtenberg*, Benjamin entertains the listeners with playful scenes of prosthetic speaking and listening. In both dramas, the new medium, to a large degree, becomes its own message.

And yet due to their underlying didacticism, Benjamin's plays clearly eschewed more radical conceptions of radio as a means of exploring sound in terms of a purely acoustical event. Unlike the products of Weimar radio avant-gardists such as Alfred Braun, Hans Bodenstedt, Hans Flesch, Eduard Reinacker, and Walter Ruttmann, Benjamin's radio plays remain essentially plot driven. They employ noise or music as mere handmaidens to a particular story line, theme, or semantic agenda. Rather than collecting random sound bites on Weimar streets, Benjamin wrote his radio contributions at a desk. They could be printed between the covers of a book, and by using sound to set dramatic scenes, they ultimately depend on a visual aesthetic. In contrast to Ruttmann's 1928 *Weekend*, which fuses speech fragments and moments of silence into an acoustical poem, Benjamin's plays place speech entirely in the service of conventionalized meaning and signification. In spite of his bias toward cinema and the visual, Benjamin did not follow the lead of radio pioneers such as Bodenstedt and Braun, who even prior to the arrival of sound film sought to transfer cinematic techniques of transition—cuts, dissolves, montage—to the radio in order to broadcast what they called acoustical films.

In Braun's sonic portraits of German cityscapes, "images both flowed dreamily and flitted by in quickest succession, abbreviated images, superimposed images, alternating and blending close-ups and distant shots. Each of the short images was positioned on a particular acoustical place, surrounded by a particular acoustical set: 1 minute street with the loud music of Leipzig Square; 1 minute protest march; 1 minute stock market on the day of the crash; 1 minute factory with its machine symphony; 1 minute soccer stadium; 1 minute train station; 1 minute train underway, etc."[14] Braun incorporates cinematic techniques, not to remake radio as a cinema of the blind, but to free sound from serving predefined images or from simply being substituted for missing visual props. Like a rag picker, Braun sifts through the acoustical landscapes of modern life, aspiring to gather unique sonic materials and assemble them within a new kind of postautonomous artwork. His penchant for collectors and collecting notwithstanding, Benjamin clearly stayed away from such avant-gardism. In spite of their sonic effects, Benjamin's radio plays show little interest in exploring the pure materiality of contemporary speech, music, and noise. Language in his plays remains well scripted and semantically coherent; music defines scenic fore- and backgrounds without drawing attention to itself; and urban noises, while supplying visceral textures, remain subordinate to the course of dramatic action. Unlike those of the Weimar avant-garde, Benjamin's radio plays remained thoroughly based on literary models. If silent film, for Benjamin, was "the school in which one could best learn the script of cinema,"[15] then radio in Benjamin's eyes provided an opportunity to reassess the contours of writing in industrial culture without leaving the realm of textuality. Reading and seeing, not listening, defined the basic coordinates of Benjamin's radio work. Trying to beat Brecht at his own game, Benjamin assigned political meanings to radio at the cost of subjecting the new medium to a general process of literarization.

III

At the same historical moment, then, when synchronized sound conquered German movie theaters, Benjamin repeatedly turned to the acoustical in order to assess its political and aesthetic potentials. As we have seen, however, Benjamin's discussion of sound remained deeply ambivalent. He resorted to various strategies of visualization and literarization so as to take the edge out of modern sound production. Though endorsing distracted perception as the principal mode of modern experience, Benjamin textualized acoustical events or transmuted noise in order to ward off unwanted sonic distractions. Unlike the visual stimuli of the modern metropolis, the cacophonous sounds of industrial culture clearly disturbed Benjamin's perception; he had to translate them into scripts or images to make them manageable.

We will therefore do well not to underestimate the absence of sound in Benjamin's film theory as a mere accident. His silence on sound was systematic; it had been in the making, in various guises, all along. What is equally important to recognize, on the other hand, is that Benjamin's repression of sound decenters the critical thrust of his theory of film and fascism in at least two dimensions. First, by rendering silent film as the most authentic formulation of the medium, Benjamin moves along argumentative positions markedly at odds with his explicit political agenda. By defining film—like Arnheim—as an essentially visual medium and by understanding visual montage—like the early Eisenstein—as the medium's innermost logic, Benjamin ended up joining the chorus of those who rejected sound film because they hoped to protect film art against what they considered the detrimental effects of modern mass culture. While popular audiences embraced sound film quickly as a new standard of representation, leading German film critics battled against it well into the 1930s. Silent cinema, for these critics, served as a twentieth-century manifestation of the bourgeois public sphere; it opened a space of public discourse based on the educated reception and edifying valorization of aesthetic artifacts. Sound, on the other hand, was seen as poisoning artistic integrity and formal rigor. It transformed film into an impure medium, undermined the structural possibility of public discourse, and hence led to a precarious leveling of high and low art. Benjamin's artwork essay, of course, argued that with the arrival of mechanical reproduction such distinctions between art and mass culture were no longer valid. In repressing sound from film, however, Benjamin revealed the extent to which he continued to read modern mass culture through the lens of more esteemed cultural practices. In spite of his endorsement of the popular, Benjamin viewed films solely as if they made for theorists and critics. Eager to define film as a visual and homogeneous art form, Benjamin in the end failed his own objective, namely, to illuminate how mass audiences actually made use of filmic events.

Second, as a result of the omission of sound, Benjamin's theory of film—in spite of its attempt to demystify the fascist aestheticization of politics—lacks critical tools for understanding the ways in which Nazi cinema coordinated emotion and engineered assent. Nazi film practitioners embraced sound film as a means to integrate word, music, and image into one impressive work of art. Nazi film scores aspired to seduce and lull the mind, but they also, and as importantly, wanted to astound and overwhelm the viewer, as well as to grant access to the mythic sources of national belonging. Film, for Nazi directors and theorists such as Wolfgang Liebeneiner,[16] was music with other means. Dialogue and music were meant to complete the rhythmical structure of the image track instead of simply to illustrate emotions or stitching together narratives. It was therefore only with the coming of film sound that German cinema, according to Liebeneiner, could finally fulfill that "old Germanic longing to include the whole world into one artwork and to combine all art forms into one powerful experience."[17]

Benjamin's artwork essay, in spite of its critical aspirations, does not offer enough to theorize how Nazi soundtracks advocated the viewers' desires so as to beat audiences into submission. Fascism indeed, as Benjamin maintained, tried to colonize modern sense perception so as to break older bonds of solidarity and establish some new kind of community; it made use of film to mobilize people's feelings and neutralize their senses. In order to do so, it relied not only on powerful images but also on mesmerizing sounds; it redefined heterogeneous media, including the sound film, as organically integrated wholes that would not only rouse powerful affects but also control all possible effects. By understanding film exclusively as a visual mode of expression, Benjamin in turn deprived himself of the possibility of recognizing the full spectrum of fascist media practice. Strangely out of synch with the developments of film technology, Benjamin mobilized the past—silent film—against the present and thus forfeited his own claim that technological developments change not only the content of aesthetic practices but also the entire concept of art.

Although Benjamin's combined theory of film and fascism must be seen as one of the most original contributions to twentieth-century thought, Benjamin's silence on sound clearly limits its historical and critical use value. Synchronized sound had simply no place within a theory that sought to join surrealist intoxication and Brechtian distanciation, aesthetic formalism and proletarian populism, viewing and reading, into one ground-breaking formula. There is little reason to believe, on the other hand, that we can mend Benjamin's conceptual exclusion of sound and simply let the acoustical in through the backdoor. As always, the repressed is most likely to return in the form of a monstrosity.

Notes

1. Walter Benjamin, *Illuminations: Essays and Reflections*, ed. Hannah Arendt, trans. Harry Zohn (New York: Schocken, 1969), 217–52; subsequently referenced in the text as "Ill."
2. Sergei Eisenstein, *Film Form: Essays in Film Theory*, by Sergei Eisenstein (San Diego: Harcourt Brace Jovanovich, 1977), 259.
3. Mel Gordon, "Songs from the Museum of the Future: Russian Sound Creation (1910–1930)," in *Wireless Imagination: Sound, Radio, and the Avant-Garde*, ed. Douglas Kahn and Gregory Whitehead (Cambridge, MA: MIT Press, 1992), 197.
4. Christopher Schiff, "Banging on the Windowpane: Sound in Early Surrealism," in *Wireless Imagination*, ed. Kahn and Whitehead, 139–90.
5. James Thrall Soby, *Giorgio de Chirico* (New York: Modern Museum of Art, 1955), 245–46.
6. Georges Ribemont-Dessaignes, "Musique eventail et le serin crocodile," *391*, no. 10 (1919): 3.
7. André Breton, "Introduction to the Discourse on the Paucity of Reality," in *What is Surrealism? Selected Writings*, ed. Franklin Rosemont (New York: Monad, 1978), 24.
8. Walter Benjamin, "Surrealism," in *Selected Writings: Volume 2, 1927–1934*, ed. Michael W. Jennings, Howard Eiland, and Gary Smith (Cambridge, MA: Harvard University Press, 1999), 215; subsequently referenced in the text as "SW."
9. Josef Fürnkäs, *Surrealismus als Erkenntnis: Walter Benjamin—Weimarer Einbahnstraße und Pariser Passagen* (Stuttgart: Metzler, 1988); Margaret Cohen, *Profane Illumination: Walter Benjamin and the Paris of Surrealist Revolution* (Berkeley: University of California Press, 1993).
10. Walter Benjamin, *Gesammelte Schriften*, ed. Rolf Tiedemann and Hermann Schweppenhäuser (Frankfurt am Main: Suhrkamp, 1972), 4:243; subsequently referenced in the text as "GS."
11. Tom Gunning, "An Aesthetic of Astonishment: Early Film and the (In)Credulous Spectator," in *Viewing Positions: Ways of Seeing Film*, ed. Linda Williams (New Brunswick: Rutgers University Press, 1995), 114–33.
12. Jonathan Crary, *Suspension of Perception: Attention, Spectacle, and Modern Culture* (Cambridge, MA: MIT Press, 1999), 138.
13. Bertolt Brecht, "Radiotheorie," in *Gesammelte Werke in 20 Bänden* (Frankfurt am Main: Suhrkamp, 1967), 18:117–34; Roswitha Mueller, *Bertolt Brecht and the Theory of Media* (Lincoln: University of Nebraska Press, 1989).
14. Quoted in Mark E. Cory, "Soundplay: The Polyphonous Tradition of German Radio Art," in *Wireless Imagination*, ed. Kahn and Whitehead, 339–40.
15. Norbert Bolz and Willem van Reijen, *Walter Benjamin*, trans. Laimdota Mazzarins (Atlantic Highlands, NJ: Humanities Press, 1996), 77.
16. Wolfgang Liebeneiner, "Die Harmonie von Bild, Wort und Musik im Film," *Film-Kurier*, 13 March 1939, 4–5.
17. Ibid., 5.

Chapter 8

DEAFENING SOUND AND TROUBLING SILENCE IN VOLKER SCHLÖNDORFF'S *DIE BLECHTROMMEL*

Elizabeth C. Hamilton

This chapter explores the nexus of sound and subjectivity in twentieth-century Germany. At issue are the ways in which sound has contributed to the construction and recognition of the human subject, and, by extension, to the rights and privileges afforded the human subject within specific historical contexts. I am concerned with the uses and abuses of sound, specifically, the political appropriation of the voice in the service of National Socialism and again in the resulting years in which West Germans struggled, in varying degrees, to deal with the legacy of the Third Reich. This essay will show how notions of the voice and hearing during the Nazi years continued to thrive during the postwar years. I shall address the several ways in which speaking and hearing influenced both Nazi and postwar West German conceptualizations of the self and the other, the subject and the object.

Before Ernestine Schlant so convincingly articulated that silence is constructed within historical narrative contexts and constitutes a substantial part of language surrounding the Holocaust,[1] Volker Schlöndorff had already offered one artistic exposition of silence as a language and problematized its historically changing roles in shaping the German subject. Twenty years after the appearance of Günter Grass's 1959 novel *Die Blechtrommel* (The Tin Drum),[2] Schlöndorff's eponymous film found corresponding public resonance. Within West Germany, the film drew not only critical and popular acclaim but also accusations of indecency and sometimes unfavorable comparisons with the esteemed, if not entirely beloved, literary work. Today, twenty years after the film's debut, its place in film history is secure even as the manner in which it contributes to *Vergangen-heitsbewältigung*, or, as it is often expressed in English, "coming to terms with the past," continues to be debated.

Although several critical studies of Schlöndorff's *The Tin Drum* subordinate the study of sound in the film to analysis of its visual images and narrative structure, sound merits more critical attention for the insight it offers in three broad areas. First, an analysis of sound sheds light on the process of filmic adaptation of the original literary work. For example, through sound, a device that a printed text does not have at its disposal, Schlöndorff conveys the type of split between the body and voice of the film's protagonist, Oskar, that Grass's novel conveys through the shifting first- and third-person narrators. Second, an analysis of sound sheds light on film history. *The Tin Drum* contains two pivotal scenes that make use of early silent film techniques, such as expanding and contracting iris shots, and footage from a hand-cranked camera. Schlöndorff does not merely honor film tradition through the use of such quotations; he also expands the grammar of film and makes his most profound statements through the very juxtaposition of older and newer techniques. Third, an analysis of sound sheds light on a primary problem of *Vergangenheitsbewältigung*, namely, the capacity of language to express the horrors of the Nazi era. Like the novel, the film exposes the economic and social structures that provided fertile ground for planting Nazi ideas. I shall argue here that even though the characters embedded within the diegesis "miss" Oskar's message and dismiss him as an inconsequential child, the pointed used of sound in the film prevents the film audience from being lulled into comfortable spectatorship. Stated bluntly, *The Tin Drum* is largely a very loud film intermittently interspersed with sequences of silence. All of the sound structures that Schlöndorff has built into the film have a particular function,[3] and they work together to confront public silence surrounding the legacy of Nazi murder. In short, Schlöndorff examines the historical route (and roots) of National Socialism by exploiting the tension between the sonic and the visual. Juxtaposing terrifically noisy sounds with silence, Schlöndorff's film reveals what is at stake when a population "overhears" silence and does not recognize its potential as a critical voice of resistance, opposition, and healing. Schlöndorff also elevates silence as a component of his art. Because he makes use of many available tools of filmmaking and elevates the interplay among acoustic and visual elements of film, it is fair to regard silence as a color on this filmmaker's palette.

Several interrelated trends in social history and film history have established a framework for interpreting Schlöndorff's use of sound in the film and for assessing his achievement. Both the content and the style of *The Tin Drum* are informed by social Darwinism, particularly by Darwinist notions of the role and hierarchy of language. Scientific and pseudoscientific theories of evolution were increasingly accepted after the middle of the nineteenth century in the form of social Darwinism and were widely applied to explain language development and to justify educational and cultural policies.[4] Broadly stated, in terms that Schlöndorff would ulti- mately call into question in his film, spoken language was thought to be the highest form of expression for human beings; but signs—expressed in silence—were thought to be for savages. Educators and philologists com- monly held that "it was through the process of natural selection and sur- vival of the fittest that the voice has gained the upper hand."[5] Within this so-called linguistic Darwinism is the assumption that spoken discourse is the highest form of language and that silence constitutes an absence or a lack of language, rendering it therefore devoid of meaning, potentially devoid of value, and arguably detrimental to a speaking population as a whole. Linguistic Darwinism had a substantial impact on the education of deaf people in oralist language and justified efforts to discourage and eventually forbid the use of sign language.[6] Carried to its extreme under National Socialism, this notion served to justify the extermination of "life unworthy of living," which for the Nazis included deaf people, among so many others.[7] Extreme linguistic Darwinism under the Nazis also shaped aesthetic sensibilities, elevating bold rhythm, militaristic music, frenzied "motivating" speeches, and jubilant, noisy crowds over more contempla- tive, introspective, or individualistic modes of expression.

Although Schlöndorff cannot be said to engage in the debate over lin- guistic Darwinism per se, he clearly delves intensively into the problem of language and signs in *The Tin Drum*. He also warns his audiences about the damaging conceptual continuities from the Nazi period. He problematizes the inability of the German language to convey sufficiently what Oskar Matzerath can communicate through a drum, a scream, and silence, namely, the damaging interpersonal and socioeconomic structures that will repro- duce themselves indefinitely unless met with substantial resistance. In other words, Schlöndorff attempts to shape a public consciousness that would ideally dislodge what psychologists Alexander and Margarethe Mitscherlich describe as a collective West German cultural denial of the Nazi past. In their 1967 work, *Die Unfähigkeit zu trauern* (The Inability to Mourn),[8] the Mitscherlichs assessed the postwar inability to mourn the loss of the war and the loss of Adolf Hitler, the leader with whom most Germans had grown to identify. Predicting widespread mourning and melancholy, the Mitscherlichs were struck instead by the lack of any sus- tained public confrontation with the Nazi past in postwar German society. Instead, they found within the West German population psychological defense mechanisms of striking emotional rigidity; a widespread, little- challenged practice of identifying oneself as a victim; and an enormous collective effort of reconstruction at the expense of considering one's own involvement with the past.[9]

Many New German Cinema filmmakers such as Schlöndorff saw them- selves not only as the inheritors of this psychological burden, but as artists who were particularly obliged to engage the public in confronting the past. Inherent in the New German Cinema project of developing a new film language to replace *Papas Kino* (daddy's cinema) was the imperative to uncover what had come before. Silent cinema from the turn of the century until the Weimar era offered surprisingly meaningful strategies for grappling with contemporary issues as well as safe and fertile ground for reestablishing a German film tradition.

These early films shared with the printed word an absence of sound, if we look away temporarily from the musical accompaniment, lecture-narration, or reading of intertitles, produced and enacted separately from the projected moving picture, that took place in cinemas themselves. Popular cinema after 1927, however, usually addressed the audience through sound, an invention that was more often hailed as signaling the demise rather than the growth of cinema as an art form. It must be noted, however, that sound itself was not what "purists" were worried about; rather, it was synchronous dialogue and speech. Talk, not sound, presented the problem. Spoken words "posed a threat to a figurative language that had evolved to a state of near-perfection during the silent era."[10] Asynchronous sound was believed to hold the most potential for new methods of expression, for film images could still be created with a moving camera. Synchronous sound, including speech, precluded the use of a movable camera, for the earliest synchronic recording equipment required a fixed microphone. All scene composition would be determined by the location of the microphone and therefore the camera, severely limiting actors' movements as well as the scope of the camera lens. Thus, at its best, synchronous sound was felt to restrict the cinema to the simple recording of theatrical performances. The silent film was widely held to offer the most promise as a new art form given its elevation of movement and visual symbols over synchronous sound and speech.[11]

Volker Schlöndorff, working under the assumption that the absence of vocalized language does not imply the absence of language itself, reclaimed not only silent film language, but also silence to refute the tenets of linguistic Darwinism. The following examination of *The Tin Drum* identifies the silences and the sounds within it as fully human language and, as such, assertions—if subversive—of human subjectivity.

A few words about Grass's novel are in order here. *The Tin Drum* tells the story of Oskar Matzerath's decision to stop growing at the age of three because he does not want "his shadows to be measured against those of his parents" (der seinen Schatten nicht mit ihrem Schatten messen wollte).[12] Even at birth, Oskar protests the self-centeredness of the lower middle class into which he is born, sensing that the very class and family structures he inhabits will lead to the murderous violence of National Socialism. Yet Oskar also represents that same capacity for exploitation and violence. Much scholarship on the novel, including my own, draws attention to the shifting narrative perspective and concludes that this shift is where Grass's commentary of West Germany's tenuous moral foundation is to be found.[13] The changing narrative perspective of the novel prevents Oskar from being perceived solely as an opponent, a victim, or a perpetrator of Nazi ideology.

Schlöndorff, in my estimation, carries Grass's important work to a clearer and more effective conclusion. Whereas Grass's novel indicts the social and economic structures of the lower middle class for having advanced National Socialism, Schlöndorff's film emphasizes parent-child relationships within the smaller family unit, underscoring more than the novel that fascism begins at home. The film speaks directly to the generational conflict played out in public and artistic realms in West Germany in the wake of the student movement during the late 1960s and 1970s. After years of silence about the Nazi era and the Holocaust, mounting pressure from *den Nachgeborenen* (those born later) culminated in often extremely painful, interpersonal dialogues in which children asked their parents what they had done during the Third Reich. Schlöndorff's extraordinary level of craftsmanship and independent vision, combined with his comprehensive understanding of both literature and of the cultural function of cinema, led to a film that most clearly confronts the German Nazi past and urges the public—in very specific ways—to come to terms with it. Schlöndorff was well aware of the magnitude of the novel and of the imposing stature of its author. Known as an artisan rather than a film auteur, Schlöndorff intended to make a film faithful to the qualities of the novel, if not faithful to the narrative itself. Schlöndorff insisted that the film not become a simple "staging of literature."[14] Although this ultimately pleased Grass,[15] other reviewers were at first lukewarm in their assessment of the film with respect to the novel.[16]

Schlöndorff's film treats only the first two sections of Grass's novel, alluding to the emerging West German capitalist state of the novel's third section in the final scene of the film. Other changes were made as well, yet Schlöndorff retained the qualities of Oskar as both a metaphor and an active critic in the same proportions in which they appear in the novel. He could have used the split forms of narrative that Grass used, but he reasoned that on film this would have been too confusing and too disjointed, even for a film about societal confusion and historical disjuncture. Schlöndorff notes Grass's approval of this change in his film journal: "It would have required constant flashbacks, complicated ones, like going around the same corner three times. What a semicolon can do for writing is too complicated for a film."[17] Schlöndorff conveys the novel's complicated narrative positions through the juxtaposition of silence and sound. By placing silent scenes next to extremely noisy ones, Schlöndorff calls into question the notion that spoken and heard discourse is of a necessarily higher order than images expressed silently. Many moments from the film suggest quite the opposite. *The Tin Drum*'s noise-filled scenes most often convey violent commotion and the capacity for language and sound to corrupt and coerce. Indeed, the noisiest sequences reveal the fascist tendencies of the characters.

Many deafeningly loud scenes feature a wide range of characters who, for a variety of reasons, subscribe to Nazi ideology and commit their voices to Nazi agitation, and Oskar himself often appears at these moments. The complexity of the film's sound matrix is compounded by the very slipperiness of Oskar Matzerath. If Schlöndorff recalls the silent film and teases viewers to imagine, he also provokes viewers with a noisy, disturbing, sound-filled film that barely leaves room to imagine. Instead, viewers meet a loud, screaming, drumming boy (and later, a young man in a boy's body) who demands to be heard but is often so loud that he cannot be heard. Viewers are presented, then, with multiple and competing sounds and silences.

Upon a first encounter, Oskar appears to be an extraordinarily loud character. He is recognizable above all for his tin drum, which he pounds rather than plays; he is also known for his glass-shattering screams[18] and for throwing loud and destructive tantrums whenever he does not get his way. Oskar's noisy drumming and screaming must be understood in two competing ways: they link him not only to the destructive, exploitative actions that found their ultimate expression in Nazi crimes and murders, but also to witnessing and resisting those same actions. Oskar's noise, in short, aligns him with both the perpetrators and the victims of Nazi violence. Consider, for example, the sequence at the doctor's office. Taking Oskar against his will to Dr. Hollatz after an outburst at school, Agnes pleads with the doctor to explain her son's screaming and stunted growth. Refusing to be examined, Oskar erupts in a piercing, specimen-jar-shattering tantrum. Three shrill, high-pitched screams emerge from Oskar's lips, accompanied by a nondiegetic, dissonant chord from an organ. Falling from the top of tall cabinets, the broken jars spill various bodily organs onto the office floor. The commotion ends in the motionless bewilderment of the characters on screen. Dr. Hollatz breaks the silence with an authoritative, if stunned, assessment—"Extraordinary. Extraordinary"—and immediately asks Agnes for permission to write about this "voice phenomenon" in a medical journal. He completely disregards the question of Oskar's diminished height.

This scene is pivotal for what it reveals about Oskar's simultaneous objectification by medical science as well as his efforts to assert himself as a social subject. Oskar has been brought to the doctor, after all, so that he might be *cured* of the condition that signals his act of resistance and self-definition. Corrective measures would thoroughly reconstitute his social as well as his physical identity. Is Oskar not then a potential victim of a society that demands uniformity? Perhaps, yet sound in this scene invites qualification. Screaming and nondiegetic music work against the images portrayed. Organ chords amplify Oskar's vocal chords, portraying Oskar to be dangerously out of control. His facial expressions, however, indicate that he is in complete control. Oskar's knowing, upturned eyes seem to recognize and even endorse the way the doctor will exploit his findings.

Oskar's capacity to act as a subject is not compromised, but is in fact disturbingly enhanced by the capacity he shows here to control and manipulate others. In earlier scenes, Oskar has exposed the self-serving actions of the people around him; here, he exposes his own, rather large, capacity to exploit and manipulate other people through the phenomenon of his voice.

It might surprise an audience to note, however, that at least in purely quantitative terms, Oskar is far more often silent than noisy. Oskar rarely speaks on-screen; I counted only ten brief exchanges. Schlöndorff's *Tagebuch* confirms this in a summary of the postproduction synchronizing process: "Oskar Matzerath speaks as little as Gary Cooper in a Western."[19] Another early screening yielded the comment that the character speaks so little that he seems like an extra.[20]

Oskar's voice-over narrations add another dimension to the sound matrix that further complicates his already questionable position among perpetrators and victims. Asynchronous voice-overs often separate Oskar's body from his voice, giving him at these moments an all-knowing presence that often belies the visual images of Oskar. When viewers see him, in other words, they are seeing a child. Simply hearing Oskar's voice-overs, viewers encounter a wiser, older Oskar, who assumes the role of the *Hofnarr*, or court jester. The court jester, who speaks the truth but finds no believers, has long been a common literary trope for a dwarf, and Schlöndorff had decided early in preproduction that he would cast an adult dwarf as Oskar. Despite this intention, twelve-year-old actor David Bennent was chosen instead for the other qualities he could bring to the part. Bennent, who received the role because of his eyes, his mature facial expressions, and his general precociousness, was cast in order to lend "credence to the idea that Oskar—far from being an ugly dwarf or gnome—was a child who of his own volition and as an act of protest simply decided to stop growing."[21] Schlöndorff has said that one does not reproduce a child's perspective simply by lowering the camera. He wanted instead to capture the emotional impact that the behavior of adults has in a child's eyes. The choice of Bennent was intended to promote audience identification, for Schlöndorff felt that it would be easier for most audience members to identify with a child than with a dwarf. If this is true, then we see again the slipperiness of Oskar that the sound of the film effects: if the visually represented Oskar is a child, but the voice of Oskar is much more mature, with which Oskar should viewers identify?

Audience identification with Oskar is most often invited at times when Oskar is silent on screen, observing the people around him. In those moments when Oskar acts as the court jester or witnesses the bad behavior of adults, viewers can comfortably identify with him as though they were witnesses as well. Viewers can see Nazi ideals taking root, and they can see, as Oskar sees, how routine selfishness allowed National Socialism to flourish. Viewers watch, for example, as Alfred Matzerath unveils the new radio in the household and replaces a portrait of Beethoven on the wall with a portrait of Hitler. The radio and the voice of Hitler are the visual and auditory signals of a new militarism, while the image of Beethoven is simply and quietly removed.

The audience, at the moment of identification with the silent Oskar, is afforded a comfortable distance from the growth of Nazism. Yet if viewers identify with Oskar at moments when he is silent, how can viewers justify not identifying with him at moments when he is loud and reveals his own protofascist tendencies? Schlöndorff has filled the film with nearly imperceptible seams where the potential victim Oskar becomes the bystander and then the perpetrator of Nazi violence. After a sequence in which Oskar silently observes yet another weekly sexual encounter between his mother and Jan Bronski, Oskar begins to drum feelings of disappointment that ultimately take the shape of a deeper, more genuine sense of abandonment. The ambiguity of this sequence emerges during its transition into the next. Oskar is pictured in the bell tower, and after his window-shattering screaming ends, a radio broadcast of Hitler bridges the scene. The transition from Oskar's destructive outburst into Hitler's speech likens Oskar to the tyrant in unmistakable ways, casting doubt on the pitiable Oskar presented only moments earlier. Through the very intertwining of seemingly disparate sound positions with visual images, Schlöndorff reveals the breadth and depth of National Socialism.

Schlöndorff offers his best hope for meaningful engagement with the Nazi past through the sound of silence. One particularly significant sequence of Oskar's silence occurs directly after the notorious eel/horse's head scene on the beach and takes place after Alfred has tried, unsuccessfully, to persuade Agnes to eat the eel that he has just prepared. The sight of eels slithering out of the horse's head has already made her vomit, and she claims that the thought of now eating one of those eels nauseates her. The adults—Alfred, Agnes, and Jan—shout at one another at a fevered pitch, and Oskar steps backwards toward the hall closet, his wide, unblinking eyes expressing fear at the commotion. Agnes throws herself onto her bed and sobs uncontrollably; Jan enters the room, stretches out beside her on the bed, and sexually stimulating her with his hand, helps her to stop crying. During this part of the sequence, the adult characters are cast in a series of frames. Agnes and Jan are framed by the bedroom doorframe; the door slowly opens, and the mirror mounted on the hallway closet door reflects Alfred in the kitchen. Alfred appears on the screen several times removed by the bedroom doorframe, the mirror frame, and the reflection of the kitchen doorframe in the mirror. Only at the end of the scene can viewers conclude that Oskar has pushed the mirrored door open, for Oskar and his reflection in the mirror finally appear in an extended shot as he observes the activity from the hall closet. Although Oskar does not speak here, he is not without language at this point in the film. Quite to the contrary, I submit that at this moment, Oskar steps outside of oralism and into the *language* of silence. Silence here is reconstituted as the beginning stage of language *acquisition* and a building block in the formation of identity.[22] The constant framing and reframing of the window panes and the mirror reflect volatile familial relationships and underscore the questionable parameters of Oskar's lineage: although Oskar has alternately claimed both Alfred Matzerath and Jan Bronski as his father, here he begins to separate himself from all three prominent adults in his life. The psychological confusion depicted suggests that Oskar's future identity will hinge upon his ability to continue to act independently from the role models whom he judges to have failed him.

Silence in *The Tin Drum* both depicts and enables mourning as a necessary component of identity formation. Oskar must not only mourn the loss of stable moral foundations described above, he must also mourn the subsequent loss of his mother and of Sigismund Markus, the Jewish shopkeeper who supplies Oskar with tin drums. After Markus's death on *Kristallnacht* (Night of Broken Glass), Oskar gently touches Markus's face and closes his eyes. This tender gesture is made in silence.[23] Silent mourning also occurs when the family gathers for Agnes's funeral. Shot with a hand-cranked Askania camera,[24] this scene is included in the film not simply for the sentimental quality that its "historical" appearance suggests; it is also structurally significant for Schlöndorff's overarching message about the importance of silence in attempting to come to terms with the past. The vigorous card playing, eating, and talking depicted in the scene indicate that this family will try to return to its typical forms of engagement as soon as possible with as little overt grieving as possible. Despite one brief instance when Jan Bronski might be overcome by grief, he quickly suppresses his cry, regains his composure and returns to his card game. Oskar, in contrast, seeks refuge in his grandmother's skirts, and together they sit in silence and appear to reflect on Agnes's death as the fire reflects in their faces. This is a productive and healing silence that I understand to address the contemporary public issue of *Vergangenheitsbewältigung*. For Oskar, as for Schlöndorff and for many others, the work of coming to terms with the past begins with mourning. The search for stable foundations necessitates a return to the generation of the grandparents, since the efforts of the parents to restore quickly any semblance of normalcy had proved to come at the cost of an oppressive and a damaging silence. Schlöndorff clearly condemns the generation of the parents for their oppressive silence even as he mourns their loss.

In *The Tin Drum*, Volker Schlöndorff mitigates sound and silence within West German culture through the sounds of Oskar Matzerath. Unlike many filmmakers before him, Schlöndorff uses silence as a rhetorical system capable of providing a level of meaning that spoken language does not provide. Juxtaposing silence with the deafening sounds representative of National Socialism, Schlöndorff's cinematic narrative interrupts the troubling silence that limits any meaningful attempts to come to terms with the Nazi past. Incorporating techniques reminiscent of silent films to represent family history and mourning, Schlöndorff return to a language of signs and visual symbols to confront postwar cultural silence. Ultimately, this moving film about a young boy's growing awareness of his parents' untoward, selfish behavior contains a deep exploration into the processes of identity formation and subjectivity. Schlöndorff uses silence to reveal what West German cultural silence all too often conceals, and in doing so, he opens a new discursive channel for hearing, understanding, and coming to terms with the Nazi past.

Notes

1. Ernestine Schlant's study, *The Language of Silence: West German Literature and the Holocaust* (New York: Routledge, 1999), identifies "how the silences enveloping the Holocaust speak the language of ambiguity, indeterminacy, instability, and absence, but speak a language nonetheless" (15).
2. For the remainder of this essay, I shall use the English title, *The Tin Drum*, rather than the German title.
3. Split into different facets such as dialogue, voice-overs, music, or sound effects mixed to form the soundtrack, the creation of film sound takes place during the production and postproduction phases. Sound in cinema is "built," not simply recorded. John Belton, "Technology and Aesthetics of Film Sound," in *Film Sound: Theory and Practice*, ed. Elisabeth Weis and John Belton (New York: Columbia University Press, 1985), 70. In the case of *The Tin Drum*, sound is rebuilt: after three and a half months of shooting, Schlöndorff felt that none of the sound takes that had been completed in three countries, France, Yugoslavia, and Poland, were good enough to keep. At about the same time, sound engineer Peter Kellerhals suddenly abandoned his work on the film altogether, and Schlöndorff consequently decided on a postsynchronization of those many months' worth of filming.
4. Although "the direct influence of [Charles] Darwin himself was small, Darwin's thought was mediated by a host of scientific popularizers, who, from the 1860s on, produced a flood of lectures, magazine articles, and best-selling books." Alfred Kelly, *The Descent of Darwin: The Popularization of Darwinism in Germany, 1860–1914* (Chapel Hill: University of North Carolina Press, 1981), 5.
5. Douglas C. Baynton, "'Savages and Deaf-Mutes': Evolutionary Theory and the Campaign Against Sign Language," in *Deaf History Unveiled: Interpretations from the New Scholarship*, ed. John V. Van Cleve (Washington, D.C.: Gallaudet University Press, 1993), 99.
6. Early-nineteenth-century deaf education in Europe and particularly in Germany saw a standoff between manualism, the use of sign language, and oralism, the use of lip-reading and speech, with oralism "rapidly gaining the upper hand by the 1860s." Günther List, "Deaf History: A Suppressed Part of General History," in *Deaf History Unveiled*, ed. Van Cleve, 118.
7. Horst Biesold has undertaken the most in-depth study to date of deaf people during National Socialism. According to Nazi logic, deafness resulted from hereditary disease that must be eliminated for the good of the German race. Instead of casting deaf people solely as victims of Nazi violence, however, Biesold details their many associations and identities, including the resistance efforts of people who were at risk because they were both deaf and Jewish. He further chronicles the involvement of some deaf people as

bystanders and collaborators. Horst Biesold, *Crying Hands: Eugenics and Deaf People in Nazi Germany*, trans. William Sayers (Washington, D.C.: Gallaudet University Press, 1999).

8. Alexander Mitscherlich and Margarethe Mitscherlich, *Die Unfähigkeit zu trauern: Grundlagen kollektiven Verhaltens* (1967; Munich: Piper, 1991).

9. Susan Linville's *Feminism, Film, Fascism: Women's Auto/Biographical Film in Postwar Germany* (Austin: University of Texas Press, 1998) acknowledges the profound contribution that the Mitscherlichs' study has made to scholars concerned with postwar Germany while at the same time illuminating the male-centered bias of the Mitscherlichs' psychological theory. Linville "insist[s] … on the complex status of the Mischerlichs' work as a cultural product" (4). I share this understanding of their work and retain it for this analysis precisely because it is a cultural product. This essay seeks to demonstrate that Schlöndorff makes conscious use of notions produced in culture to examine the very process of cultural construction.

10. Belton, "Technology and Aesthetics of Film Sound," *Film Sound: Theory and Practice*, 75.

11. Many national cinemas use the term "mute" instead of "silent" to describe film with asynchronous sound and speech. Michel Chion, *The Voice in Cinema*, trans. Claudia Gorbman (1982; New York: Columbia University Press, 1999), 7. The German word to indicate "silent film" is also "mute"—*Stummfilm*—yet the actors in these films were not mute, nor did they portray mute characters. The plots of early soundless films clearly contained characters who spoke, and viewers were called upon to imagine the voice and to identify with the characters on largely visual terms. The aesthetics and narrative strategies of the *Stummfilm* addressed hearing and nonhearing, speaking, and nonspeaking audience members alike. The striking affinity of sign language with cinematic language helps to explain the equalizing function of silent cinema. William Stokoe observes that "in a signed language … narrative is no longer linear and prosaic. Instead, the essence of sign language is to cut from a normal view to a close-up to a distant shot to a close-up again, and so on, even including flashback and flash-forward scenes, exactly as a movie editor works…. Not only is signing itself arranged more like edited film than like written narration, but also each signer is placed very much as a camera: the field of vision and angle of view are directed but variable. Not only the signer signing but also the signer watching is aware at all times of the signer's visual orientation to what is being signed about." Quoted in Oliver Sacks, *Seeing Voices: A Journey into the World of the Deaf* (New York: Harper Perennial-Harper Collins, 1989), 90. Indeed, silent films offered people who were deaf a rare opportunity to participate in a public discourse, cinema, on equal terms with hearing people. The emergence of sound film effectively separated deaf from hearing audience members once again. If linguistic Darwinists regarded the addition of sound to film as progress, the advent of synchronous sound had a regressive effect on deaf audience members, for it once again promoted the notion that speech is the sign of a more highly developed human being. See John S. Schuchman's "Silent Movies and the Deaf Community," *Journal of Popular Culture* 17, no. 4 (1984): 58–78, for a detailed examination of cinema in the lives of people who were deaf.

12. Günter Grass, *Die Blechtrommel* (1959; Neuwied: Luchterhand, 1971), 64. All translations from the German are mine.

13. Hanspeter Brode, "Die Zeitgeschichte in der 'Blechtrommel' von Günter Grass. Entwurf eines Textinternen Kommunikationsmodells," *Günter Grass Materialienbuch*, ed. Rolf Geißler (Darmstadt: Luchterhand, 1976) 86–114; Hildegard Emmel, *History of the German Novel* (Detroit: Wayne State University Press, 1984); and Elizabeth C. Hamilton, "Disabling Discourses in German Literature from Lessing to Grass," Ph.D. diss., Ohio State University, 1998.

14. David Head, "Volker Schlöndorff's *Die Blechtrommel* and the 'Literaturverfilmung' Debate," *German Life and Letters* 36, no. 4 (1983): 353.

15. Upon viewing the film, Grass said, "I forgot the book and saw only the film." Volker Schlöndorff, ed., *Die Blechtrommel: Tagebuch einer Verfilmung* (Darmstadt: Luchterhand, 1979), 121.

16. Henry Pachter, for example, bemoaned the film's differences from the book in his 1980 review in *Cineaste*, disparaging Schlöndorff's decision to portray a sex scene that does not appear in the novel: "Schlöndorff has yielded to temptations, some of which I register with regret. Thus, there is too much sex without justification in the story; a very explicit bed scene between Oscar's mother and her lover is not in the book, and it is not justified as Oscar's fantasy; it certainly is not his own observation or experience." Harry Pachter, "*The Tin Drum*," *Cineaste* 10, no. 4 (1980): 31. To be sure, this scene is neither Oskar's fantasy, nor his observation, nor his experience. It does occur, however, with his knowledge but without his approval, prompting one of the most memorable outbursts of drumming and glass-shattering in the film. If Schlöndorff used artistic license to "authorize" this scene, he did so completely in keeping with the tone and message of the novel.
17. Schlöndorff, *Die Blechtrommel*, 23.
18. German cinema recently featured another screaming, glass-shattering character: Lola, in Tom Tykwer's *Lola rennt* (1998).
19. Schlöndorff, *Die Blechtrommel*, 117.
20. Ibid., *Die Blechtrommel*, 115.
21. Richard Kilborn, "Filming the Unfilmable: Volker Schlöndorff and *The Tin Drum*," in *Cinema and Fiction: New Modes of Adapting, 1950–1990*, ed. John Orr and Colin Nicholson (Edinburgh: Edinburgh University Press, 1992), 35.
22. This scene enacts a pivotal concept of Lacanian psychoanalytic theory to explain the psychological dimensions of social organization, namely, the moment of identity formation as the child finds himself separated from the parental figures. For Lacan, this separation takes place at the moment of language acquisition. This occurs when the child, leaving the "mirror stage," formulates a notion of the self as separate from the other, as Oskar does in this scene.
23. Schlöndorff's inclusion of this scene constitutes an important departure from Grass's novel, which contains no such gesture of commemorating Jewish victims of the Nazis. I thank my colleague Heidi Thomann Tewarson for this insight.
24. David Head, "Volker Schlöndorff's *Die Blechtrommel* and the 'Literaturverfilmung' Debate," *German Life and Letters* 36, no. 4 (1983): 347–67.

Chapter 9

SILENCE IS GOLDEN?
The Short Fiction of Pieke Biermann

Christopher Jones

I

Crime fiction has always had a love affair with the world of sounds: muffled footsteps in a dense fog, the creaking of a door in the middle of the night, a sudden shot that breaks a tense silence. Who can forget Holmes and Watson hearing the hissing of the swamp adder in Arthur Conan Doyle's "The Adventure of the Speckled Band," or the terrible and unnatural scream in Agatha Christie's *Hercule Poirot's Christmas*? The recent collection of Pieke Biermann's short stories, *Berlin, Kabbala*,[1] has provided an excellent opportunity to reconsider the role of sound and noise in her crime fiction. The two earliest stories are "3'21'," originally from *Mit Zorn, Charme und Methode*, a 1992 collection of short *Frauenkrimis*[2] that Biermann herself edited for Fischer, and "7.62," taken from *Wilde Weiber GmbH*, a similar collection that Biermann edited the following year for the same publisher.[3] In both stories, sounds play a vital role in the crimes that are depicted, but of equal significance is the manner in which Biermann weaves the sounds into her tapestry of contemporary Berlin life.

In 1937 in Seattle, the composer John Cage made a prediction about the future of music: "I BELIEVE THAT THE USE OF NOISE TO MAKE MUSIC WILL CONTINUE AND INCREASE."[4] Whether that prediction holds true for music per se is not something that can be discussed here. What is certain is that Biermann has chosen to create a female composer, interested in the sounds and noises of Berlin, as the central character of her first published short story "3'21'."[5] The deliberate connection to Cage's 4'33" (1952) in the provocative title is the reader's first indication that the world of sound will play a role of above-average importance in this *Frauenkrimi*.

Notes for this chapter begin on page 150.

Through this explicit reference to a milestone in twentieth-century music, Biermann is inviting the reader to recall the significance of this piece and then to relate that significance to her own story. Influenced by the white paintings of Robert Rauschenberg, Cage took the painter's observation that "a canvas is never empty"[6] and applied a similar notion to what we hear, creating a piece without any notated music or sounds at all, forcing the audience to spend four minutes and thirty-three seconds reconsidering its concept of silence in the face of so much ambient noise.

However, Biermann's composer is not only influenced by Cage the philosopher but also by Cage the advocate of using noise as a concrete building block of music: "Wherever we are, what we hear is mostly noise. When we ignore it, it disturbs us. When we listen to it, we find it fascinating. The sound of a truck at fifty miles per hour. Static between the stations. Rain. We want to capture and control these sounds, to use them not as sound effects *but as musical instruments*."[7] The chosen medium of Biermann's narrator is urban noise which she records, selects, and assembles from the city of Berlin in which she lives in order to create a portrait in sound. However, the death of her close friend Lisi breaks into her life and changes its direction dramatically, not merely through the loss of a friend but also through the manner in which she died. Lisi's motorcycle had been tampered with, and she crashes to her death outside the narrator's home. Although there is no recording of the actual event, the unusual sound of the motorbike, which the narrator hears just before the crash, is enough to prompt a personal investigation into the truth, with the key sound going round and round her mind like "ein innerer Bandschnipsel" (an internal snippet of tape).[8] It is at this stage that the reader realizes that it is not only the title of "3'21"" that is reminiscent of other well-known works in the field of sound and music. Although the allusion to Cage's 4'33" is telling, it is the debt that the story pays to Brian De Palma's 1981 film *Blow Out*[9] that allows Biermann to build on the use of sound as a clue to a crime that must be investigated and, by extension, to develop a parallel narrative in which an investigator searching for a clue is also searching for a deeper truth.

In *Blow Out* John Travolta plays Jack Terry, a soundman who manages to record the sound of a car crash one night. Not only does the car crash result in the death of one of its occupants, the dead man is also a presidential candidate. From a close listening to the tape, Terry draws the conclusion that the crash was no accident but was caused by a shot fired at the car, which hit a tire, producing a "blow out." The links to Biermann's "3'21"" are clear in the two central characters, both involved professionally in the recording of sound, and in the crashes, both of which were deliberately caused but meant to appear as accidents. However, the differences between the two works are also significant for an understanding of Biermann's intentions. Unlike De Palma's Jack Terry, the narrator in "3'21"" does *not* get a recording of the key moment, and it is this regret that, among other things, drives her to explore every avenue to solve the crime. The political current in *Blow Out* with its many references to painful incidents in recent United States history,[10] is also absent in Biermann's work with its sharp focus on the personal sphere. Finally, the downbeat ending of *Blow Out* is nothing like the ending of "3'21"," in which the narrator can toast a successful outcome to her investigation and the reader can bear witness to her reintegration into the real world after her artistic isolation.

Part of this reintegration process is illustrated in a highly visual fashion, and it is perhaps not without significance that the narrator is in her apartment when she hears the crash. From her descriptions we learn that she lives high up in her apartment block "oberhalb der Baumgrenze" (above the tree line).[11] Her investigation of the crime will then take her quite literally to street level, representing a movement from an ivory tower existence concerned primarily with aesthetic considerations to an involvement with the material life of the city. The distinction that Michel de Certeau makes in "Walking in the City" between voyeurs and walkers is also illuminating in this respect. The former are characterized by the desire to achieve an objective, detached view, often from a high vantage point, but at the expense of being a part of the city. The latter are the people at ground level who experience and indeed write the "urban 'text'"[12] without being able to understand it fully. It is possible to see in the narrator's progress in "3'21"" a movement away from a life as a voyeur (or perhaps more properly an *écouteur*) to one as a walker, implying in her case a turn from detachment to involvement. At first, this change is not of her own volition, since the death of her friend forces her into the role of a detective, which also means that the understanding, rather than the portrayal, of the city becomes of central importance to her.

Inevitably, through the creation of a detective character in a major city, Biermann invites comparison with the rich tradition of metropolitan detectives, from Edgar Allan Poe's Dupin onward.[13] There have been readings of the American hard-boiled private investigator (PI) and his or her attempts to solve mysterious crimes as an allegory for attempts to understand a modern city, something that has come to be regarded as ever more complex and resistant to understanding.[14] The detective's search for clues in an attempt to unravel a particular mystery is therefore representative of the desire to understand the supercomplexity of the city itself. For Biermann's composer this task is made particularly difficult, because one of the key clues, the sound of the moment before the crash, is lost forever: "Mir wurde plötzlich klar, daß ich das einzige wirklich Bedeutende nicht hatte" (I suddenly realized that I didn't have the one thing that was really significant).[15] This realization causes her depression and doubt in her chosen vocation, yet forces her away from a preoccupation with secondhand experiences, as symbolized through her work with the tape recordings, and makes her deal with reality more closely.

Biermann's choice of career for her narrator enables her to intertwine a number of threads related to the use of sound in this story. On the one hand, she is an artist attempting to create a sound portrait of Berlin: "Seit ich hier lebe, bin ich besessen von dem Traum, diese Symphonie hörbar zu machen. Dafür sammele ich die O-Töne" (All the time I've lived here I've been obsessed by the dream of making this symphony audible. That's why I collect the original sound recordings).[16] Yet on the other hand, the killing of her friend throws her work into a new relief, as she is forced to deal not only with the sounds of the crashing motorcycle but also with the cacophony of the arriving police and ambulance services: "Es folgt Gerenne, Geklapper von metallenen Koffern und Geräten, knapp gezischte Kommandos, Rolltüren, Funkdurchsagen, ein dichtes feingesponnenes Netz aus Tönen.... Nichts, was ich kenne, geht über die Klangwelt in diesen Blechkästen, in denen alles scheppert, klappert, kreischt, piept" (Then comes running, the clatter of metal cases and equipment, quickly hissed commands, sliding doors, radio messages, a dense, finely spun network of sounds.... There is nothing that I know of which surpasses the sonic world in these tin crates, in which everything rattles, clatters, screeches, and beeps).[17] As this example shows, Biermann employs a narrative style that draws on devices such as onomatopoeia and alliteration to approximate the aural sense impressions of her narrator. Yet this is never unnatural, since the reader expects a close attention to sounds from an artist working with them as a concrete medium. There is also justification within the story itself, although from a different angle, as the female narrator is always listening out at night for suspicious sounds. This is, of course, a common feature of the *Frauenkrimi*, which attempts to emulate a woman's view of the world, seeking an element of recognition from female readers and affording male readers an opportunity to experience that different view of the world.

It is not just Cage's exhortation to raid the world of noise for the raw materials of composition that finds a reflection in "3'21""; Cage's keen attention to silence also forms a strong feature of the story. Central to this area of Biermann's work is the association that she establishes between silence and death, accomplished through the use of contrasts. Biermann's characterization of Lisi, at least through the narrator's eyes (and ears), relies heavily on the use of sound, specifically, Lisi's incredibly loud voice. In one anecdote the narrator recalls how Lisi had shouted at a man with such a loud voice that "in dieser stillen, engen Einbahnstraße alle Fenster hätten aufgerissen werden müssen" (in this silent, narrow one-way street every window should have been thrown open).[18] But then in death Lisi "war absolut still" (was absolutely silent).[19] This contrast creates an emotional effect by juxtaposing the vibrant, louder-than-life Lisi with a literal silence of the grave. When reviewing the tape that had been recording during her discovery of Lisi's body, the narrator once more focuses on silence. Here, among all of the other sounds that had been recorded, it is silence that is key, achieving a meaning and status far above the mere absence of sound through the narrator's emotional response to it: "Das Unheimlichste aber war die Stille" (But the most unsettling thing was the silence).[20] The circle of associations is completed: sound and noise representing the dynamic city of Berlin, silence representing death and loss.

Another feature of Biermann's style in this story, the almost fetishistic use of brand names and abbreviations, is reminiscent of much science fiction, but cyberpunk in particular. William Gibson's *Neuromancer* set the tone for the whole subgenre by stripping sentences, such as the following, of all verbs in order to force a focus on the objects: "The Ono-Sendai; next year's most expensive Hosaka computer; a Sony monitor; a dozen disks of corporate-grade ice;[21] a Braun coffeemaker."[22] Gibson's mix of genuine brand names and invented ones allows him to construct a bridge between a concrete present and an extrapolated future, which the reader will recognize and accept through familiar products and the persistence of market forces. However, Biermann makes somewhat different use of this technique in "3'21"," in which the constant allusion to the narrator's Sony DAT, for example, is employed not to bring authenticity to an imaginary world, but rather to complement her chosen vocation as a composer. It may be regarded as a similar affection for an object that a photographer might feel for a Nikon or Leica or a guitarist for a Gibson or Fender. These objects define and enable chosen careers. In the case of "3'21"," it can, of course, also be argued that this reference to a tape recorder is an additional link to *Blow Out*.

As the story progresses, the search for sounds for purely artistic reasons becomes supplanted by the search for the truth surrounding Lisi's murder. Depressed at first for not having captured the critical sound on tape, the narrator starts to question the value of her own work. Yet her involvement in the investigation gives her a new purpose and perhaps also brings her closer to reality after her purely aesthetic work, achieving a clear value by the end of the story: the crime has been solved and at least some of the solution is sitting on her beloved Sony DAT—four minutes and thirty-seven seconds, to be precise, which end with the "melodiös-knödelige Lalülala" (melodiously strangled nahnaw-nahnaw)[23] of the arriving police.

It has certainly not been the intention of this study to imply that Biermann is merely following in Cage's (or De Palma's) footsteps in this short story. The context of Cage's work with sound and music, which he clarifies through the lectures collected in the *Silence* volume, reveals a passionate desire to dismantle the notion of a musical hierarchy with the genius composer at the top and then the performers taking the middle ground above the audience. The use of various techniques, often involving coin-flipping or the imperfections in a sheet of paper, to achieve a random result are a vital component of this process of democratization. Biermann's composer, in the final analysis, does *not* share these goals, either in her work or in her investigation of the sonic clues. Her compositions, although drawing on the noises that Cage felt would become an increasingly important part of twentieth-century music, are shaped by her intellect (or *psychology* as Cage would have said), which chooses and arranges those noises into a work of art. She is a far more traditional composer than Cage. Her investigative work, too, is predicated on the belief that there is a hidden order or meaning to what she has heard, that the sounds which anticipated the death of her friend are *not* meaningless but susceptible to analysis and solution. In this fashion Biermann takes Cage's somewhat rarefied aestheticism and gives it a more worldly application.

II

There is, of course, another, darker side to the pervasiveness of sound and noise in the urban environment: "The development of technology, urbanization, and the increase of road and air traffic has led us to the current situation where noise has become an environmental pollutant affecting the majority of the population; it is estimated that in the OECD countries there are over 130 million people affected by very disturbing environmental noise."[24] What makes this situation at all tolerable is the resilience and adaptability of human beings to cope with such extremes of noise: "We are not receptive to all of the multimedia attack because of our natural self-protection mechanism, which has the ability to tune out all the information that is superfluous to our concerns."[25] But what were to happen to someone whose self-protection system did not function in the normal way? That individual would experience, perceive, and react to the sonic environment in a very different way to the rest of the population: "Fortunately for our well-being's sake, we adapt ... and start hearing less, seeing less, smelling less; *otherwise the result would be madness.*"[26]

It is into this very world of madness that Pieke Biermann guides us in the second of the stories under consideration here. "7.62" provides a very bleak contrast to "3'21"," as the female composer/investigator gives way to a female sharpshooter with a murderous streak. Indeed, the title is an explicit reference to the caliber of her weapon of choice, a Mauser SP66 7.62. Turning from one side of the law to the other is not the only change between the two stories, as there is also a marked contrast in style, tone, and message. Biermann is drawing rather less on the tradition of the hardboiled city-dwelling PI here and rather more on aheroic *noir* crime fiction, in which the experience of the city can lead to paranoia,[27] and in which our moral reaction to the central character is at best ambivalent and at worst condemnatory.

The Berlin that the narrator in "3'21"" had felt compelled to capture in sound for other people to experience has also changed, transformed by a view from someone living very close to the edge. Sounds have become a symptom of a violent, threatening city; Biermann presents a character who has been pushed to the edge by aural assault. The narrative techniques which had been exploited in "3'21"" here reveal a high de-gree of adaptability, as they are now used to develop a very different sort of story. The use of onomatopoeia, which in the first story had been an indication of the narrator's focus on the sounds around her, has a far more specific task in this story, where it is reserved almost exclusively for the sound of the motorcycles that the narrator hates so much: "Braaammm-brrraaammm! Immer lauter. Immer näher. Der ist doch völ-lig gaga! Höraufduarsch! Mirplatztderkopf!" (Vrooom-vrooom! Louder and louder. Nearer and nearer. He must be off his rocker! Stopyoubastard! Myheadsexploding!).[28] This example also reveals the extent to which Biermann, through her narrator, is prepared to bend standard German in her efforts to accurately mirror a disturbed state of mind. The highly evocative descriptions of noise achieve even greater efficacy through the use of contrast. The sound/silence combination that was a part of "3'21"" returns here particularly through the recurring phrase "himmlische Ruhe" (heavenly peace),[29] which represents the narrator's ideal.

Although Biermann has once again chosen a female first-person narra-tor, the style of "3'21"," which draws the reader both into the investigation and into the sensorium of an artist keenly attuned to the sounds of the city around her, is replaced here by an interior monologue that, by turns, excludes the reader through its dense network of impenetrable detail, only to then become accessible, but this only to a manic, paranoid vision of the city. Most of the difficulties in understanding the text are a result of Biermann's uncompromising use of the stream of consciousness tech-nique, which makes no allowances for the reader's ignorance of anything the narrator takes for granted. Naturally, weapons technology is one such area, and Biermann peppers the text liberally with appropriate brand names and techniques, such as the special preparation of the bullets.[30] Once more her character's profession achieves at least a partial definition through the association with a particular tool of the trade, in this case, her Mauser SP66 7.62. Again, however, Biermann's choice of career for her central character is ideal, allowing her to marry the narrative style, with its concatenation of sense impressions, to the person, a sharpshooter trained in detailed observation.

In "3'21"," motorcycles play a key function, since Lisi has died on one and the narrator has subsequently been obliged to learn as much about their technology as possible in order to understand how the crime could have been committed. Interestingly, motorcycles also play a role in "7.62," but here they are primarily representative of noise: "Da kommt so'n gottver-dammtes Dreckstück auf 'ner dicken Maschine und rammt mir sein durch-gedrehtes Rammm-Raaammm-Brrraaam in die Ohren!" (Then along comes some goddamned dirtbag on a fat bike and rams his raging vroom-vroom-vroom in my ears).[31] Some research has classified sounds such as these as masculine sounds.[32] In Honkasalo's work there is an explicit reference to young boys who "like driving mopeds without exhaust pipes" and a conclusion that loud noise "acts as an efficient sign of strength, danger, and power."[33] Quoting from the work of Davis and Cornwell, Honkasalo refers to a violation of "acoustic privacy" by subjecting someone to unwanted noise. The fact that the motorcycle riders in "7.62" are male, therefore, has the effect of almost transforming these incidents into sonic rape.

As a weapons expert, the central character is, of course, far from helpless and soon begins a one-woman vigilante crusade, shooting down the motorcyclists without a hint of conscience: "Einer reißt dir das Ohr auf und päng! Weg ist er!" (Someone rips your ear open and bang! He's a goner!).[34] Naturally, Biermann's choice of an interior monologue allows her to present her central character's delight at the killings without any obligation to turn a moral light on the action. This is also very much in the tradition of *noir* fiction and filmmaking, wherein "the opposition between good and bad, light and dark, is blurred. The collapse of boundaries may lead to an uncertainty or ambiguity of response on the part of the audience."[35] This is seen clearly here, as our sympathies are unlikely to lie with either the killer or the anonymous, noisy motorcyclists. Although we may find it difficult to identify or sympathize with its central character, the story does afford Biermann an excellent opportunity to explore the darker side of big city life, in which sound and noise can have an enormous impact on the well-being and sanity of its inhabitants. The difficulties facing governments attempting to pass legislation regulating noise levels have been well documented, argues Nils Lennart Wallin, citing the example of cutting the speed of commuter trains to reduce noise levels, which would compromise the efficiency of the transit system.[36] Indeed, given that such levels of noise are likely to increase with some regularity,[37] Biermann's vision becomes less a nightmare than a prediction.

However, there is a further possible interpretation that also does not involve a moral reaction to the shootings. If we, following Donatella Mazzoleni, equate the city with the body, then we can regard the activities of Biermann's psychopathic narrator in quite a different manner, for if the city becomes "the body's Double,"[38] then her actions may be seen in a somatic light. Her madness becomes the symptom of an attack on the city's health, and her killings are the reactions of an antibody to an intruder into the city's biosphere. This view of the city and its inhabitants as a living, symbiotic organism addresses the notion of murder as an event demanding a moral judgment and pushes it beyond the boundary of good and evil into the realm of necessity. The narrator becomes a helpless agent, predetermined to carry out an act of cleansing against the cause of the city's sickness by ridding it of a pollutant, in this case of polluting agents. Regarding "7.62" in this fashion does not imply an acceptance of vigilantism, but it does acknowledge a view of the city as a shared communal space, in which the actions of the few can reduce the (mental) health or quality of life for the many.

The question posed in the final chapter of *The Naked City*, "do 'noir' crime fiction and images of decline encourage the acceptance of social responsibilities and the search for social justice?"[39] receives a partial answer through a story that focuses on the potential outcomes of neglecting social responsibility. Biermann is thus no more an advocate of or apologist for cold-blooded shootings than Heinrich Böll is with his female killers, Johanna Fähmel and Katharina Blum.[40] Instead, "7.62" is a cautionary tale, designed to highlight the precarious balance between conflicting interests in a large city, where a disruption of that balance can lead to torment for the individual and danger to the collective.

III

Originally appearing in collections of other short *Frauenkrimis*, these two stories share an understanding and a concern for the urban environment and its future, which gives them continuing validity and a relevance beyond their original boundaries. The decision to investigate two extremes of noise pollution—represented on the one hand by a desire to employ it as a concrete medium for capturing one particular essence of the city in an art form, and on the other as a source of such stress and irritation that it can literally drive someone mad—means that the stories demand treatment as antithetical companion pieces with a message about noise that can be synthesized only from a reading of both texts. That message reveals Biermann as a genuine city-lover with a keen awareness of the delicate balance between personal liberties and the sanctity of the personal sphere.

Notes

1. Pieke Biermann, *Berlin, Kabbala* (Berlin: Transit, 1997). It is from this edition that all quotations from "3'21''" and "7.62" are taken.
2. *Frauenkrimi* is the German word for crime fiction written by women authors for a mainly female audience.
3. Pieke Biermann, ed., *Mit Zorn, Charme & Methode* (Frankfurt am Main: Fischer, 1992); Pieke Biermann, ed., *Wilde Weiber GmbH* (Frankfurt am Main: Fischer, 1993).
4. John Cage, *Silence* (1961; Cambridge, MA: MIT Press, 1966), 3 (capitalized in the original).
5. Coincidentally first published in the same year that Cage died (1992).
6. Cage, *Silence*, 98–108.
7. Ibid., 3 (emphasis added).
8. Biermann, *Berlin*, 13–14.
9. Which of course owes its own debt to Michelangelo Antonioni's *Blow-Up* (1967).
10. The assassination of President John F. Kennedy, Watergate, and the Chappaquiddick incident.
11. Biermann, *Berlin*, 9.
12. Michel de Certeau, "Walking in the City," in *The Cultural Studies Reader*, ed. Simon During (London: Routledge, 1993), 153.

13. Introduced in "The Murders in the Rue Morgue."
14. Ralph Willett, *The Naked City: Urban Crime Fiction in the USA* (Manchester and New York: Manchester University Press, 1996).
15. Biermann, *Berlin*, 21.
16. Ibid., 12.
17. Ibid., 11.
18. Ibid., 16.
19. Ibid., 10.
20. Ibid., 11.
21. Intruder countermeasures electronics.
22. William Gibson, *Neuromancer* (London: Grafton, 1986), 61.
23. Biermann, *Berlin*, 25.
24. Antero Honkasalo, "Environmental Noise as a Sign," *Semiotica* 109, no. 1–2 (1996): 29.
25. Claire Taylor, "Noise Is O.K.," *Semiotica* 52, no. 3 (1984): 277.
26. Ibid. (emphasis added).
27. Willett, *The Naked City*.
28. Biermann, *Berlin*, 37.
29. Ibid., 28 and 34.
30. Kalaschnikow, Makarow, Mauser, Siminow, Stetschkin, Strela.
31. Biermann, *Berlin*, 37.
32. Honkasalo, "Environmental Noise," 29–39.
33. Ibid., 33.
34. Bierman, *Berlin*, 37.
35. Willett, *The Naked City*, 89.
36. Nils Lennart Wallin, "The Modern Soundscape and Noise Pollution," *UNESCO Courier* (April 1986): 31–33.
37. Rex Keating, "Cuando el sonido se enfurece," *Folia Humanistica* 285 (1986): 631–35.
38. Donatella Mazzoleni, "The City and the Imaginary," *New Formations* 11 (Summer 1990): 97.
39. Willett, *The Naked City*, 133.
40. In *Billard um halbzehn* and *Die verlorene Ehre der Katharina Blum*, respectively.

Part IV

TRANSLATING SOUND

Chapter 10

BROADCASTING WAGNER

Transmission, Dissemination, Translation

Thomas F. Cohen

… I think that the river
Is a strong brown god—sullen, untamed and intractable,
Patient to some degree, at first recognised as a frontier;
Useful, untrustworthy, as a conveyor of commerce;
Then only a problem confronting the builder of bridges.

— T. S. Eliot, "The Dry Salvages"[1]

I

Communications theorist Claude Shannon once described "the fundamental problem of communication" as one of engineering rather than semantics.[2] Successful communication, for Shannon, meant transmitting the symbols of communication from one point to another. I picture him standing on the bank of Eliot's river, planning the most efficient way to transport these "goods" to the other side. In Eliot's poem, it is this crossing that transforms the sacred river-god from a frontier into a profane commercial medium.[3] Such "disenchantment," note Max Horkheimer and Theodor W. Adorno, is a consequence of the technological domination of nature. With the historical shift from magic to science, "the holiness of the *hic et nunc*," gives way to "universal exchangeability."[4] In such an economy, a single standard of efficiency determines the worth of both river and bridge, and the latter renders the convenient yet unreliable waterway obsolete. I would like to point out the error, however, in mistaking the bridge as any less "untrustworthy" than the river it traverses, for the problem stems not from the medium's reliability but from transmission itself—in short, everything expressed by the prefix *trans-*, including transportation and translation. Derived from the Latin preposition signifying *over*, *across*, or *beyond* and fairly rendered by the German *über*, the English *trans-* is the prefix that fails to respect geographic and linguistic borders.

Kurt Weill, speaking of Richard Wagner as much as Richard Strauss, declared that musical drama based on outdated myths fails to engage youth occupied with "technical questions, with airplanes, automobiles, radio installations, and bridge construction."[5] Here, too, the modern engineer displaces the ancient *cultor*, who not only cultivated but occupied the land and revered the local gods. Indeed, Wagner's tales of magic rings and holy grails contain something inimical to the networks of canals, railroads, radio, and television that comprise the modern media of communication. In the case of the Wagner cult, mass dissemination serves to demystify or to exorcise the hodgepodge of art, mysticism, and politics that the composer represented.

The present chapter examines a clash between two rival communications networks as radically different as Eliot's river and the bridge spanning it. One encompasses the American motion picture industry, along with the media for wireless and wire transmission and communication. Under this heading fall Paramount Pictures, Hollywood, the cartel comprised of the NBC networks, RCA, the AT&T system, and radio manufacturers Westinghouse and General Electric, as well as governmental regulatory bodies such as the Federal Communications Commission and its predecessor, the Federal Radio Commission.[6] The other consists of the ordained performers of Wagner's art. The first network desires to market culture as a cosmopolitan phenomenon free from those racial associations and national interests that the second network considers essential for an authentic art of the people. Such a notion of culture as the careful cultivation of the soil contrasts with the view of dissemination as the indiscriminate scattering of seed. This difference extends to the operations of the communications media themselves: one seeks to advertise its product as broadly as possible to any and all through diverse media such as film, radio, and television; the other strives to transmit a mission through apostolic succession that precludes any type of media self-awareness.

II

This essay begins with an instance of how the U.S. entertainment industry tried to steer between the "useful and untrustworthy" aspects of broadcasting just prior to World War II. During this critical period in history, film and radio managed to exploit Wagner's work as entertainment while keeping its political significance at arm's length. My discussion focuses on how a short segment from the popular movie *The Big Broadcast of 1938* served not only to publicize the star of the Metropolitan Opera's Saturday afternoon radio broadcasts but also to defend against the menace of contamination, foreign invasion, and sedition.

Since the late 1830s, the transmission of electromagnetic waves through wires and especially through the air has continually disturbed our comfortable sense of being at home. In the 1930s, radio broadcasting inspired the type of awe expressed by James Watson, head of the Interstate Commerce Commission, who describes this mysterious force "projected through 500 feet of firm rock and a dozen feet of solid lead ... by means of which the voice of the orator and of the prima donna may be heard across the continent swifter than the coming light."[7] Radio transmission, electromagnetism—indeed, the whole idea of "action at a distance"—implied that barricades, trenches, and even natural boundaries such as mountains and oceans could no longer secure national borders. During World War I, in the prebroadcast days of 1917, Oswald Garrison Villard, president of the New York Philharmonic, a German-American and a pacifist, could proclaim in a speech at Carnegie Hall that "the pitiful waves of sound that beat across oceans moaning of bloody, unreasoning death pass by this temple of art. No strife can enter, for here is sanctuary for all and perfect peace."[8] Invisible radio waves, on the other hand, easily pass through thick, solid walls, and, by tuning in, listeners often invited news of the European conflict into their homes along with their favorite musical program. As Europe's political situation worsened throughout the decade, news flashes interrupted regular programming with increasing frequency. According to Robert J. Brown, this coverage played no small part in infecting high culture with profane politics: "The sounds of air raid sirens and bomb explosions in London turn American public opinion away from its traditional isolationism and towards a more active anti-fascist foreign policy."[9] Yet in 1938 many Americans—in particular, many German-Americans anxious to avoid the anti-German backlash typical of World War I—hoped that Europe's problems would remain on the other side of the Atlantic.[10] This was not to be, however, as distant events traveled across the ocean faster and more frequently due to electronic media, which rapidly replaced print media as the primary source of news. Radio provided extensive coverage of Germany's annexation of Austria in the spring of 1938 and of the Munich crisis later that fall. Ronald Garay reports that, following the latter event, "radio was named as the preferred news source by more than two-thirds of all Americans."[11]

The decade also represented the peak of Hollywood's involvement with radio programming. Like other Hollywood studios, Paramount ached to exploit the medium and, in fact, had toyed with establishing its own broadcasting network, the Keystone chain, in 1927. Although this project failed to materialize, continued negotiations with CBS resulted in the 1929 stock merger between Paramount and that network. To showcase "crossover" talent, such as Bing Crosby and George Burns and Gracie Allen, who could work both radio and movies, Paramount inaugurated its

"Big Broadcast" series in 1932. Sequels followed in 1936, 1937, and 1938, when Paramount released the fourth and final installment in this series, *The Big Broadcast of 1938*, a banal, if entertaining, movie starring Bob Hope, W. C. Fields, and Martha Raye. Like its predecessors, the movie offers up the thinnest of narratives, this one involving a transatlantic race between rival luxury ocean liners. The plot, however, merely provides the vehicle for a radio variety show supposedly broadcast from sea. Paramount talent thus shares the spotlight with the wireless medium itself, which gained initial prominence in ship-to-shore communications. Aside from comedy segments, the film featured popular musical numbers such as Hope's trademark "Thanks for the Memories," an upbeat tour de force by Martha Raye called "Mama, That Moon Is Here Again," and the utterly forget-table, though much preferred, "You Took the Words Right Out of My Heart."[12] Conspicuous among these light songs and corny skits is a seg-ment featuring soprano Kirsten Flagstad, in Viking armor and brandish-ing a spear, performing Brünnhilde's battle cry from the second act of Richard Wagner's *Die Walküre*. Flagstad's appearance seems calculated to impart an air of "culture" to the program. So compelling is the allure of "high art," that *Variety* paid lip service to Flagstad's performance, pro-nouncing it both "the outstanding moment of the film" and "the season's high mark in screen song," even though its pages generally reflected pop-ular taste on movies and music.[13]

The *Walküre* segment is noteworthy because it offers not filmed opera but a filmed opera *broadcast*. Moreover, Flagstad's appearance depicts events in the world outside the film's diegesis. Specifically, it invokes the Metropolitan Opera's Saturday afternoon broadcasts on NBC, which be-gan earlier that decade, and which often featured the Norwegian soprano as the Met's most brilliant new star. Although the Italians had ruled pre-viously at the Met under director Giulio Gatti-Cassazza, Flagstad's per-formances proved immensely popular and profitable. *Opera News* claims that her reputation influenced Texaco's decision to sponsor the show beginning in 1940.[14] Teamed with conductor Arthur Bodanzky, she spe-cialized in "Teutonic" offerings such as Beethoven's *Fidelio*. But above all, her fame depended on her renderings of Wagner. She sang the role of Isolde from *Tristan und Isolde* seven times for these broadcasts, and, while this role remained her specialty, she portrayed other Wagnerian heroines as well. In fact, she made her Saturday matinee debut in 1935 in *Die Walküre* (as Sieglinde, however, not Brünnhilde) and reprised the role in December 1937. This latter event most likely provided the model for the *Big Broadcast* segment.

When the segment resurfaced in the 1995 compilation *The Art of Singing*, which aired on various PBS stations, Flagstad's forced histrion-ics elicited virtually unanimous negative critical response, prompting one critic to comment cynically that, after all, few opera stars "could sing and act."[15] This unfavorable criticism may not proceed entirely from Flagstad's deficient acting abilities, however, but from the difficulty in translating Wagner's opera from one medium to another. In fact, by combining visual staging effects with the broadcast of a musical performance, the segment looks beyond film to television broadcasting—particularly anticipating the *Voice of Firestone* show, which, beginning in 1949, featured performances by popular opera stars, including Flagstad's successor at the Met, Helen Traubel. Flagstad's departure in the spring of 1941 gave Traubel the opportunity to become a major Wagner interpreter. Previously, Traubel's on-stage experience singing Wagner heroines had been scant. Nearly forty years old when she assumed Flagstad's mantle, she lacked the latter's virtuosity, regularly singing Brünnhilde's battle cry a half step lower than originally written. That critics found this adjustment significant reveals how transposition represented a failure to communicate the original mission unchanged—the measure of a worthy apostle.

Certainly, not everyone was happy with Flagstad's replacement. Conductor Erich Leinsdorf called Traubel untalented, lazy, and "bovine."[16] Yet Traubel, American-born and -bred, was free from those associations that had plagued Flagstad—associations that had once constituted strengths but had become liabilities. Traubel's numerous screen appearances suggest that she had a "personality" well suited for postwar film and television. One segment from the 1950 *Firestone* season shows Traubel performing a selection from *Die Walküre*.[17] Instead of the warrior maiden's call to arms, she sings Sieglinde's love song to her brother Sigmund, "Du bist der Lenz." Whereas many of the *Firestone* segments modestly attempted to render costume and settings, this one has Traubel appearing *sans* costume, clad in a simple black dress. All possibly offensive Wagnerian props have been extracted, leaving only vague signifiers of "high culture."

Marshall McLuhan might argue that Wagner's art could not survive the translation from a "hot" medium such as radio to a "cool" one such as television. Recall McLuhan's controversial comment on media and Nazism: "Had TV occurred on a large scale during Hitler's reign he would have vanished quickly. Had TV come first there would have been no Hitler at all."[18] Perhaps McLuhan's point that the archaic tribal magic so readily propagated by radio could not survive television applies equally well to Wagner as to Hitler. Certainly, *Big Broadcast* director Mitchell Leisen's decision to adapt the traditional Bayreuth costumes and staging of *Die Walküre* is in part to blame for the segment's awkwardness. The opera's original mise-en-scène was received rather poorly when it was introduced in 1876.[19] If, as a tableau regarded from a distance, these sets and costumes already struck many audience members as ridiculous, they look especially silly rendered in the series of medium-long shots, medium close-ups, and close-ups that Leisen uses to shoot the scene. Yet they no doubt fulfilled audience expectations of what a Wagner opera should look like. One wonders how audiences in the 1930s could have missed the militarist and racist connotations in these trappings, especially when combined with Flagstad's robust Aryan looks. Yet even today's critics dismiss Flagstad's cinematic performance as a mere novelty without value for the serious study of music drama. This essay contends, on the contrary, that the *Big Broadcast* segment raises important questions about the meaning of programming and broadcasting Wagner on the eve of World War II.

In contrast to the World War I era, when New York opera houses either banned German operas or recast them in English, enthusiasm for Wagner increased in the 1930s. In fact, Paul Jackson calls the decade "the heyday of modern Wagner performances at the Metropolitan."[20] Wagner's appeal appears curious, as does Flagstad's fame, for the résumé that legitimized her status as bearer of the Wagnerian tradition also linked her with Nazism. During both the 1933 and 1934 seasons she sang at Bayreuth, which by that time resembled a National Socialist Party rally more than a music festival. Frederick Spotts describes the transformation of the festival:

> From the first summer, in 1933, what had been a Wagner festival became an outright Hitler festival. On arriving in the town, visitors were greeted by swastika banners hanging on every flagpole and from every house. Storm troopers crowded the streets and cafes resounded to the Horst-Wessel-Lied, the Nazi anthem. Shops that since 1876 had displayed illustrations and miniature busts and other souvenirs of Richard Wagner now featured photographs and mementos of Adolf Hitler.... The street [Adolf-Hitler-Strasse] was lined by SS guards and tens of thousands of onlookers heralding—and heiling—the arrival of government and party leaders.[21]

By 1937, the year that *The Big Broadcast* was in production, music critic Alfred Einstein could declare that the Bayreuth festival "has ceased as an artistic institution and has become an agency of Nazi propaganda."[22] Surprisingly, these menacing developments did not sour American tastes for Wagner's operas nor stall Flagstad's career. After auditioning for Giulio Gatti in 1934, she was hired for the Met's 1935 season. Flagstad arrived by boat in New York in January 1935 and proceeded to enjoy meteoric success. After five seasons, she returned to her native Norway in 1941 to join her husband, a Nazi collaborator who was denounced and arrested after the war. Although postwar investigations exonerated the singer herself from any wrongdoing, her husband's reputation cast a shadow over her return to the United States in the 1950s. In regard to these events, *The Big Broadcast* seems uncannily prescient. The film presents Flagstad broadcasting from an ocean liner at sea, beyond American borders, and heading away from the United States toward Europe. The plot expresses the desire to refuse delivery, to return the package from Bayreuth, to counter the initial transatlantic crossing with one that would restore things to their proper places on the other shore.

III

In the 1930s, no one could predict how telecommunication might transform Wagner's work and music in general. In 1941, Adorno concluded that radio broadcasting distorts the work and that "symphonic music and the radio are incompatible."[23] Radio, Adorno maintained, promotes a kind of listening that reduces an integrated work such as a Beethoven symphony to a patchwork of melodies heard as isolated quotations. Such criticism certainly suits *The Big Broadcast*, in which Wagner's dramatic dialogue becomes operatic "aria"—the term Bob Hope employs to introduce the segment. The effect of editing on the narrative as well as the musical context here is significant. *The Big Broadcast* severely truncates the second act's overture to begin instead at measure 54 and then jumps eighteen measures to two bars before Brünnhilde's vocal entry. This cut omits entirely the presence of Brünnhilde's interlocutor Wotan, who would have been instructing her to ensure Siegmund's victory in his fight with Hunding. At this point, Brünnhilde sings her famous battle cries ("hojo-to-ho"), which are interrupted as she alerts her father, Wotan, to the immanent arrival of his pugnacious wife, Fricka: "Dir rath' ich, Vater, rüste dich selbst; harten Sturm sollst du besteh'n" (Take heed, father; prepare yourself; a hard storm must you withstand). Removing Wotan transforms the scene from a dialogue between two mutually present speakers into an apostrophe to a missing addressee. Consequently, Brünnhilde's words assume a fortiori the character of dissemination, of *writing*, which, as Jacques Derrida notes, has traditionally been treated as a "poor orphan" in contrast with speech, which can claim legitimate filiation to "a father that is present, standing near it, behind it, within it, sustaining it with his rectitude, attending it in person in his own name."[24] Without the presence of the addressee—without the father's attendance—the message cannot be delivered *in person* but must rather be relayed and hence suffer the effects of dissemination.[25]

Wagner's operatic works, packed with mythological symbols and figures, especially invite exegesis and lend themselves to various interpretations. Consider Flagstad's Brünnhilde, trumpeting her warning, "[I]n solchem Strausse streit' ich nicht gern, lieb ich auch muthiger Männer Schlacht, drum sieh wie den Sturm du bestehst" (In strife like this I take no delight, though sweet to me are the battles of men; therefore take now thy stand for the storm). Back in 1870, as hostilities between the nascent German empire and France began, German audiences had responded to the warrior maiden's battle cry with enthusiastic applause.[26] Likewise, throughout the 1930s, the Wagner festivals in Bayreuth became increasingly transformed into jingoistic displays in which the singing of the national anthem often followed performances. To audiences in the United States just prior to World War II, would Brünnhilde's words sound like a plea for peace or a call to arms?

The question of whether or not Wagner's music would foment pro-German sentiment among German-Americans is a typical "problem" for communications theory. Writing in the late 1940s, information theorist Warren Weaver lists three levels of such problems: (A) How accurately can communication signals be transmitted; (B) How precisely do the transmitted signals convey the desired meaning; and (C) How effectively will this meaning influence audience conduct? Weaver sought to meliorate the purely technical approach of his colleague at AT&T, Claude Shannon, who confined his investigations to the first level. Yet a rigorous concept of broadcasting as dissemination renders levels B and C fundamentally in error. A theory of communication should account for how Brünnhilde's battle cry can signify in different contexts, yet communications theory in general tends to treat chronic "problems," "improbabilities," and "infelicities" as anomalous situations or "noise" rather than as structural conditions.[27] Nevertheless, such "problems" occupied American intelligence before and during the war. Although the Communications Act of 1934 prevented the FCC from directly censoring program matter, after 1942 agencies such as the War Problems Division, the Radio Intelligence Division, and the Foreign Broadcast Intelligence Service increasingly treated foreign language as an enemy code and translation as a means for breaking it. The U.S. Office of Censorship's statement to broadcasters in January 1942 instructed programmers to "broadcast only foreign-language programs that are accompanied by full English-language transcripts." Yet such safeguards proved ultimately ineffectual, since even "an innocent-sounding song or combination of words could convey a message to the enemy." The solution was to restrict traffic on the airwaves' channels: "[A]ny access to an open microphone is dangerous.... Do not accept public service announcements by telephone."[28] The U.S. government recommended maintaining a vigilantly suspicious attitude toward telecommunications apparatus such as the microphone and the telephone. Regulating the message's source made sense since broadcasters cannot control the destination nor determine for certain the message's semantic content.

Regulation, however, had traditionally proved difficult because broadcasting ostensibly differs from the post or any other delivery service. The Interstate Commerce Act of 1887 placed "common carriers" such as the railway and waterways under the Interstate Commerce Commission's jurisdiction,[29] and the Mann-Elkins Act of June 1910 extended the term to "include all pipe-line companies; telegraph, telephone, and cable companies operating by wire or wireless."[30] Henceforth, ICC regulations would cover both transportation via locomotion and the "transmission of intelligence through the application of electrical energy ... by means of wire, cable, radio apparatus, or other wire or wireless conductors or appliances."[31] The ICC, however, soon balked at this responsibility, pointing out that broadcasting lacked "the boy in the blue uniform who rings the door bell and who brings the message itself."[32] In 1934, the Federal Communications Act contradicted the Mann-Elkins's classification of broadcasters as common carriers.[33] Common carriers operate station-to-station and deliver to specific addresses whereas broadcasting addresses anyone. The Communications Act legislated this distinction by defining broadcasting as "the dissemination of radio communications intended to be received by the public, directly or by the intermediary of relay stations."[34] By doing so, claims John Durham Peters, the 1934 act "installed the ancient notion of dissemination in the heart of a modern technology in the guise of broadcasting."[35]

In *Speaking into the Air*, Peters elaborates a theory of dialogue and dissemination as two distinct types of communication: one consists of conversation between mutually present interlocutors; the other involves the indiscriminate scattering of the message. Peters contrasts the example of communication as exchange in Plato's *Phaedrus* with Jesus's parable of the sower in the synoptic gospels. Although Peters presents a compelling argument regarding the stubborn privileging of dialogue over dissemination, I believe his reading of the sower parable overemphasizes the accessibility of Jesus's teachings to anyone or everyone, for although the message may be available to all, it is addressed to an elite—those who are saved through grace.

Perhaps the most convincing argument for exclusivity asks why Jesus speaks in parables in the first place. Peters acknowledges that this strategy serves "to keep people from understanding the doctrine," but he places the onus for discovering meaning almost entirely on the receiver. Peters interprets Jesus's proclamation, "who hath ears to hear, let him hear," as a command for the addressee to assume the "interpretive burden ... the responsibility to close the loop without the aid of the speaker."[36] Such a reading, however, ignores the role of election. "To you it has been given to know the secrets of the kingdom of heaven," Jesus tells the twelve, "but to them it has not been given."[37] Interpretive ability is a divine gift, not a skill acquired through diligent application.

Peters also claims that "the sower engages in a purely one-way act: no cultivation of the fledgling plants occurs, no give-and-take, no instruction as to intended meaning."[38] This statement may suit the sower or missionary but not Jesus himself, who employs parables when addressing the multitude, but speaks plainly when alone with the twelve, to whom he "expound[s] all things."[39] Here, contra Peters, Jesus appears as *cultor* rather than sower. Moreover, the twelve make up a privileged secret society, trained by the master and charged with delivering his message. Jesus reminds them that "it is not you who speak, but the Spirit of your Father speaking through you."[40]

Peters's notion of dissemination differs from Jacques Derrida's more radical use of the term, which implies the impossibility of limiting, determining, or "saturating" the linguistic or semantic context.[41] Any ideal of faithful transmission disappears when the identity of the senders and receivers themselves is put into question. "I cannot be assured that an appeal or an address is addressed to whom it is addressed," Derrida observes. There are, then, aleatory or chance elements at work in every kind of message, every type of letter, all mail, if you will. When Derrida speaks of the "post," he envisions a technology that encompasses the ancient courier *and* wireless telephony. According to Derrida, "every envoi is postal," that is, subject to a series of relays and switches. Like writing in the narrow sense, the capacity of broadcasting to extend the voice's range cannot produce a shared horizon where the exchange of intended meanings between interlocutors takes place. On the contrary, the concept of range or horizon fades away, making it difficult to distinguish near from far and up from down. In fact, telecommunication more often makes us lose our bearings than helps us find our place.

Anxiety over the effects of dissemination lies behind efforts to concentrate Wagner's art in Bayreuth, where audiences attend performances given under rigorous control of dramatic and musical elements. Restricting performances of *The Ring* and *Parsifal* to this place made sense before electronic recording and broadcasting technology allowed people to bring Wagner's music into their living rooms. For example, the protagonist of J.-K. Huysmans's 1884 novel *À Rebours* complains that ardent Wagnerites might as well stay home if they "could not or would not travel to Bayreuth."[42] The alternative would mean enduring second-rate conductors "massacring disconnected snatches of Wagner to the huge delight of an ignorant crowd." Such a compromise was anathema to the connoisseur, who understood that "there was not a single scene, not even a single phrase, in any of the mighty Wagner's operas that could be divorced from its context with impunity."[43]

IV

Many believed Wagner's message should not be dispersed indiscriminately but personally delivered by the chosen to the faithful. "His art," writes Friedrich Nietzsche in "Richard Wagner in Bayreuth," "is not to be embarked on the ship of the written word, as the philosopher's must be: art wants performers as transmitters, not letters and notes."[44] Neither literature nor musical notation but rather voices and gestures should serve as means of conveyance. Although R. J. Hollingdale renders Nietzsche's "Könnende als Überlieferer" as "performers as transmitters," it would be more precise to say that Wagner's art wants connoisseurs as messengers. The archaic term *Könnende* is related to the verb *können*, to be able, to know, to understand. Gary Brown translates *Könnende* as "capable men,"[45] while Richard T. Gray prefers "skilled people."[46] Although Hollingdale's choice of "transmitters" adequately renders *überliefern*, which means to hand down or to pass on (as a tradition) and whose stem, *liefern,* means to deliver, familiarity may have dulled the vivid sense of a "carrying over" that the word suggests for English readers.

When Nietzsche raises the timeworn question of "whether a culture can be transplanted to a foreign soil," he employs the term *übertragen,* a rich and complex word that, in short, means to transmit or transport. Hollingdale's rendering of Nietzsche's phrase—"ob eine fremde Cultur sich überhaupt übertragen lasse"—offers more a reading than a translation,[47] yet it supplies that sense of uprooting (more literally conveyed by the German *verpflanzen*) appropriate to questions of culture. *Übertragung* can signify a medium carrying a communicable disease—and thus contagion. In *The Gay Science,* Nietzsche rails against the modern "man of letters," whom he characterizes as "der Ladendiener des Geistes und 'Träger' der Bildung"—the "carrier" of culture.[48] In technical jargon, *übertragen* means to carry a force such as an electromagnetic wave, hence, to transmit or broadcast a radio or television program. The problem Nietzsche refers to, then, concerns whether a distant culture can be successfully broadcast. Nietzsche regards the question as tiresome; it is more crucial to grasp one's role in history as a culture passes through phases of expansion and contraction. Nietzsche believed that the period of Orientalization begun by Alexander's conquests and culminating in Christianity's ascendancy had started to wane. The time had come to gather the "spirit of the Hellenic culture [that] lies endlessly dispersed over our present-day world."[49] In this historical process, Wagner would play the role of a "counter-Alexander." He would cultivate and harvest rather than sow. Nietzsche regards Wagner's "demonic transmissibility"[50] not as a gift for broadcasting but as a drive for communication as mutual exchange. The greatness of Wagner's nature lies in its capacity both to give and to receive. Unfortunately, Wagner's plea for communication meets with baffled silence: "[N]o one answered, no one understood the question."[51] As a remedy, Wagner offers his *Schriften,* which Nietzsche denounces as an improper medium. During the frustrating period of inactivity following the first Bayreuth festival, Wagner establishes the *Bayreuther Blätter* as the organ for his anti-Semitic rants and engages as editor the fawning Hans von Wolzogen, who was expected in many ways to fill the apostate philosopher's shoes.

Wolzogen considered Bayreuth "a power station of the spirit";[52] it served indeed as the source of Wagner's "demonic transmissions." The first issue of the paper carried a short piece by Wagner on his plan for maintaining a "school" for pilgrims, who would be able to receive instruction at the master's feet.[53] He gives the *Blätter*'s raison d'être as the need to establish interconnection among the network's stations: "[T]hese Leaves were originally to be the channel for communications from the school to the outlying members of the *Verein*."[54] Wagner's rhetoric leaves no doubt concerning the exclusive nature of this mission:

My friends will see that I was aiming at a thoroughly practical intercourse with those who were *to derive their instruction from that intercourse itself*. Now admittedly these "Blätter," in which we must take our refuge for the present, cannot help us to instruction in that sense. It therefore only remains for us to mutually instruct ourselves upon the causes of those hindrances to a noble cultivation of the German artistic faculty on the field which we have entered, and the exertions it will need to triumph over them. The execution of my Bayreuth *Bühnen-festspiels* [stage festivals] has shown, on my side, that I had in mind the fostering of this faculty through a living example.[55]

The text clearly presents dialogue as the preferred pedagogical method and broadcasting as an expedient and temporary compromise. Writing—telecommunications—cannot substitute for the "living example."

Unfortunately, the composer considered even his handpicked lieutenants incompetent without his watchful supervision. In an 1879 letter to Wolzogen, Wagner laments: "There is not a single soul ... to whom I could trust to perform my work correctly, nor any singing actor whom I could count upon to give a correct performance ... unless I first went through the part with him, bar by bar and phrase by phrase."[56] Such insistence on transmission through actual contact is consistent with apostolic ordination. The analogies between the hierarchical ordering of Wagner's "church" and the Roman Catholic apostolate suggest that Wagner borrowed from Catholicism more than merely subject matter for his final opera, *Parsifal*. Strictly speaking, the mission belongs to the founder—Christ or Wagner— and must be communicated through means such as the laying on of hands. Hence, "no lacuna can be allowed, no new mission can arise; but the mission ... must pass from generation to generation through an uninterrupted lawful succession."[57]

To ensure the legitimacy of succession, Wagner gathered around him a group of dedicated young apostles in Bayreuth throughout the decade of the 1870s. This company included the Hungarian Anton Seidl, a Richter protégé, who would remain in Bayreuth as Wagner's student and assistant for six years before moving to the United States to replace Leopold Damrosch at the Metropolitan Opera. Seidl's wife, soprano Auguste Seidl-Krauss, had sung at the Metropolitan Opera when *Die Walküre* debuted there under Damrosch's baton. This genealogy suggests the extent to which the Wagner ministry was spreading the gospel abroad. One may read the words Auguste chooses to describe her husband's impression of New York Harbor as aesthetic observation or tactical report: "The moment he saw the harbor he was delighted; the elevated railroad he found imposing; even the large telegraph poles seemed to him beautiful."[58] Like any good strategist, Seidl pays primary attention to the channels of communication—the waterways, the railroad, and the telegraph. In any case, it was Seidl who established the standard for conducting Wagner at the Met.

Given Wagner's extreme care in appointing conductors, a legacy carried on by his heirs at Bayreuth, what are we to make of Wilfred Pelletier conducting the orchestra in *The Big Broadcast*? A French-Canadian, Pelletier did not belong to the Met's German fleet. On the contrary, he specialized in French opera: Verdi, Gounod, Delibes, Massenet. In fact, Pelletier never conducted a Wagner opera for the Saturday afternoon broadcasts. Perhaps Bodanzky's increasing ill health prevented him from undertaking the rigors of traveling and filming. In any case, the consequences of Pelletier's presence are clear. He disturbs the homogeneous Germanness of the segment and changes the performance to a cosmopolitan affair whose atmosphere smacks more of Paris or New York than Bayreuth or Munich. This effect is evident in Bob Hope's careful pronunciation of the conductor's name: Wilfred Pel-let-tee-ay. In contrast, one could imagine the effect if Hope had introduced instead Bodanzky's assistant, Erich Leinsdorf.

It would be enlightening to compare Pelletier's tempos with music performed under these men's direction, for Wagner considered the art of finding the right tempo the true measure of a conductor's worth,[59] and he ranted vehemently against conductors who failed to follow his tempo indications. For Wagner, the communication of musical ideas becomes enmeshed with the difficulties of translation. When the composer stopped giving metronome markings for his compositions, he was dismayed to find conductors unable to comprehend tempo indications expressed in German. "The gentlemen, accustomed to the old Italian labels," he complained, "are all at sea as to what I mean by 'Mässig' [moderate]."[60] We might joke that Pelletier is literally "at sea" in *The Big Broadcast*, but, more to the point, he lacks the grounding from which to comprehend the tempo's meaning. For Wagner, understanding tempo requires membership in a community comprised of "those who parley in a language mutually intelligible."[61]

In this chapter, I have called attention to certain "defense mechanisms" springing not from the psychological struggles of the individual human consciousness but from the interaction between two communications networks: one that seeks to broadcast its message to the widest possible audience, and one that strives to transmit its mission to a select few by means of direct contact. Telecommunications technology brings strangers into uncomfortable proximity, and, because these two networks promoted different cultural values, encounters between them naturally caused tension. Ironically, these rivals shared an aim—to minimize broadcasting's unsettling effects. Such efforts must ultimately prove futile, however, because broadcasting, as McLuhan notes, "is not only a mighty awakener of archaic memories, forces, and animosities, but a decentralizing, pluralistic force."[62] Concerns over whether or not a message reaches its destination matter little once the very notion of destination—including that destination called "home"—is called into question. The practice of extending ourselves in space changes our relation to the land and culture, and the wanderer returns from the quest to find everything familiar yet different.

Notes

1. T. S. Eliot, "The Dry Salvages," in *The Complete Poems and Plays 1909–1950* (New York: Harcourt, Brace & World, 1971), 130.
2. Claude Shannon and Warren Weaver, *The Mathematical Theory of Communication* (Urbana: University of Illinois Press, 1949), 3.
3. In similar terms, Maurice Blanchot describes early Soviet space exploration as "sacrilegious." As Blanchot points out, the Russian cosmonaut Yuri Gagarin joked on his return to earth that he had been to heaven and had not met God there. Maurice Blanchot, "The Conquest of Space," in *The Blanchot Reader* (Cambridge: Blackwell, 1995), 271.
4. Max Horkheimer and Theodor W. Adorno, *Dialectic of Enlightenment*, trans. John Cumming (New York: Continuum, 1995), 10.
5. Quoted in Alexander Ringer, *Arnold Schoenberg: The Composer as Jew* (New York: Oxford University Press, 1990), 92.
6. On the history of this cartel, see Michele Hilmes, *Hollywood and Broadcasting: From Radio to Cable* (Urbana: University of Illinois Press, 1990), chaps. 1 and 2; David A. Cook, "The Birth of the Network," *Quarterly Review of Film Studies* 8, no. 3 (1983): 3–8; Armand Mattelart, *Networking the World, 1794–2000*, trans. Liz Corey-Libbrecht and James A. Cohen (Minneapolis: University of Minnesota Press, 2000); and N. R. Danielian, *A.T. & T.: The Story of Industrial Conquest* (New York: Vanguard, 1939), esp. chap. 7. On Paramount's incursions into radio, see Hilmes, *Hollywood Broadcasting*, chaps. 2 and 3.
7. Quoted in Hilmes, *Hollywood and* Broadcasting, 9.
8. Quoted in Joseph Horowitz, *Wagner Nights: An American History* (Berkeley: University of California Press, 1994), 330.
9. Robert J. Brown, *Manipulating the Ether* (Jefferson, N.C.: McFarland and Company, 1998), xii.
10. On the treatment of German-Americans during World War I and World War II, see La Vern J. Rippley, *The German-Americans* (Boston: Twayne, 1976), esp. chaps. 14 and 15.
11. Ronald Garay, "Guarding the Airwaves: Government Regulation of World War II American Radio," *Journal of Radio Studies* 3 (1995–96): 131.
12. The 12 January 1938 issue of *Variety* gives the following number of station "plugs" for songs from the film: "Thanks for the Memories," 8; "Mama, That Moon Is Here Again," 21; and "You Took the Words Right Out of My Heart," 24. On 26 January, the last song was #1 on *Variety's* charts with 39 "hits."
13. *Variety*, 14 February 1938.
14. Robert Tuggle, "Clouds of War," *Opera News* 60, no. 1 (July 1995): 10–17.
15. Marc Shulgold, "Encore with Greatness: PBS Special 'Art of Singing' Takes Measure of Cinematic Opera Stars," *Denver Rocky Mountain News*, 25 March 1998, 9D.
16. Paul Jackson, *Saturday Afternoons at the Old Met: The Metropolitan Opera Broadcasts 1931–1950* (Portland: Amadeus Press, 1992), 267
17. *The Great Sopranos: Voices of Firestone Classic Performances*, prod. Video Artists International and New England Conservatory (Fort Lee: Video Artists International, 1995), videocassette.
18. Marshall McLuhan, *Understanding Media* (Cambridge: MIT Press, 1994), 299.
19. Frederic Spotts, *Bayreuth: A History of the Wagner Festival* (New Haven: Yale University Press, 1994).
20. Jackson, *Saturday Afternoons*, 22.
21. Spotts, *Bayreuth*, 171–73.
22. Ibid., 236.
23. Theodor Adorno, "A Social Critique of Radio Music," *Kenyon Review* 7 (1945): 209, 217. Adorno's piece on the radio symphony complements his 1938 article "On the Fetish Character in Music and the Regression of Listening," in *The Essential Frankfurt School Reader*, ed. Andrew Arato and Eike Gebhard (Oxford: Basil Blackwell, 1978), 270–99. Careful reading of these works reveals that Adorno does not propose a crude cause-and-effect relation between the medium and aesthetic appreciation; rather, the regression

of listening typical of the radio audience is merely one aspect of the thorough commodification of art.

24. Jacques Derrida, "Plato's Pharmacy," in *Dissemination*, trans. Barbara Johnson (Chicago: University of Chicago Press, 1981), 77.

25. As Derrida points out, a message's destination is always uncertain. For Derrida, all writing is telecommunication and subject to the "postal principle." Jacques Derrida, "Envois," in *The Post Card*, trans. Alan Bass (Chicago: University of Chicago Press, 1987), 121.

26. Robert W. Gutman, *Richard Wagner: The Man, His Mind, and His Music* (New York: Harcourt Brace Jovanovich, 1990), 308.

27. I speak of "communications theory in general" in the interest of time and space. The present essay is informed significantly by Claude Shannon and Warren Weaver, *The Mathematical Theory of Communication* (Urbana: University of Illinois Press, 1949), which could be compared with Niklas Luhmann's work, in particular, *Essays on Self-Reference* (New York: Columbia University Press, 1990) and *Ecological Communication*, trans. John Bednarz, Jr. (Chicago: University of Chicago Press, 1989). These works can be read along with—or against—Derrida's critique of J. L. Austin's notion of communication. For a historically informed and provocative overview of communications theory, cybernetics, and systems theory, see N. Katherine Hayles, *How We Became Posthuman* (Chicago: University of Chicago Press, 1999).

28. U.S. Office of Censorship, "Code of Wartime Practices for American Broadcasters," in *Radiotexte*, ed. Neil Strauss and Dave Mandl, *Semiotext(e)* 16 (1993): 229.

29. John Durham Peters, *Speaking into the Air: A History of the Idea of Communication* (Chicago: University of Chicago Press, 1999), 209; and Joshua Bernhardt, *The Interstate Commerce Commission: Its History, Activities and Organization* (Baltimore: Johns Hopkins University Press, 1923), 26.

30. Quoted in Bernhardt, *The Interstate*, 64.

31. Ibid., 65.

32. Quoted in Peters, *Speaking into the Air*, 209.

33. Section 3 (h) states that "a person engaged in radio broadcasting shall not … be deemed a common carrier." Section 3 (i) defines "person" as "any corporation, joint-stock company, or association." United States, 73rd Congress, "The Communications Act of 1934," in *Documents of American Broadcasting*, ed. Frank J. Kahn (New York: Appleton-Century-Crofts, 1973), 56. The situation is complex. AT&T's wire service would still maintain its status as a common carrier although individual broadcasters, the stations, and the networks would not.

34. "Communications Act," 57.

35. Peters, *Speaking into the Air*, 210.

36. Ibid., 52–53.

37. Matthew 13:11, New Revised Standard Version (hereafter NRSV).

38. Peters, *Speaking into the Air*, 53.

39. Mark 4:34, NRSV.

40. Matthew 10:20, NRSV.

41. Jacques Derrida, "Signature Event Context," in *Margins of Philosophy*, trans. Alan Bass (Chicago: University of Chicago Press, 1982), 316. See also *Positions*, trans. Alan Bass (Chicago: University of Chicago Press, 1981), 45, 86.

42. J.-K Huysmans, *Against Nature*, trans. Robert Baldick (New York: Penguin, 1959), 205.

43. Ibid., 204.

44. Friedrich Nietzsche, "Richard Wagner in Bayreuth," in *Untimely Meditations*, trans. R. J. Hollingdale (Cambridge: Cambridge University Press, 1997), 247. Friedrich Nietzsche, *Werke* (Berlin: Walter de Gruyter, 1967), 4:72.

45. Friedrich Nietzsche, "Richard Wagner in Bayreuth," *Unmodern Observations*, trans. Gary Brown, ed. William Arrowsmith (New Haven: Yale University Press, 1990), 298.

46. Friedrich Nietzsche, "Richard Wagner in Bayreuth," *Unfashionable Observations*, trans. Richard T. Gray (Stanford: Stanford University Press, 1995), 321. Nietzsche, *Werke*, 4:18.

47. Recall Walter Benjamin's words: "Any translation which intends to perform a transmitting function cannot transmit anything but information—hence, something inessential." Benjamin calls such work "the hallmark of bad translations." Walter Benjamin, "The Task of the Translator," in *Illuminations*, trans. Harry Zorn (New York: Schocken Books, 1968), 69. It would be interesting to read Benjamin's statement against Claude Shannon's ideas on transmitting information quoted at the beginning of the present essay.

48. Friedrich Nietzsche, *The Gay Science*, trans. Walter Kaufmann (New York: Vintage, 1974), 323. Nietzsche, *Werke*, 5:297.

49. Nietzsche, *Untimely Meditations*, 209.

50. Brown prefers "daimonic infectiousness" (275); Gray offers "demonic transferability" (291).

51. Nietzsche, *Untimely Meditations*, 231.

52. Quoted in Spotts, *Bayreuth*, 131.

53. Richard Wagner, "Introduction to the First Number of the Bayreuther Blätter," in *Religion and Art*, trans. W. Ashton Ellis (Lincoln: University of Nebraska Press, 1994).

54. Ibid., 23.

55. Ibid., 24.

56. Richard Wagner, *Selected Letters of Richard Wagner*, trans. and ed. Stewart Spencer and Barry Millington (New York: Norton, 1988), 890.

57. "Apostolicity," *New Advent Catholic Encyclopedia*. Available from http://www.newadvent. org/cathen.

58. Quoted in Horowitz, *Wagner Nights*, 88.

59. Richard Wagner, "About Conducting," in *Art and Politics*, trans. W. Ashton Ellis (Lincoln: University of Nebraska Press, 1995), 304, 314.

60. Ibid., 305.

61. Wagner "What Is German?" in *Art and Politics*, trans. Ellis, 152.

62. McLuhan, *Understanding Media*, 306.

Chapter 11

SOUNDS FAMILIAR?

Nina Simone's Performances
of Brecht/Weill Songs

Russell A. Berman

I

The conventional admonition to keep quiet in a library can be taken as a motto for deep-seated expectations regarding literature: when serious, it is silent, and its enemy is noise. "Reading aloud" is an activity associated with children, who themselves are directed to overcome the immaturity of moving their lips and to begin to "read to themselves." There are, of course, "poetry readings," although fewer than one might imagine, and they are not always easily distinguishable from promotional tours (a commercial and a therefore presumably degraded form of literary life). In any case, the implicit assumption of the genuine scene of literary reception is the isolated reader, engrossed silently in a text. T. S. Eliot's women "talking of Michelangelo" stand as a contemptuous marker of chatter, a Heideggerian *Gerede*, at odds with the mute gravity of art.

Yet the normative expectation of silence stands at odds with competing phenomena, which indicate how acoustic dimensions may in fact be constitutive of the possibility of literature despite the conventional imperative of quiet. The incantatory mission of poetry, the unsevered linkage of drama to performance, and the residual dynamic of narration and readership in the structure of prose fiction all point to an inherent, acoustic aspiration of literature, which, if not strictly teleological for all literature, is surely present as a possibility in all writing. In other words, the silence in which literature is indeed read—as if always in a library, so to speak—has to be considered in relation to potentials of vocalization, be they inscribed in the specific texts themselves or implicitly in the overlay of institutional

Notes for this chapter begin on page 182.

settings, for example, genre expectations, cultural-historical conventions, and material and technological conditions. Literary culture—if not in general, then at least since the invention of writing—depends on the particular potential of displaced vocalization or imminent intonation. What force is required to keep sound at bay and the library silent? What voices threaten to disturb it? The silence of the written text always implies *ex negativo* the sounds marginalized at its borders. Theater can provide an additional, telling analogy to the library invoked at the outset: the simultaneity of the silenced public and the privileged recitations of the actors—disciplined speechlessness on the one hand, formal oratory on the other.

Sound accompanies literature in a variety of modalities, not mutually exclusive, frequently overlapping, but nonetheless distinct enough to allow for ideal-typical separations. The written text itself may foreground particular acoustic features, for example, alliterative phrasings or rhyme, independent of any empirical likelihood of an oral performance but presumably resonant in the mental act of reading.[1] The written text thereby presumes its own silent reading but projects into it an acoustic texture to be realized solely in the mind of the reader. Alternatively, the capacity of the written text to build on the tension between the silence of writing and the potential for sound can also become even more demonstrative, through the invocation of sound within the medium-specific silence. Fredric Jameson has pointed to the mute character of Edvard Munch's *Scream*, in relation to the painting's iconic standing within modernism.[2] A similar conundrum is posed, for example, by the conclusion of Franz Kafka's "The Judgment": the narrative leaves Georg hanging from a bridge until the noise of the traffic can muffle the sound of his fall. The ambiguity of that *Verkehr* and the conclusion of the story surely stand in relation to the intermedia competition between writing (the letter sequence that dominates the first half of the story) and speech (the conversation with the father in the second half). The general problem is one of acoustic ekphrasis: not the description of works of visual art but rather moments of sound within the literary text. If visual ekphrasis stages the tension between the written word and visual art, acoustic ekphrasis underscores the silence of writing and the specific exclusion of sound.

Acoustic ekphrasis references sound within the soundlessness of the writing. Alternatively, sound may shadow the written word externally, for example, in the form of accompanying music or a soundtrack. This is the traditional field of "music and literature," that is, music composed to support a literary text, whereby the relationship between the music and text can be seen in terms of either an affirmative doubling or a contrapuntal subversion, or in fact a range of intermediate positions. In the first case, the music asserts and emphasizes the text, underscoring and amplifying an intentional meaning; in the second, the music undermines a literary intention, commenting on it, or calling it into question. The distinction is central to Bertolt Brecht's account of epic drama and the opera. In his notes on *The Rise and Fall of the City of Mahagonny,* he distinguishes emphatically between the dramatic opera, in which music heightens the text, and the epic opera, in which music provides a commentary.[3] "Heightening" the text implies a romantic strengthening of the emotional coloration, in contrast to which the commentary music of the epic opera—according to Brecht—prevents emotional identification and therefore bolsters the audience's critical acuity. Brecht's particular political evaluation of modes of reception aside, his focus on the function of nondiegetic music points to a complexity of the multimedia aesthetic object, leading to the particular appropriation of Brechtian nonidentity postulates in the cinematic work of Hans-Jürgen Sybergerg. The soundtrack can function as a dimension of citation and allusion, commenting on both other dimensions of film: the visual display and the verbal scripts—particularly, but not exclusively, those of the narrator.

Sound also accompanies literature in the form of vocal performance: as recitation, spoken text in drama, or song, for example. Performance may imply accompanying music, but it is separate from it; it involves the appropriation of the written script by the human voice. This phenomenon entails a "secondary orality," that is, speaking a text that was specifically written to be spoken or sung.[4] At stake, therefore, is not primarily the commentary that the music may be providing, as discussed above. Rather it is the character of the rendering provided by the speaker/singer. On this point, too, Brecht provides a useful distinction. In the epic opera: "Der Sänger wird zum Referenten, dessen Privatgefühle Privatsache bleiben müssen" (The singer becomes objective reporter whose private feelings have to remain a private matter).[5] Building on the distinction between the traditional "dramatic opera" and the epic variant, Brecht insists on the nonidentification of the performer with the text and hence on a colder, more analytic stance. Nonetheless, no matter how the individual characteristics of a performer might remain "private," as Brecht would have it, any oral performance necessarily moves from the unrealized potential of the written text to a very specific rendition that is performed by an individual performer in a particular context. The performance is therefore close to a project of translation, moving the reception of the text from the silence of the page to a new and concrete venue, at the very least, a new historical context (since the performance is by definition subsequent to the moment of production of the original), and possibly to a new cultural context as well (through a displacement to a different location, a translation into a new language, etc.). Therefore, the implicit acoustics of any text and, in particular, the potential for a performative vocalization (for some texts, more than others) pose the question of the specificity of any reception, raising issues of both individuality and cultural particularity.

Nina Simone's performances of Brecht/Weill songs are especially interesting examples insofar as all of these aspects of the literature/sound relationship come to the fore. "Pirate Jenny" is itself a staging of performance and hence an ekphrastic invocation of sound. In fact, it invokes a proliferation of performance: Lenya playing Polly playing Jenny playing to her customers, as well as a foregrounding of the tension between silence—"wird es still sein am Hafen"—and aleatory sound—"Hoppla." Furthermore, the external relationship of text to music, namely, the problem of music as either affirmative amplification or analytic subversion, is at the core of the Brechtian theory of epic theater. Most importantly, however, the distinction between Lenya's and Simone's performances is embedded in deep cultural structures, pertinent not only to Germany and the United States, but also to the capacity of American German studies to recognize the complex diversity of American receptions of German culture. Thus, to examine how a text travels from German verse to German voice and from a German performance to an African-American performance highlights how the question of performance—as one version of the relationship of text to sound—quickly involves the critic in a recognition of cultural particularities, their internal complexities, and the possibilities of translation. In examining Simone's Brecht, therefore, we touch not only on her implicit criticism of Brecht and Lenya but also on the need to diversify the community of American Brecht recipients. The definition of that community of readers is interrupted by an attention to sound, which replaces the abstraction of the written text with a potential plurality of voices.

II

Any literary criticism focused solely on the written text is necessarily predisposed to ignore context. The question of sound, particularly in light of the implicit vocalization inscribed in a literary text, promises to disrupt a narrowly grammatological reading and thereby to open up a dialectic between written and sonic, generalizing and particularizing vectors. Sound underscores particularity because of its relation to performance, which is always particular. Consequently, the emerging attention to sound may serve as a corrective to the bias of academic criticism to formulate ever more abstract, and therefore less particular, statements. Yet this methodological universalism tends to undercut the study of particular traditions, a problem currently acute within American German studies. On the one hand, a frantic effort to "Americanize" the field and thereby avoid the association with "German particularity" defines German Studies as just one among many ultimately interchangeable national literatures and therefore in no way specifically German—a strategy designed to avoid difficult questions about tradition and historical legacy. On the other hand, the agenda to Americanize German studies retains a nearly consistent blindness to the breadth of what "American" might mean. The overly dramatic polarization of American German studies versus German *Germanistik* typically leaves the composition of American identity unexamined (just as it surely oversimplifies, for polemical purposes, the range of literary scholarship in Germany). Exhortations to overcome a putative disciplinary isolation and to join a larger American discussion—this is one of the recurrent topoi of the discourse—idealize that American discussion, refuse to inquire into its own shortcomings, and certainly fail to ask how German perspectives might contribute to correcting those shortcomings, just as they avoid the plurality of American subject positions. This narrow and exclusionary idealization of American identity, coupled with a desperate effort to flee particularity, German or otherwise, effectively excludes any thematization of ethnic or racial specificity. In other words, the Americanization program within American German studies tends to posit a uniformly "American" reception of German material, the implicit alternative to an equally illusory uniform Germany. For all of its political correctness (because it is a variant of anti-Eurocentrism), Americanization promises to make a difficult situation worse by occluding diverse American voices.

That the Americanization of German studies turns out to be deaf to the African-American reception of German culture is particularly striking against the background of the study of German in the United States. From its inception, the field was intertwined with an outspoken abolitionism, from the Pastorius protest of 1683 through Charles Follen's involvement in the 1830s; his contract at Harvard was terminated evidently due to his antislavery politics. Meanwhile, at least since Frederick Douglass, the movement for black freedom and equality has been marked by encounters with German culture and politics. During his sojourn in Berlin, W. E. B. Du Bois wrote back to the college newspaper at his alma mater, Fisk, in Nashville, that students should study Goethe "for the rise of the Negro people."[6] Far from some essentialized "Americanization," the study of German has always involved processes of cultural transfer and a transatlantic dialectic, in which critical reflection on Germany could elicit critical thinking about the United States. Critiques of *die deutsche Misere* hardly necessitate an affirmation of the status quo in the United States. On the contrary, the same emancipatory spirit of inquiry can, we know, continue its project by posing similar questions in a new context. As an intellectual project, "Americanization" threatens to undermine this interaction: Germany would become less a source of ideas or a provocation to criticism. Instead, it would be reduced to a distanced and reified object of inquiry, which is observed and measured from an unquestioned "American" perspective, in which any residual critical thought disappears in a tidal wave of universalist triumphalism that disallows genuine cultural differences.

There are, however, other American perspectives, including the history of African-American reception of German material, notably, the interest in German musical traditions. The lineage stretches from W. E. B. Du Bois's treatment of *Lohengrin* in his seminal volume, *Souls of Black Folk*, through Marian Anderson's reinterpretation of the *Lied* tradition, and Jessye Norman's elaboration of Anderson's legacy in a series of concert performances with a mixed repertoire of high European art songs and black spirituals. Indeed, one of the more striking overlaps between German and African-American culture involves the willingness for each to ascribe a privileged position to music. The point is not to assert that all members of the two populations are somehow essentially more musical; that would indeed be a strange and counterfactual claim. However, in each tradition there is abundant evidence of a frequent self-definition in explicitly musical terms. Thus, in addition to his fascination with German high music culture, Du Bois also posited an equation between spirituals and German folk songs, a Herderian gesture that compounded the Hegelian agenda of *Souls of Black Folk*: the popular musical idiom was treated as the carrier of emancipatory substance. Consequently, in contrast to the high-art tradition from Du Bois's Wagner to Norman's Mahler, there are also examples of an explicitly political art. Although plans for an all-black performance of *The Threepenny Opera* (in which Paul Robeson was to star as Macheath) were not realized, two Brecht/Weill songs played a crucial role in the performance repertoire of Nina Simone, whom Stokely Carmichael referred to as "the true singer of the civil rights movement."[7] Her reworkings of two classic texts of German modernism—"Seeräuber-Jenny" (Pirate Jenny) and "Moon of Alabama"—represent a significant cultural transfer between the left-wing modernism of Weimar Germany and the culture of American protest music.

III

The songs undergo telling transformations, pointing to important questions regarding political art, posed against the background of the complexity of German-American interactions. At stake are assumptions about the character of political art and the cultural-political differences and similarities between Weimar Germany and civil-rights-era United States. The Brechtian agenda of distanciation does not travel well through the geographical displacement, and Simone's performances are therefore readable as critical responses to key tenets of left modernist aesthetics.

Some of the transformations that characterized Simone's performances were in fact not specifically musical or even performative but derived instead from distinctly literary elements, particularly differences between the original Brecht text and the Marc Blitzstein translation of "Pirate Jenny." The locational ambiguity of the German poem, suggesting a grotesquely fairy-tale-like sensibility to the Jenny of the play (a typical Brechtian device that works against specific identification possibilities), was replaced by Blitzstein with a decisive repositioning within an American geography. Thus, Lenya sings Polly singing Jenny in an indeterminate harbor town, while Simone's Jenny is unambiguously located close to home. For example, the third and fourth verses,

Und Sie geben mir einen Penny, und ich bedanke mich schnell
Und Sie sehen meine Lumpen und dies lumpige Hotel,[8]

become:

Maybe once ya tip me and it makes ya feel swell
In this crummy Southern town/In this crummy old hotel.

This translation relocates the abstract class struggle of the German people into the specific context of the civil rights movement: however one might evaluate the focus on the South (does it, for example, minimize issues of race in other regions?), its deployment here is certainly not just a matter of atmospherics. On the contrary, the text takes on a very precise referentiality, which is underscored by elements of the performance, for example, the inclusion of several interjections such as "I'll tell you," in the mode of African-American gospel singing. These vocal signals of Southernness work quite differently from Lenya's southern German/Austrian accent, with its exaggerated clarity of enunciation, which may be interpreted as the overcorrecting of a regional accent in order to strive for conventionality. Simone, instead, marks her speech with flaunted signs of regional, racial, or class specificity, for example, dropping final g's: "grinning" becomes "grinnin'." The precision of Lenya's enunciation signals a repression of a particular accent, even if it thereby marks it; Simone's approach highlights the dialectic's nuance.

Translation is not an issue for "Moon of Alabama," of course, yet a literary change takes place here as well, insofar as Simone would frequently perform it in medley with her own signature protest song, "Mississippi Goddam." That song, written in response to the assassination of Medgar Evers and the Birmingham church bombing, represented Simone's breakthrough to political performance. Intertwining the Brecht/Weill song with her own composition imputes a more emphatic engagement and a specificity of reference, namely, to "Alabama" (which was surely absent in the original); thus, Simone relocates Brecht's imaginary Alabama of Mahagonny into the politicized South of the civil rights movements. As in "Pirate Jenny," an imaginary location, Mahagonny, suddenly becomes quite recognizable in an anti-Brechtian process of refamiliarization that is quite the opposite of the aesthetic principle pursued by Brecht. It is not distance and abstraction but proximity and precision that Simone targets. Making matters even more complex, in at least some performances, Simone would gloss this linkage with interjected references to Brecht and Weill writing in Berlin in 1932—an inaccurate dating, by the way, but one that suggests a metaphoric relationship between the American South and the collapse of German democracy. The connection builds on a comparison that had been elaborated as early as the 1930s by Du Bois and which involves two distinct, if interrelated, issues: the comparability of racial politics in Germany and the United States, namely, the Jim Crow and the Nürnberg laws, and the anxieties regarding the instability of democratic institutions in general. By invoking Weimar-era Germany, particularly at its end in 1932, Simone dramatizes the American situation as an eleventh-hour emergency with a threat of looming fascism. On this point, she was, of course, participating in the preferred register of political rhetoric of the time.

This locational transposition of the German content—whether due to the Blitzstein translation or the linguistic/dramatic elements of Simone's own performance—resonates with a prior transition in Simone's career, which also double-exposed German culture onto the United States: her initial musical aspiration involved becoming "the first Black concert pianist"; she writes of her "beloved Bach"; and she attended Juilliard.[9] Aside from church performances during her childhood, her genuine entry into a popular musical idiom was not at all a career goal but purely a vehicle to finance her classical training. Yet this experience provided her with the opportunity to explore a generic hybridity that would eventually mix German musical material and popular American forms of entertainment:

> Before I started at the Midtown Bar [in Atlantic City] my musical life was sep-
> arated into two halves. The tuition I gave at my storefront was simply a way of
> earning money to keep up my studies; I didn't even think of it as music—it was
> just a job. Because I spent so long accompanying untalented students I came to
> despise popular songs and I never played them for my own amusement—why
> should I when I could be playing Bach, or Czerny or Liszt? That was real music,
> and in it I found a happiness I didn't have to share with anybody. So the only
> way I could stand playing in the Midtown was to make my set as close to clas-
> sical music as possible without getting fired. This meant I had to include some
> popular music and I had to sing, which I'd never thought of doing. The strange
> thing was that when I started to do it, to bring the two halves together, I found
> a pleasure in it almost as deep as the pleasure I got from classical music.[10]

This position between genres and styles continued to characterize her self-understanding and her reception. She would later comment on the response to her Town Hall concert of 1959: "So saying what sort of music I played gave the critics problems because there was something from everything in there, but it also meant I was appreciated across the board—by jazz, folk, pop and blues fans as well as admirers of classical music."[11]

By transporting the Brecht poems into a specifically American setting, Simone politicized them, or politicized them in a new way. Instead of the imaginary locations of Brechtian struggle, a very specific identity emerges through Simone's increasingly engaged stance. This metamorphosis is not only literary but pertains to the music as well, combining a more strident politics with greater emotionality. Unlike Lotte Lenya's normative performance, which largely refrains from affective engagement, maintaining instead a cool distance from the narrated events, Simone's voice is dramatic and emotional, vengeful and threatening. The powerful performance, therefore, stands at odds with underlying precepts of epic theater. Perhaps the most salient example of musical change involves tempo; Lenya's recordings of "Pirate Jenny" last about four minutes, while Simone takes six minutes and forty seconds—65 percent longer. Lenya's crisp, mechanical sound, conveying the pressured time of the harried maid as well as her dismissive disregard for the victims of the imaginary slaughter, gives way to a much more nuanced subjectivity in Simone's rendition, which takes the time to savor the affective complexity of submission and revolt. In turn, that dialectic loses Lenya's harsh objectivity and becomes itself more subjective, running the risk of sliding into the sort of introspection that redefines the personal as the political and the only political. In any case, the distinction between the two rhythms is, of course, not absolute: Lenya also slows down at the refrain, and she retards the progress through the final stanza. Simone, however, stretches the material out to a much greater extent, thereby gaining the flexibility for brilliant additions, such as the threatening laughter after, "And you see me stepping out in the morning/Looking nice with a ribbon in my hair," or the minatory repetition of "nobody" in, "Cuz there's nobody gonna sleep here, honey/Nobody/Nobody!" Here the ironic usage of "honey" resonates with the heightened danger of Blitzstein's translation. Brecht's straightforward "Und das Bett wird gemacht/Es wird keiner mehr drin schlafen in dieser Nacht" becomes a grimly playful: "But I'm counting your heads/as I'm making the beds."

The affective complexity corresponds to a greater range of vocal registers. At points, Simone comes close to a classical *Sprechgesang*, at others, she falls into a whisper. While close attention to Lenya's singing can detect a variation from assertive phrasing to moments of emotive tremolo, nothing approaches Simone's dramatic emotionality and rich texturing of the sound. The (in more than one sense) high point of the performance is the final refrain in which Simone sings "the ship" for the last time, holding it at a high falsetto (in contrast to her otherwise deep voice) for a considerable length of time. Within the tradition of African-American reception of German music, this high note, conveying mourning rather than the triumph suggested by the text, points back to Du Bois's use of a similar note from *Lohengrin*. It therefore not only establishes an intertextual continuity between *Souls of Black Folk* and civil-rights-era protest songs, it also appears to pose a Wagnerian question to Brechtian aesthetics: How do we explain Simone's distance from distanciation?

Simone challenges the stability of Brechtian political aesthetics on multiple levels. The first involves the question of individualization. The distance between Simone's subjective version of "Pirate Jenny" and Lenya's "epic" objectivity reflects distinct political cultures. It is the difference between—in simplified terms—an American individualism and Brecht's antisubjectivism, which, for all of the radical gesturing he placed around it, was surely deeply indebted to long-standing German reactions against

Romanticism. (Indeed, Brecht's antisubjectivism may have been more Goethean than he would have conceded.) Simone rescues particularity, and especially individual particularity, from the mechanical uniformity that signaled Brecht's own proximity to the New Sobriety of the Weimar period. This, at least, is the answer that is suggested, intentionally or not, by the Alabama/Mississippi entwinement. Brecht's familiar text stages a collectivity, no matter how degraded, while Simone's dwells on a private and subjective response to political events: "Alabama's gotten me so upset/Tennessee made me lose my rest." These personal reverberations issue into a shared consciousness: "And everybody knows about Mississippi Goddam." This self-reflective dialectic between Simone's "me" and her "everybody"—how she moves from her individual response to collective knowledge—makes Brecht's group search for the next whiskey bar seem all the more crude. Yet in the context of "Mississippi Goddam," Brecht's "Moon of Alabama" also turns out to provide a political analysis: whiskey, dollars, and conformism explain the bombings and assassinations in such a way that the record of subjective response inherent in "Mississippi" might not. Brecht's analysis, in its identification of an economic cause of the cultural distortions, remains more radical, but Simone is more engaged by insinuating a rage to the political judgment—hence, presumably, her decision to link the two. The Brechtian text supplements her own song by implying a trenchant social analysis that she did not provide on her own.

Intertwined, the two texts, and the two analyses, threaten however to merge into one; it is therefore important for Simone's verses to foreground individuality precisely in order to prevent her "everybody"—as in "everybody knows about Mississippi"—from collapsing into Brecht's "us"—as in "show us the way." This urgent staging of individuality within the hybrid lyrics reflects and depends upon two opposing historical tendencies. On the one hand, Simone sings against the background of the appropriation of African-American music, especially jazz, as an icon of individuality during the Cold War. Her efforts to maintain her individualism against Brechtian collectivism fit neatly into an American cultural politics of anti-Communism, which she would hardly have endorsed, even while participating in it. On the other hand, the civil rights movement as whole, undergoing radicalization, was fraught with tensions between a focus on individual civil rights and aspirations for collective, social change (these terms continue to underlie contemporary debates over affirmative action). Her singing represents an initial effort to think through this problem, which can be traced along the fault line between the two intertwined songs and their variations on social vision: Brecht's Communist collectivism and Simone's commonsensical "everybody," "upset" about the news. The sonic corollary is the contrast between the intentionally routinized singing of "Moon of Alabama" and Simone's expressive mourning.

Secondly, beyond these primarily literary and political categories, Simone's distance from *Verfremdung* can be understood as a result of a specific performative strategy. Simone programmatically pursues a distinct relationship to her audience that cannot be subsumed under the tenets of Brechtian aesthetics:

> It was at this time, in the mid-sixties, that I first began to feel the power and spirituality I could connect with when I played in front of an audience. I'd been performing for ten years, but it was only at this time that I felt a kind of state of grace come upon me on those occasions when everything fell into place.... It's like being transported in a church; something descends upon you and you are gone, taken away by a spirit that is outside of you.... It's like electricity hanging in the air. I began to feel it happening and it seemed to me like mass hypnosis—like I was hypnotizing an entire audience to feel a certain way.[12]

Such is the description of auratic performance in the context of the 1960s counterculture; Simone concedes that it sounds "a little Californian and wired,"[13] but the main point is the establishment of an identification between performer and audience, precisely the opposite of classical Brechtian theater. In this light, her rendition of "Pirate Jenny" must be seen less as an American or African-American version of the song than as an updating of Lenya into the new sensibility of the 1960s counterculture era. To the extent that the latter is reasonably understood as the heir to certain neo-Romantic cultural traditions, Simone is in effect redefining the Brechtian texts, especially "Pirate Jenny," in Wagnerian terms.[14] Her goal is evidently not to hone rational criticism, but rather to appeal to emotion, to the terror and pity that characterize the Aristotelian poetics for which Brecht reserved only contempt. Indeed, Simone's Wagnerian emotionalism links her precisely to the Peachum of *The Threepenny Opera* and his efforts to deceive the public by providing the beggars with disguises designed to evoke pity. In other words, from a strictly Brechtian viewpoint, Simone's radical sounds imply an inadequate politics; the sentiment is correct, but, as sentiment alone, it is strategically wrong. While a Brechtian critique of Simone's sentimentalism is surely imaginable and could possibly explain her own slide into outsider positions—tax resistance and exile—Brechtian orthodoxy was not a plausible position in the American civil rights movement. On the contrary, the aesthetic success of Simone's "Pirate Jenny" demonstrates the power of a non-Brechtian treatment of song. The political routinization of the New Sobriety had already failed once in the Weimar Republic and hardly represented a viable strategy in the American 1960s.

Yet while Simone's performance certainly underscores the aging of Brechtian aesthetics and, therefore, the obsolescence of the categories of the historical avant-garde, her singing also displays its own historicity and therefore the historicity of the political moment. The specific character of her performance is not only a version of engagement—more Wagnerian and Aristotelian than Brechtian, but engaged nonetheless—but also an indicator of objective conditions, a "philosophical sundial telling the time of history" in its own right.[15] Her liminal position among the musical options of the 1960s—never exactly blues or soul, jazz or folk—is as much an expression of her unique creativity as it is of the coming-to-an-end of a lineage of political music. The protest song, as an expression of the 1960s, may have been the end of musical politics, at least in the conventional mode of a topical ballad or chanson. New forms of music were emerging. Politicized jazz, with Mingus, could offer a more compelling treatment of the dialectic of improvisational freedom and organizational necessity; new rock—the Doors' "Alabama," for instance—could engage a mass public in a different sort of popular cultural discourse, far beyond Simone's liberal and urban audience. However one understands subsequent popular musical developments, such as rap, it is surely no longer a matter of the radical individualism that pervades Simone's singing. Did the conclusion, the mournful high note, of her "Pirate Jenny" announce the end of the genre, the departure of political song? And of which politics? Simone transposes the structures of Brechtian radicalism from Weimar Germany into the context of the contradictions of the civil-rights-era, so the performance is doubly historical. It navigates through the poles of German-American critical theory, investigating the texts of epic theater but representing them in a post-Brechtian mode. Simone's performances recall a moment when avantgarde aspirations and popular idiom briefly appeared to coincide.

Notes

1. Cf. Garrett Stewart, *Reading Voices: Literature and the Phonotext* (Berkeley: University of California Press, 1991).
2. Fredric Jameson, *Postmodernism or, The Cultural Logic of Late Capitalism* (Durham: Duke University Press, 1999), 11–16.
3. Bertolt Brecht, "Zu Aufstieg und Fall der Stadt Mahagonny," *Gesammelte Werke* (Frankfurt am Main: Suhrkamp, 1967), 17:1011.
4. Walter Ong, *Orality and Literacy: The Technologizing of the Word* (London and New York: Methuen, 1982), 136.
5. Brecht, "Zu Aufstieg und Fall," 17:1011.
6. David Levering Lewis, *W.E.B. Du Bois: Biography of a Race* (New York: Holt, 1993), 139.
7. Nina Simone, *I Put a Spell on You: The Autobiography of Nina Simone*, with Stephen Cleary (New York: Da Capo Press, 1993), 98.
8. Bertolt Brecht, *Selected Poems*, trans. H. R. Hays (New York and London: Harcourt Brace Jovanovich, 1947), 66.
9. Simone, *I Put A Spell on You*, 34; 45.
10. Ibid., 51.
11. Ibid., 68.
12. Ibid., 92.
13. Ibid., 93.
14. Cf., on the neo-Romanticism of the counterculture, see Martin B. Green, *The Mountain of Truth: The Counterculture Begins, Ascona: 1900–1920* (Hanover, N.H.: University Press of New England, 1986).
15. Theodor W. Adorno, "On Lyric Poetry and Society," in *Notes to Literature*, trans. Shierry Weber Nicholas (New York: Columbia University Press, 1991), 46.

Chapter 12

ROLL OVER BEETHOVEN! CHUCK BERRY! MICK JAGGER!
1960s Rock, the Myth of Progress, and the Burden of National Identity in West Germany

Richard Langston

> The politics of rock and roll is not the production of an identity but the constant struggle against such identities.[1]

I

Constructing a postwar national identity devoid of fascism assumed a central role in the early political, economic, and cultural life of the Federal Republic. In contrast to the 1950s, when the production of an affirmative Germanness flourished, identity politics in the 1960s shifted away from stabilizing a national sense of self and toward deconstructing this fledgling national discourse. In an essay aptly titled "Am I German?" from 1964, Hans Magnus Enzensberger reported that "for Germans, the extinction of *Nationalität* as an objective, socially galvanizing force is comparatively near at hand."[2] While Enzensberger excluded himself from the growing inclination toward "national exorcism," his forecast described perfectly the rise in antinationalism that saturated the later 1960s, especially within the politicized student population. From the oblique censure of national identity through an alignment with victims of Third World oppression to unbridled hatred and even violence, anti-German sentiment within this small yet influential group manifested itself in diverse forms and intensities. Writer and counterculture guru Rolf Dieter Brinkmann channeled one extreme of this antinationalism through the protagonist in his 1968 novel *Keiner weiß mehr*: "It would have been better if the others after Hitler would have simply eradicated this place. And hopefully some-one will make up for that soon and erase everything here, finally, once and for all.... Just imagine it. There would simply be nothing left of us, we would simply no longer exist. That's why Germany should rot in hell."[3] Such apoc-alyptic fantasies were the exception to the rule. Nevertheless, Brinkmann's invective captures, albeit hyperbolically, not only the increasingly unbear-able burden of being German in the 1960s, but also the sudden turn toward violence as the only suitable response to an undead German past.

The seeds of this battle over nation and identity at the close of the 1960s lay neither in the sudden activation of a political consciousness in West German literature around 1960, nor in the crystallization of a recognizable student opposition by mid-1965. The desire to escape Germanness dates back to the 1950s, and was firmly rooted in how youths consumed imported popular culture and wielded it against acceptable values and codes of behavior. American rock-and-roll à la Bill Haley and Elvis Presley, for example, had proven to be an effective weapon against a budding West German culture ever since rock arrived in the second half of the 1950s. As Uta Poiger recently demonstrated, dominant West German culture depicted rock-and-roll as a decadent force capable of corrupting German youths both sexually and racially, a threat that the *Halbstarken* (young hooligans) and their female counterparts instrumentalized in their quest to rearticu-late the meanings and feelings in their everyday lives.[4] Although their actions did bear political consequences in hindsight, their chief interests in rock-and-roll lay elsewhere. As Lawrence Grossberg has argued, the plea-sure of rock-and-roll lies primarily in its ability "to mark a difference, to inscribe on the surface of social reality a boundary between 'them' and 'us.'"[5] Access to this pleasure of difference depended on one's ability to make correct aesthetic choices between Elvis and his German look-alike Peter Kraus, or between "Jailhouse Rock" and its German adaptation "Hafenrock," for example, choices that certified one's affiliation with a musical and cultural vanguard. This ability to demarcate the good from the bad, the genuine from commercial imitations, and by extension, insiders from outsiders assumed an added significance in the West German context. Those who made a distinction between "them" and "us" according to musical alliances also delineated the German from the non-German. To seek out the pleasure of difference through rock-and-roll quite possibly entailed a border-crossing beyond the reaches of official German culture.

By the end of the 1960s, rock-and-roll's initial politics of pleasure gave way to a growing exploration of the pleasures in rock's politics. Pleasure and the creation of sonic sanctuaries of otherness morphed into a convic-tion that the triumvirate "sex, drugs, and rock" was politically significant and that the production of difference through the pleasures of rock was an explicitly political act capable of deconstructing dominant notions of West German identity.[6] Infused with a concentrated dose of oppositional poli-tics, this emergent rock ideology quickly found itself taking on a daunting discourse about history, one that not only publicized how the Third Reich seeped into the West German present but also sought to exorcise the fascist element once and for all.

II

Assumptions abound that rock music played an active role in the international student movement, but upon close inspection we find that the West German architects of the extraparliamentary opposition awarded it little attention. For theoretician and spokesman Rudi Dutschke, the West German student revolts had little need for a soundtrack. Anti-imperialism at home and abroad was best achieved, he asserted, through spontaneous acts of resistance, a rigorous theorizing of past and present pitfalls in (pre)revolutionary praxis, and a symbiosis between the revolutionary masses and an intellectual caste. While Dutschke did acknowledge, albeit in a cursory fashion, the Rolling Stones' association with the battle against false consciousness, his formula for emancipation had nothing pertinent to say about rock in the revolution.[7] For those of Dutschke's colleagues who were especially interested in matters of aesthetics and politics—members of the think tank dubbed Kultur und Revolution (Culture and Revolution)—Anglo-American rock music warranted no consideration in their spin on Max Horkheimer and Theodor W. Adorno's treatise on the culture industry.[8] Less inclusive than Dutschke and more outspoken than the collective, fellow spokesman Bernd Rabehl—dismayed by the movement's increasingly unfavorable public image—went so far as to cast off rock fans ("die Beat-besessene Jugend") and other subcultural riffraff from the earnest core of activists.[9]

While the movement's vanguard intellectuals may have granted rock music short shrift, its biographers recall rock enjoying a far more prominent position among the students themselves. For example, in Uwe Timm's novel *Heißer Sommer* (1974), the music of Bob Dylan, the Beatles, the Rolling Stones, and Frank Zappa's Mothers of Invention sounds forth between the story's account of the murder of Benno Ohnesorg, the sit-ins at the University of Munich, news of the assassination attempt on Dutschke, and the dogmatic and militaristic devolution of the extraparliamentary opposition.[10] Such discrepancies between the intellectual elite's disdain for rock and rock's seemingly audible place in the actual student movement were not ignored. On the contrary, debate over the status of rock's power weighed heavily on the minds of many 68ers. Leftist publications such as *konkret* warned its readers, for example, not to conflate the political gestures in agitprop rock songs such as "Street Fighting Man" by the Rolling Stones, since "it is still just rock-and-roll, still one-dimensional revolution, still entertainment, and rock cannot take the place of politics."[11] Instead of dismissing rock on the grounds that it emanated from a manipulative entertainment industry, leftists argued that politically engaged rock redeemed itself because it benignly reflected the realities of the anti-authoritarian struggle.

Unburdened by the League of Socialist German Students' (SDS) obligations to wed revolutionary politics with popular culture, West Germany's budding literary underground identified rock as a model for reviving an avant-garde impulse in literature. Long before he penned his manifesto, "Der Film in Worten" (1969), Rolf Dieter Brinkmann explored the fractured link between poetry and everyday life. In his poem "Gedicht am 19. März 1964," he enumerates, for example, the poet's vocational tools, the sights and sounds shaping his creative place, and the sensory organs involved in the writing process:

> A pencil
> a piece of paper
> a cup of coffee
> a cigarette
>
> the last hit
> by the Rolling Stones
> the coming spring
> the family photo
>
> a hand
> a few words
> an eye
> a mouth.[12]

As if to catalogue a poem's ingredients without yielding the aesthetic product that it foreshadows, Brinkmann emphasizes with his poetic inventory the aesthetic process, an experience that eludes the representational capabilities of the poem itself. What prevents his poem from succumbing to artistic elitism is the central position of rock music. The popular, here the rhythm-and-blues inspired rock of the early Rolling Stones, saturates the experience that the poem refuses (or fails) to reconfigure into poetic language. Roughly four years later, when Brinkmann and friend Ralf-Rainer Rygulla announced the arrival of West Germany's literary underground with their groundbreaking anthology *Acid: neue amerikanische Szene* (1969), Brinkmann infused his former aesthetic concerns with a dose of counterculture politics. In his aforementioned manifesto, which was included in *Acid*, he not only reiterated the written word's long-standing disregard for "everyday sensory experience," but also foresaw—in a new, multimedial aesthetic incorporating rock, cinema, photography, and literature—the possibility of a radicalized and expanded consciousness. This new realm of consciousness presupposed the social utopias endorsed by West Germany's political opposition. This aesthetic movement, Brinkmann argues, "creates a little piece of emancipated reality that helps to facilitate the use of violence on the part of the oppressed, underprivileged, shut-out, and outsiders against … standardized reason." "The culture of rock music,"

Brinkmann further maintains, "must be affirmed" on the grounds that it "creates the social rituals of the future."[13] Rock and social revolution converged, according to this subcultural aficionado, precisely on account of their identical utopian moments.

Scholarship on the Federal Republic's emergent literary subculture, however, usually casts its cadre as naive, charging that they failed to grasp both the insidious nature of the recording industry and the appropriate avenues for progressive change. Early detractors such as Martin Walser, who viewed the subculture as protofascist due to its apparent inward escapism via drugs and rock, paved the way for others to portray the extraparliamentary opposition and the subculture as being diametrically opposed to one another.[14] While the SDS did accuse the subculture with infantilism, and vocal members of the subculture did chastise the SDS for its joyless theoretical asceticism by emphasizing how these two factions radically differed from one another, these detractors ignored not only their shared interests in rock but also the possibility of intermediary, hybrid positions. Even though evidence abounds that both groups disagreed on what constituted good rock music—whereas organs such as *konkret* encouraged readers to align themselves with ostensibly political bands including the Rolling Stones, the counterculture showered an array of performers with praise—their musical sensibilities intersected according to how their alliances stood in unified opposition to pop music. Rock mattered for both extremes within the overarching antiauthoritarian movement because it presumably reflected in its sounds and lyrics an authenticity, a sense of immediacy to everyday realities, and a politically useful vitality. In short, rock was progressive. Conversely, pop music and its commodified cultures smacked of artifice; served up transitory, private pleasures; and, worst of all, failed to signify anything beyond itself.

III

"When I talk with friends about music," exclaimed writer and filmmaker Uwe Brandner, "then it is foreign music ... the German *Schlager* is not my friend."[15] Roughly translated into English as "hit" or "pop" song, the word *Schlager* refers in this strict sense to a song's lucrative popularity. And yet, as Brandner noted in 1971, the concept is more semantically overburdened than any simple translation may disclose: "'Something' in me hesitates to describe Jimi Hendrix as a *Schlagerinterpreten* [pop artist], even if he did make hits."[16] That "something" is Brandner's unease with how the term advanced in common parlance to designate a specifically German phenomenon. One of West Germany's most outspoken rock advocates, music journalist Rolf-Ulrich Kaiser, remarked in 1969 that *Schlager* no longer described the entire class of popular music as it once had. Instead, English derived words such as "Folk," "Beat," "Pop," and "Rock" entered the German language to accommodate the emergence of new forms of popular music that reflected the real world. The expanded pop music vocabulary provided the likes of Kaiser and others with the linguistic possibility of categorizing and describing in stark contrast to *Schlager* the semiotic peculiarities of "foreign music," such as that of the Jimi Hendrix Experience.[17] Accordingly, the designation *Schlager*, while applicable to a panoply of international stars, was reduced by its adversaries to describing a narrow genre of West German popular music identifiable according to its distinct musical forms, content, and corpus of performers.

Dissecting German *Schlager* became a favorite pastime among liberal intellectuals beginning in the early 1960s. In his *Einleitung in die Musiksoziologie* (1962), Adorno extended his earlier dismissals of jazz to include *Schlager* on the grounds that its standardized structures engendered in its listeners a false sense of individual and collective identity.[18] Unlike Adorno, who attributed the *Schlager* to a ubiquitous American culture industry, Wilfried Berghahn contended in his influential essay of 1962 that the popularity of *Schlager* was a historical function of its ability to accommodate the psychosocial concerns of the German nation.[19] The pervasive thematic complex of homelessness, homesickness, and broken hearts pointed, according to Berghahn, to an irrational unhappiness among many West Germans with the material prosperity underlying the Federal Republic's rapid ascension. With the advent of the antiauthoritarian movement, the critique of German *Schlager* ranged from Adorno's manipulation theory to Berghahn's diagnosis of the West German psyche, or, in rare moments, comprised both impulses. While leftist singer-songwriters such as Franz Josef Degenhardt and Rolf Schwendter publicly rejected German *Schlager* stars such as Reinhard Mey and Roy Black on the grounds that their songs disseminated reactionary ideologies inconsistent with the spirit of the revolts, others such as Brandner denounced the genre for producing a suspicious discourse on West German identity.[20]

At the close of the 1950s, when Elvis's spell over West German youths faded and rumors of the death of rock-and-roll began to circulate, *Schlager* stars such as Freddy Quinn reclaimed control of the star cult, and the South Pacific figured prominently in the texts of domestic and imported hits.[21] Often attributed to the explosion in West German tourism and the popularity of Italy and other Mediterranean destinations, the wave of exotic *Schlager* coincided with an influx of foreign performers, representatives of the very southern lands so often fantasized about by their German counterparts. This preponderance of otherness on the German airwaves proved for rock zealots at the close of the 1960s the German *Schlager*'s waning cultural credibility. Rolf-Ulrich Kaiser postulated, for example, that because less than a fourth of all titles to appear on the West German top ten were of German origin, the German recording industry had lost touch with the concerns of its consumers.[22] In his short essay on the *Schlager* entitled "Exotik," Uwe Brandner goes further by observing how "a relatively large percentage of German *Schlagerinterpreten* somehow have foreign-sounding names," yet speak German fluently and without an accent.[23] Accordingly, Brandner formulates an initial working thesis—"The German *Schlager* is alienated from itself"—which after several revisions finally becomes "The German *Schlager* is made *for* the Germans *against* the Germans." Brandner's seemingly ambivalent hypothesis about the cultural function of the *Schlager* comes into focus when he later asserts: "[I]t would be interesting if one would move to create a completely foreign *Schlager* performer as embodied image and have it exclusively dubbed by German *Schlager* performers."[24] The vulgar discrepancy between the German *Schlager*'s ethnic sign (the foreign body) and its domestic referent (the German voice), which Brandner exaggerates by exposing the ideal *Schlager*'s use of ventriloquism, serves an ideological function, one that seeks to obscure the Germanness of the *Schlager* through its visible otherness, while simultaneously producing an affirmative sense of national identity through the disembodied native voice.[25] In short, Brandner's disgust for the genre lies squarely with its production of a veiled Germanness.

IV

Not all vitriol leveled at the *Schlager* in the late 1960s was as sophisticated as Brandner's. Rolf Dieter Brinkmann merely griped that the music of Frank Sinatra and Udo Jürgens repeated "the same old crap over and over again."[26] Brinkmann's aforementioned conviction that rock predicated "the social rituals of the future" rested on an uncomplicated opposition that associated rock with a social and aesthetic avant-garde and *Schlager* with its reactionary antipode. Brinkmann's assertion about rock's forward progression complements Brandner's case against *Schlager*, inasmuch as rock yearns to move beyond the domestic territories that Brandner exposes in German pop music. As if afraid that detailing them would spoil their realization, Brinkmann never elaborated on those future possibilities that rock ostensibly anticipates. His reticence speaks not to any shallowness in his articulation of rock's power, but rather to how the music's futurity is less a vision of what should come than of what should not be. The flip side of rock's progressiveness—a desire to venture forth, away from the here and now—was a destructive character, not unlike the spirit of Brandner's strike at German pop, that was committed to obliterating all that stood in its way. Rock's progressive violence spared not even its forefathers: "Roll over, Chuck Berry!... Roll over Beethoven. And Jerry Lee Lewis. Pretty *verse*! Hunted down by amplifiers."[27] Referring to a conviction among bands of the late 1960s that louder was better, Brinkmann emphasized how new rock exploited technology to dethrone its rock-and-roll predecessors who had invoked similar revolutionary decrees only a decade earlier. Committed to capturing a sense of rock's progressiveness in his own aesthetic program, Brinkmann literally pumped up the volume in order to drown out West Germany's tired literary establishment. In his response to the West German intelligentsia's firm rejection of American Leslie Fiedler's unprecedented ideas on the postmodern, Brinkmann pondered: "Should I join in this sad and boring litany? I write this, while an album by the DOORS plays on my Dual record player ... should I not just turn up the music a few more notches and give myself to it entirely instead of typing on."[28] Less than a week later, Brinkmann surpassed rock's power to silence by threatening literary critics Marcel Reich-Ranicki and Rudolf Hartung in person: "'If I had a machine gun, I'd shoot you dead right now.'"[29]

The idea of progressive violence became particularly germane among those antiauthoritarians convinced by the shootings of Ohnesorg and Dutschke that any forward momentum intent on breaking through existing political, social, and cultural barriers had to contend with repressive power.[30] "Violence against things not people" and "Destroy that which destroys you" became the principal mantra of the West German student movement on the occasion of its attack on the Berlin headquarters of the Springer Verlag, precipitated by claims that media mogul Axel Springer provoked neo-Nazi Josef Bachmann's assassination attempt on Dutschke. In the case of the Springer blockades, real violence wielded by students in the name of progress targeted contemporary West Germany as well as its fascist predecessor. While some held that Molotov cocktails, riots, and even terrorism were the last and only agents capable of disengaging the contemptible past and its contemporary manifestations from the liberating future, writer Günter Herburger contended that the destructive campaign against German history was equally imaginary as it was real. In a poem from 1970 entitled "The End of the Nazi Era," Herburger dreamt up a fantastic death for Germany's painful past, one administered by the annihilating power of rock.

> When the Rolling Stones, the Rolling Stones
> ...
> When the Rolling Stones, in the rubble
> on the grounds of the Nuremberg Party Days,
> finally begin to play and Mick Jagger,
> before one hundred thousand German students
> sitting in flowers and sucking on grass,
> shows his mega-amplifiers and sings,
> and on the same day, when Rudolf Hess is released
> and floats over the stadium in a white airplane
>
> Then we wink for the last time to the memory
> of the fragile, silvery geezers
> who directed concerts in a deadly way
> and again want to breed gelatinous culture
>
> Then the Rolling Stones play in the rubble
> on the grounds of the Nuremberg Party Days,

and in the mega-amplifiers, a singing
Mick Jagger eats photos of Hitler and Hess
…
Then the Rolling Stones play, the Rolling Stones[31]

Herburger's poem is exemplary of his writerly intentions of emanci-
pating humankind.[32] Bringing together common events from the late
1960s (acts of civil disobedience such as sit-ins and outdoor rock concerts
such as Woodstock), along with impossible scenarios such as the early
release of the last of the incarcerated Nazis, Rudolf Hess, the poem reflects
the author's desire to yield a utopian moment from the tension created by
juxtaposing existing and unrealized orders. Herburger's fantastic concoc-
tion resembles a farewell concert, in which pacifist, flower-powered German students bid adieu to a Nazi past that incessantly encroached on their
present. While their peaceful occupation of the Nuremberg stadium invokes the idea of a refunctionalization of abandoned Nazi ruins, though
on this occasion for the sake of an antifascist present, the powerful image
of rock icon Mick Jagger devouring photographs representing Germany's
past suggests the wish among students to destroy leftover Nazi history.
With the dirty work of cleansing the present of the historical past completed, the concert shifts its attention back to the music: "Then the Rolling
Stones play." Rock's destructive character provides, then, the very cathar-
tic closure to the Third Reich so long forestalled by other escapist forms of
popular culture, such as the *Schlager*. As it were, the possibility of being
Germanless emerged through rock.

V

Herburger's image of Jagger ingesting images of Hitler and Hess is not,
however, without its problems. The symbolically charged gesture of swal-
lowing representations of Nazis, while surely intended as an act of violence
against fascism, exceeds the designed result of clearing the path forward of
both living and dead Nazis. In masticating and digesting images of fascism,
the antifascist hero's body absorbs the very thing his audience hopes to
destroy. Whether Herburger meant to allude to rock's own fascist predilections is debatable; nevertheless, the loophole in his fantastic vision of rocking the Nazis out of existence foretells the repudiations made by many rock
fans, who charged that rock's progressive power was a chimera.[33] In fact,
conviction in the music's power crashed just as the official West German
antiauthoritarian movement folded in the spring of 1970. In the eyes of its
most loyal fans, the rising body count of 1960s rock as well as its assimila-
tion into the entertainment industry undermined its prior integrity. In addition to the infamous fatal riots at the Rolling Stones' 1969 outdoor concert
at the Altamont Speedway in California, the untimely, drug-induced deaths

of key musicians—Brian Jones of the Rolling Stones (1969), Jimi Hendrix (1970), Janis Joplin (1970), and Jim Morrison of the Doors (1971)—exposed the cannibalistic tendency of rock to devour its own.

For Brinkmann, the steady influx of obituaries transformed the music's deterritorializing pleasures into the unbearable sound of existential agony: "The/pain is distorted on sixteen/tracks.... I/stick plugs in my ears, in order/to be able to cope with the present/20th century."[34] Brinkmann officially abandoned rock between 1971–72, not merely because he was convinced that it echoed the unbearableness of modern living, but also because rock's promise of liberation proved nothing more than a swindle in light of its commercial trendiness. In his 1975 collection of poems, Brinkmann exposed rock's crass obsession with turning a profit and accordingly declared that "the Rolling Stones' tricks are over."[35] His disgust with rock's scam moved him to want to kick the band's lead singer "in the ass."[36] Elsewhere, he goes so far as to denounce the band's hits as music for a modern-day Holocaust: "Sister Morphin, I get no satisfaction, let's spend the night together, and other melodies have been driven into the bodies of you and me, simply by a bunch of pop singers ... who say a bunch of crap in discotheques around the world that resemble gas chambers."[37] As blasphemous as Brinkmann's evocation of the Shoah is, his equation of rock music with genocide, informed by his growing obsession with American theories of behaviorism, suggests that rock had devolved to a level far below that of German pop music. Rock became, just as Herburger insinuated in his poem, the unthinking handmaiden of modern-day fascism.

With rock dead, it would logically follow that the identities of difference once culled from an operative opposition between rock and *Schlager* were at risk of collapsing. Hard-core rock fan Helmut Salzinger, who prophesied in 1969 that revolution would emanate one day soon from booming amplifiers, resisted the leveling of differences, and sought in the early 1970s to preserve rock's power by complicating the categories of valid rock and by calling on bootleggers to circumvent the recording industry's control of the reigning means of production and distribution.[38] Others bided their time and waited for the advent of postmodern pastiche in rock to rejuvenate their quest for an aesthetics of difference.[39] As for Brinkmann, his rejection of rock was symptomatic of a deeper, new-found pessimism about the possibility of articulating genuine expressions of individuality beyond the ubiquitous grasp of state- and media-controlled discourses. Instead of abandoning his earlier search for "a little piece of emancipated reality" in light of such insurmountable odds, Brinkmann intensified his efforts by developing a severe regime of negation, one that construed absolute silence as the true utopian moment.[40] Far from renouncing his vocation altogether, Brinkmann continued not only to write but also to listen, albeit privately, to rock music. Following a lengthy hiatus from publishing, his work posthumously resurfaced in 1975 with a volume of poetry entitled *Westwärts 1&2*, which Brinkmann opens with the thought: "Perhaps I succeeded sometimes in making the poems simple enough like songs."[41] That his lingering, private obsession with rock became the model for his last poems suggests that his previous abnegation was nothing more than ascetic posturing invented as the ultimate escape from the present—a posturing that was unable, in the end, to withstand the lure of listening to rock.

Brinkmann resolved the apparent incongruity between his rabid mistrust of mass media and his incorporation of rock into his poetics by renegotiating how pleasure and politics figure into rock. In a letter from the summer of 1974, he exclaimed: "[M]aking music and listening to music are better than making a revolution."[42] Previously convinced of rock's forward-looking, destructive impulse, Brinkmann's profound sense of pessimism led him to recant his earlier proclamations about rock's progressiveness. Firmly situated within his private sphere, rock's pleasures came to serve more modest needs, such as navigating the hazards of everyday life. Stripped of its revolutionary politics, rock was reduced to the immediate pleasures it offered. But because rock still conveyed a sense of authenticity and intensity and was able to transform via music otherwise cliché-ridden lyrics into genuine expressions, it remained for Brinkmann the best model for creating a poetry that eluded every hegemonic discourse that, so he claimed, anesthetized his mind and body.

One such discourse that Brinkmann sought to stave off was that of media representations of Germany's Nazi past. In the third section to his poem "Einige sehr populäre Songs" entitled "Histoire," he writes: "Tonight I thought about the love/story of Adolf Hitler./I saw the perm in the hairdo/of Eva Braun."[43] Inspired by a multitude of photos of Hitler and his mistress, the lyrical subject assembles a battery of questions intended to probe the missing, intimate details of Eva's life. Following pages of rambling questions interspersed with brief accounts of experiences, memories, and ruminations made by the lyrical subject, the piece concludes with the very photo with which it began: "Is a love story necessary, that requires/so many questions? You now have vanished from the historical/photo.... Now the story [*Geschichte*] is, broken down and over."[44] Misread by some as Brinkmann's intention to erase the memory of Germany's fascist past, the poem—unlike Herburger's which plainly advocates the obliteration of German history—actually strives to produce history. The lyrical subject clarifies his intentions toward the end: "I write this rock 'n' roll song about your/terrible insanity, Eva Braun."[45] However, the insanity that "Histoire" seeks has little to do with the Holocaust. Particularly interested in Braun's body and her sex life, the series of questions sets out to overproduce the signifiers roused by the photo of Braun. As Gerhard Lampe has argued, the subject of Brinkmann's poem focuses not on Nazi history itself, but on how representations of that history manipulated the consciousness of West German viewers and promoted amnesia.[46] The poem's indictment of the cheap visualization of history in memory work becomes especially clear when the lyrical subject claims: "I was not, I know, born in a photo./Snow fell in April/when I was born, wrapped in the/ornamental blankets of the baptism."[47] By locating his origins outside of the scopic regime responsible for the simplification of historical consciousness, the lyrical subject underscores the primacy of personal, organic memories without expunging a sense of their relation to an authentic collective history. Thought of as an act of self-preservation, the poem as rock song suggests that Brinkmann anchored his new concept of rock's pleasure in the maintenance of a sense of self fully aware of its unavoidable affiliation with a collective past, present, and future.

Listening to and writing about rock were but just two means for young West Germans in the late 1960s and the 1970s to wrestle with the burdens of their inherited national identity. Making rock proved for some a far better alternative, for it rendered the antiauthoritarian spirit of progress into a sound, a message, and a lifestyle. From dogmatic rock outfits such as Floh de Cologne and Ton Steine Scherben to the experimental, more politically ambiguous bands like Faust, Amon Düül, and Can, West Germany's rock scene took root at the end of the 1960s, reflecting both the SDS's penchant for politics and the subculture's fascination with expanding consciousness.[48] What set the literary engagement with rock and national identity apart from the efforts of most musicians, however, was both a critical distance inscribed in the fan's writerly relation to the music and a striking sense of the inauthenticity of German rock, especially when compared to its Anglo-American counterpart. As for Brinkmann, the critique that eventually evolved from his enthusiasm for bands such as the Rolling Stones, Jimi Hendrix, and the Doors revealed earlier convictions in the progressive power of rock as nothing more than myth. His final imbrication of rock with personal identity politics and collective German history revealed that rock had more in common with the *Schlager* than previously thought. Like the *Schlager*, rock was most effectual when used privately. Rock was also just as ephemeral and pleasurable as pop music. The imagined uses put to rock, regardless of their apparent Germanlessness, could neither negate the a priori national identity inscribed in them, nor thwart the flow of history passing through that identity. Above all, rock music, like the *Schlager*, was far better suited for renegotiating national identity than for obliterating it entirely. Nevertheless, as the late Brinkmann would attest, rock still differed from *Schlager* in two important ways: it retained both its potential as a vehicle of critique as well as its claim to reflect and invigorate the authenticity of everyday life.

Notes

1. Lawrence Grossberg, "Another Boring Day in Paradise: Rock and Roll and the Empowerment of Everyday Life," in *Dancing in Spite of Myself: Essays on Popular Culture* (1984; Durham: Duke University Press, 1997), 39.
2. Hans Magnus Enzensberger, "Am I German?" *Encounter* 22, no. 4 (April 1964): 17.
3. Rolf Dieter Brinkmann, *Keiner weiß mehr* (1968; Reinbek bei Hamburg: Rowohlt, 1993), 132. Unless otherwise noted, translations from the German are the author's.
4. Uta Poiger, *Jazz, Rock and Rebels: Cold War Politics and American Culture in a Divided Germany* (Berkeley: University of California Press, 2000).
5. Grossberg, "Another Boring Day," 39.
6. Rock historian Simon Frith outlines this instrumentalization of 1960s rock in Britain in his article "Rock and the Politics of Memory," *The 60s without Apology*, ed. Sohnya Sayres et al. (Minneapolis: University of Minnesota Press, 1984), 59–69.
7. Rudi Dutschke, "Die geschichtlichen Bedingungen für den internationalen Emanzipationskampf," in *Rebellion der Studenten oder Die neue Opposition*, ed. Uwe Bergmann et al. (Reinbek bei Hamburg: Rowohlt, 1968) 92. Dutschke quotes radical American journalist Andrew Kopkind, who cited the British band as a revolutionary force.
8. Kultur und Revolution, "Kunst als Ware der Bewußtseinsindustrie," *Die Zeit*, 29 November 1968, 22. The group reveals its proclivity for high culture by analyzing serial music.
9. Bernd Rabehl, "Von der antiautoritären Bewegung zur sozialistischen Opposition," in *Rebellion der Studenten*, ed. Bergmann et al., 151.
10. Uwe Timm, *Heißer Sommer* (1974; Munich: dtv, 1998).
11. "Scheiß-Beatles," *konkret*, 16 December 1968, 49. Cited in Helmut Salzinger, *Rock Power, oder Wie musikalisch ist die Revolution?* (1972; Reinbek bei Hamburg: Rowohlt, 1982), 102.
12. Rolf Dieter Brinkmann, "Gedicht am 19. März 1964," in *Le Chant du Monde, Standphotos: Gedichte 1962–1970* (1964; Reinbek bei Hamburg: Rowohlt, 1980), 45.
13. Rolf Dieter Brinkmann, "Der Film in Worten," in *Acid: neue amerikanische Szene*, ed. Rolf Dieter Brinkmann and Ralf-Rainer Rygulla (1969; Frankfurt am Main: Zweitausendeins, 1981), 381, 384, 387, 388.
14. See Walser's well-known screed entitled "Über die Neueste Stimmung im Westen," *Kursbuch* 20 (1970): 36. More venomous than Walser is Jost Hermand in his *Pop International: eine kritische Analyse* (Frankfurt am Main: Athenäum Verlag, 1971), 148.
15. Uwe Brandner, "Exotik," *Akzente*, special issue entitled "Der deutsche Schlager" 3 (1971): 226.
16. Brandner, "Exotik," 227.
17. Rolf-Ulrich Kaiser, *Das Buch der neuen Pop-Musik* (Düsseldorf: Econ Verlag, 1969), 14. See Kaiser's opening chapter entitled "'Zu satt, zu fett, zu alt': Schlager," 7–19.
18. Theodor W. Adorno, *Einleitung in die Musiksoziologie: zwölf theoretische Vorlesungen* (1962; Reinbek bei Hamburg: Rowohlt, 1968), 35–37, 44–48.
19. Wilfried Berghahn, "In der Fremde," in *Trivialliteratur: Aufsätze*, ed. Gerhard Schmidt-Henkel et al. (1962; Berlin: Literarisches Colloquium, 1964), 246–59.
20. Albrecht Koch, *Angriff auf's Schlaraffenland: 20 Jahre deutschsprachige Popmusik* (Frankfurt am Main: Verlag Ullstein, 1987), 31–35.
21. Werner Mezger, *Schlager* (Tübingen: Tübinger Vereinigung für Volkskunde e.V., 1975), 177–87.
22. Kaiser, *Das Buch*, 9.
23. Brandner, "Exotik," 227.
24. Ibid., 228.
25. For more on *Schlager* and the maintenance of a German "imagined community," see Mark Terkessidis, "Die Eingeborenen von Schizonesien: der Schlager als deutscheste aller Popmusik," *Mainstream der Minderheiten: Pop in der Kontrollgesellschaft*, ed. Tom Holert and Mark Terkessidis (Berlin: Edition ID-Archiv, 1996), 128–35.
26. Brinkmann, "Der Film in Worten," 231.

27. Rolf Dieter Brinkmann, "Notizen 1969 zu amerikanischen Gedichten und zu der Anthologie Silverscreen," in *Der Film in Worten: Prosa Erzählungen Essays Hörspiele Fotos Collagen 1965–1974* (1969; Reinbek bei Hamburg: Rowohlt, 1982), 266.

28. Rolf Dieter Brinkmann, "Angriff aufs Monopol: Ich hasse alte Dichter," in *Roman oder Leben: Postmoderne in der deutschen Literatur,* ed. Uwe Wittstock (Leipzig: Reclam Verlag, 1994), 66.

29. Horst Bienek, "Gewalt und Kritik," *Süddeutsche Zeitung,* 20 November 1968, 11.

30. For an overview of violence and the West German student movement, see Oskar Negt, *Achtundsechzig: politische Intellektuelle und die Macht* (1995; Frankfurt am Main: Zweitausendeins, 1998), 49–134.

31. Günter Herburger, "Das Ende der Nazizeit," in *Protest! Literatur um 1968,* ed. Ulrich Ott and Friedrich Pfäfflin (Marbach: Deutsche Schillergesellschaft, 1998), 401. Herburger's poem, originally entitled "The Stones rock out the Nazis," was first published in the magazine *twen* in 1970 and first reprinted in: Martin Gregor-Dellin, ed., *PEN Prosa Lyrik Essay: Neue Texte deutscher Autoren* (Tübingen: Erdmann, 1971), 152–53.

32. Cf. Gerhard Köpf, "Phantasie und Hoffnung," in *Günter Herburger: Texte, Daten, Bilder,* ed. Klaus Siblewski (Hamburg and Zürich: Luchterhand Verlag, 1991), 133–36. For a more complete understanding of Herburger's interest in music, see his essay "Erfahrungen mit Musik," in *Das Flackern des Feuers: Beschreibungen* (Darmstadt: Luchterhand, 1983), 72–81.

33. Helmut Schmiedt explores further how writers happened upon rock's illusory promises in "No satisfaction oder Keiner weiß mehr: Rockmusik und Gegenwartsliteratur," *Zeitschrift für Literaturwissenschaft und Linguistik* 34 (1979): 11–24.

34. Rolf Dieter Brinkmann, "Vage Lufe," in *Satzbau: Poesie und Prosa aus Nord-Rhein-Westfalen,* ed. Hans Peter Keller (Düsseldorf: Droste, 1972), 244.

35. Rolf Dieter Brinkmann, "Einige sehr populäre Songs," *Westwärts 1&2* (1975; Reinbek bei Hamburg: Rowohlt, 1999), 121.

36. Rolf Dieter Brinkmann, *Erkundungen für die Präzisierung des Gefühls für einen Aufstand: Träume Aufstände/Gewalt/Morde REISE ZEIT MAGAZIN Die Story ist schnell erzählt (Tagebuch)* (Reinbek bei Hamburg: Rowohlt, 1987), 124.

37. Ibid., 38.

38. Helmut Salzinger, "Das lange Gedicht," in *Super Garde: Prosa der Beat- und Pop-Generation,* ed. Vagelis Tsakiridis (Düsseldorf: Droste Verlag, 1969), 167–91. See also Salzinger, *Rock Power,* 205, 224–38.

39. See Diedrich Diederichsen, *Sex-Beat: 1972 bis heute* (Cologne: Kiepenheuer & Witsch, 1985), 17–18.

40. Brinkmann first developed his idea of silence in 1970; see "Spiritual Addiction: zu William Seward Burroughs' Roman *Nova Express,*" in *Der Film in Worten,* 203–6.

41. Brinkmann, *Westwärts 1&2,* 7.

42. Rolf Dieter Brinkmann, *Briefe an Hartmut, 1974–1975* (Reinbek bei Hamburg: Rowohlt, 1999), 93.

43. Brinkmann, *Westwärts 1&2,* 130.

44. Ibid., 139.

45. Ibid.

46. See Gerhard Lampe, *Ohne Subjektivität: Interpretationen zur Lyrik Rolf Dieter Brinkmanns vor dem Hintergrund der Studentenbewegung* (Tübingen: Niemeyer, 1983), 138–39.

47. Brinkmann, *Westwärts 1&2,* 130.

48. For a history of German rock in the 1960s and 1970s, see Koch, *Angriff auf's Schlaraffenland,* 26–63.

Chapter 13

THE MUSIC THAT LOLA RAN TO

Caryl Flinn

I

It took just a few years for Tom Tykwer's 1998 hit *Lola rennt* (Run Lola Run) to generate enough conference talks, papers, and academic referencing to effectively create even more variations of the film's already thrice-told tale. Indeed, the movie is prime academic fodder, with something for almost everyone: narratologists, Germanists interested in post-Kohl Berlin, genre theorists, game theorists, sports scholars, new media critics, chaos theorists, semioticians, historians (spot the intertexts), and the like. What remains constant among these accounts, however, is the way that the film's score has been constructed. Tykwer's impressive soundtrack is consistently cast in terms of its "driving energy" that matches Lola's own drive, determination, and frenzied rush to better her and her partner's circumstances, which she finally achieves.

Although I am reluctant to add yet another contribution to the heap of Lola readings, I am happier about the fact that the present version will *not* be one with a happy ending. For *Lola rennt*'s score, wonderful as it may be, is not nearly as hip as it seems. Its functions, I believe, ensure that a number of very traditional contracts are maintained along with the film's thematic and diegetic obsession with contracts, deadlines, and faith. Among these is the positioning of music as a form of emotional and economic Esperanto or universal language, a romantic, heterosexual affair stamped with the imprint of humanism. That this is achieved through techno, usually considered an antihumanist form of music, makes the accomplishment all the more intriguing.

Tykwer's choice of techno is at once instructive and canny. Although it emerged largely from African-American urban DJ cultures in the American

---

Midwest, techno quickly became a global phenomenon with innumerable regional variants and subgenres (Lola's city, Berlin, has an especially vibrant techno culture). That fact enables the soundtrack to bestow the apparent imprint of international viability upon a film that has, indeed, done enormously well in and outside of Germany. Yet that internationalism, I believe, is contingent upon the simultaneous assertion and denial of Germanness. Moreover, the film's music works alongside other contradictions, including freedom and containment, hipness and conservatism, spontaneity and calculation, and one I call "luck and the law."

It is easy to read *Lola rennt* as a road movie, a genre that, whether from Germany or other countries, frequently boasts memorable, engaging soundtracks, for example, *Easy Rider* (USA, 1968), *The Adventures of Priscilla, Queen of the Desert* (Australia, 1995), *Until the End of the World* (Germany, 1991). The genre and the promotion of films through tie-in soundtracks took off after World War II, with populations increasingly on the move. For prosperous residents of Western countries, there was also the larger rise in commodity accumulation, be this through the form of car ownership or the purchase of soundtracks and popular music. There was an increasing sense that vehicles and music went hand in hand. The social experience of road travel in industrialized countries confirms that music fills or kills the time through group sing-alongs, car radios, CDs, Walkmans. Yet it is important to acknowledge that music never simply accompanied people or film figures as they passed through cultural and geographical spaces. It also helped establish those very geographies, whether as spaces for youth cultures, indigenous cultures, or cross-cultural clashes. This is as true in cinematic depictions of movement "on the road" as it is of the social experiences we have of music and traveling.

Corey Creekmur argues that American road movies featuring an outlaw couple are inverted musicals, with roadside stops functioning like musical numbers, spectacles that can simultaneously put the brakes on the plot, develop character, and entertain. Both genres, he maintains, draw connections between the idea of movement and freedom (or a sense of escape); both feature a couple or partnership that teams up to "perform" musical or criminal acts, and so on.[1] Creekmur's remarks describe recent German road movies with prescience, Katja von Garnier's *Bandits* (1997) being a particularly good example. *Bandits* follows a group of singing female cellmates on the lam and actually goes so far as to fuse the genres Creekmur describes since it is a musical as well as a road story.

Tykwer's *Lola rennt* moves along similar lines, albeit with variations. First, despite an abundance of vehicles (of which nearly every one ends in an accident), Lola's "road trip" is on foot. Secondly, it appears that Lola travels on her own, violating the generic stipulation that a twosome be present. At the same time, her high-speed chase is diegetically motivated by her desire to preserve a twosome, namely herself and her boyfriend Manni. Her goal is clear: to reach Manni, to get to that telephone booth before he moves and gets himself into more trouble. Music, as we shall see, helps preserve that romance.

But the film maintains another, more significant couple nondiegetically that complicates the freedom typically associated with movement in road movies. This is the coupling of *Lola rennt*—as a German film, as a commodity, as an icon of femininity—and Tykwer, its young German director/composer/writer, the man who made Lola "run" (literally, by forcing actress Franka Potente, who has claimed she hates jogging, to do so) and who turned his film into a runaway hit.[2] Because this coupling operates on the levels of film characters, production personnel, and the finished film itself, throughout this essay I will be referring to "Lola" as an amalgam of character, film, national icon, and product.

II

Music has always had the power to define, abstract, establish, and even transform geographic, social, and cultural spaces. While noise ordinances were often designed to keep youths or ethnic musicians from laying claim to public space, house music turned abandoned warehouses into sites of ecstatic, communal raves, and Muzak transformed simple elevators into torture chambers.[3] In road movies, diegetic and nondiegetic music enables characters and audience members to move through space by providing acoustic continuity as cinematic space is chopped up and condensed.

Techno has an especially strong relationship to place and location, as its globetrotting history both asserts and denies. Most musicologists find its roots in the rhythmically rich traditional music of Ibiza, even if they argue its initial electronic incarnation was in the postdisco urban American Midwest.[4] Because it spread quickly across the U.K., Europe, and Southeast Asia in forms such as Scallydelia, hardcore, trance, and jungle, becoming associated with various places, styles, and years,[5] it would be wrong to consider techno as just one of so many "Made in USA" exports with regard to *Lola rennt* or anything else. To begin with, its origins are too diverse; influences include British punk and Germany's Kraftwerk as much as black American disco.[6] Moreover, as a musical practice and performance, techno is intimately tied to local scenes, with urban rather than national centerpoints. Even within the space of a particular city, a variety of factors (club, audience, DJ, etc.) help to produce different forms. West Berlin's hip-hop often targeted young Turkish audiences, for instance, and techno's general development in Germany proceeded very differently between the former East and West.[7]

Thus, while techno depends on "place" for its social, cultural, and economic existence, it simultaneously suggests a multitude of coterminous places. Early ravers frequently remarked on techno's seeming ability to construct a sense of location as well as an escape into a non-place. One critic, Antonio Melechi, called rave "a form of internal tourism."[8] For Frankfurt techno producer Achim Szepanski, that free-form "tourism," at least in German rave, soon became no longer anything to champion, having been appropriated and institutionalized.[9]

III

Techno poses a challenge for those who view popular music as an expression of "authentic" youthful rebellion or of a rebellious creator. In fact, scholars in the U.K., Canada, and Germany have taken a variety of positions on what to make of techno. Certain forms have led no less an icon than Brian Eno to call its fans "slaves to their machines";[10] for others, techno offered the means to "oppose the old industrial machine."[11] Among those in the latter camp, we often hear the claim that techno made a full rupture with previous musical forms, or that it was the great leveler, flattening racial, class, and gender differences, points to which I will return. Some claims relied on surprisingly old, tenacious assumptions about authorship and authenticity, concepts that inform critics who associate rock and punk with expressive "authenticity," not to mention virile white masculinity (à la Bruce Springsteen). Needless to say, such notions of musical expressivity are beholden to a Romantic ideology of individualized, subjective aesthetic production.

With all of its sampling, modulating, remixing, and looping, techno appears to deflect any claim to authorial, Romantic expressivity, authenticity, or originality, not to mention copyright. Noises and voices heard do not necessarily correspond to noises and voices ever sung; one need not have elaborate musical training to become a techno composer; it is first and foremost a dance music, not an expressive one. Philip Tagg makes the point in especially strong terms: "There is no guitar hero or rock star or corresponding musical-structural figures to identify with, you just 'shake your bum off' from inside the music ... you could say that perhaps techno-rave puts an end to nearly four hundred years of the great European bourgeois individual in music."[12] While it is hard to believe that a late-twentieth-century form of music could single-handedly undo all that humanist baggage, Tagg, who is clearly being polemical, is not alone in that view. Producer Achim Szepanski argues that "hardcore's sped-up vocals sounded like a serious attempt to deconstruct pop music.... Treating sampled voices as instruments or sources of noise destroyed the idea of the voice as an expression of human subjectivity."[13]

In a 1992 interview, Rising High's Caspar Pound stated: "The best thing about hardcore is all the soul'd been taken out. We've had 200 years of human element in music and it's about time for a change."[14] Bereft of the "human element," the running and dancing body of techno becomes a sort of rationalized machine, as techno critic Simon Reynolds argues in this description of a rave: "I was instantly entrained in a new kind of dancing—tics and spasms, twitches and jerks, the agitation of bodies broken down into separate components, then reintegrated at the level of the dance floor as a whole, each subindividual part (a limb, a hand cocked like a pistol) was a cog in a collective 'desiring machine.'"[15] As Reynolds's vocabulary of a high-tech erotic collectivity asserts, techno becomes a democratizing, even emancipatory form for consumers. The same argument is often made for its producers, given the relative facility with which it can be "composed." (The understanding here is that in the wake of the death of the Author, innumerable new ones are born, assembling, mixing, and manipulating instead of creating an original composition per se. This is not a new argument, having been made for earlier popular music such as grunge rock, or even for art music such as musique concrète.)

Conceptualizing techno as another easy-access emancipatory form stems partly from the rave culture with which the music has been historically tied. Critics and ravers alike championed raves as alternative utopian spaces that transformed dead warehouses into communal events. Many ravers, especially in the late 1980s and early 1990s, argued that the usual tensions between classes, races, genders, and, to a lesser extent, sexual orientation were effaced in raves, especially in Britain. Rave space was one in which the standard rules of the game were suspended: people experienced time and space differently; they moved and interacted differently. One raver described the scene as "a communism of emotions," a politics of feeling that was frequently enhanced by the empathetic effects of the drug Ecstasy.[16] With all of this suspension of routine life, ordinary emotions, and experiences of time and location, raves generated an interesting contradiction: space was simultaneously transformed, concrete, and specific as well as escapist, placeless, and transcendent, a point that proves important to *Lola rennt*. Techno paradoxically is grounded to region and place—for example, local rave cultures, clubs, and genres of techno of various cities—at the same time that it evades or evacuates geographical specificity. (Significantly, the "internal tourism" to which Melechi refers appears in a piece entitled "The Ecstasy of Disappearance.")

IV

The contradiction of being identified with concrete, specific place and a multi-, inter-, or even transnational abstraction often results with the "national" dropping out of the scene. *Lola rennt*, it would seem, wants to have it much the same way. Its techno tracks are certainly bound up with the geography of the film: the various streets and stairs of Berlin, its bridges, banks, and phone booths. But they also mark out a transnational space in which *Lola rennt* "ran" equally well—at the box office and music shops. In these ways, *Lola rennt*'s soundtrack delineates diegetic space while also abstracting it, suggesting both an emancipatory freedom along-side calculated control. As director Tykwer avers (at least, in the North American media),[17] he deliberately selected Berlin streets and landmarks that were not readily identifiable: "[I]t could be anywhere." That choice, I believe, is critical.

Formally speaking, techno is a perfect, if obvious, choice for *Lola rennt*. As dance music, it immediately connotes high-charged physical move-ment.[18] The film's techno tracks are closely knit to its activity, with musi-cal beats dictating much of its rhythm, pace, editing, and energy. Moreover, unlike traditional tonal music, techno has no clear beginning, patterns of development, or resolution; unchanging and energetic, it is repetitive without standing still. Like Tykwer's film, techno is a repetitively struc-tured form, organized around beats per minute,[19] not unlike the three 20-minute frames in which DM 100,000 must be found. Its compressed, hypnotic beats, sequenced loops, and harmonic stability seem the perfect accompaniment to a chase or other high speed movement, its pulsating 4/4 time and its rhythmic beats punctuating like tires (or feet) pounding the pavement.[20] *Lola rennt* even modulates the sound of a heartbeat into one section. So tight are the economic, physical, and formal connections between *Lola rennt*'s soundtrack and its depicted action that an ad in the U.K. hailed the CD as "perfect music for joggers." Tykwer had Potente, an ostensibly nonsinging actress (who actually sings quite well in Dorris Dörrie's *Bin ich schön?* [1998]), sing so that the soundtrack would be an "extension of her character," as he puts it (in this film, however, Potente's delivery leads a colleague of mine to dub it *Drone Lola Drone*). However electronic and abstract, techno, like the dance culture intertwined with it, is linked closely to the human bodies that move to it. Techno's presence in *Lola rennt* thereby highlights the materiality of the character's movement and, in different ways, the material gain she recoups in the end.

V

Given that techno is not exactly renowned for its dramatic development or its melodious peaks and valleys, it is hardly surprising that *Lola rennt*'s music does not change much over the course of the film. Chords, or rather stripped-down held notes, provide the basis on which the rhythm propels itself, and while textures shift, the fundamental beat remains unchanged. At the same time, as the film moves on to its third, artificial happy ending in which the couple and their wealth are preserved/enhanced, a number of subtle but significant changes occur. This is more apparent with the CD soundtrack than the film, since the former is divided into sections such as "Running One," "Running Two," and "Running Three." "Believe" pro-vides a central musical theme and includes lyrics such as "I don't believe in promise/I don't believe in chance/I don't believe you can resist/the

things that make no sense/I don't believe in silence/'Cause silence seems
so slow/I don't believe in energy/if tension is too low ... I don't believe
in panic/I don't believe in fear/I don't believe in prophesies that don't
waste any tears."

What kind of musical "movement" occurs over the course of the film?
For one thing, the music moves from minor to major modes. A sense of
solidity also becomes more apparent within the rhythm of the music. Initially, in "Running One," the rhythm is unstable. The fundamental beat
remains unchanged for the first few seconds, but the accent is on the
downbeat, and before long the stress starts shifting to different positions
in the four-beat divisions, achieved primarily through cross-rhythm and
even polyrhythms. By "Running Three," there is much more of an overall
sense of formal stability.

Of the three tracks, "Running Two" (which accompanies the first cor-
rected version of Lola's tale) features the "hardest" techno score, possibly including sampled material from the Chemical Brothers. "Running
Three" is softer but the most percussive—at times close to Teutonic
trance and jungle techno, reminiscent of Peter Gabriel's early solo work,
which was possibly sampled into the track. A number of nonmusical
sounds (such as sirens) are interjected throughout the score, and as the
film progresses, it uses more organic sources. The rhythm in "Running
Three," for example, is established in an electronically reverbed guitar
timbre. The trend is especially noticeable where the human voice is concerned. (Vocal work is far from proscribed in techno, but it is not an altogether standard feature, with sounds more common than actual lyrics.)
In "Running Three," Potente's incantations are joined by professional
singer Susie van der Meer, who repeats Potente's lines more melodically
and in a light, breathy style: "I wish I was a hunter/In search of different food." There is also a background of male and female vocals in the
same track that adheres to Tagg's description of human voices in techno
at large:

> You will find either a female vocalist in quite a high register singing one-bar
> phrases whose lyrics consist of short, simple repeated phrases or just single
> words or even just 'oo-s' and 'aa-s'; or, alternatively, you will find a male voice,
> often sampled, reciting—not singing—single words or short phrases at regular
> intervals. Rave numbers featuring *sung* male vocal figures are quite rare.[21]

"Running Three" features precisely the kind of aimless, angelic voices
Tagg describes. That ethereal quality is at its most pronounced as Lola
lands in front of the casino, where Indian- or Arab-influenced music fragments are introduced. What we hear evokes a clichéd, Orientalist mysticism, an unsettling acoustic signifier to say the least. Its intended function
seems more or less clear—to invoke the mystical faith required of gam-
blers and religious worshippers alike. Indeed, it is no accident that the
Berlin casino is depicted in unequivocally churchlike terms, from its

motionless inhabitants and their organized placement, their garb, their judgmental stares, their sanctimoniousness. We take in the stained glass windows, the mockingly respectful low camera angles, and the incantatory tones of the croupier, whose "rien ne va plus" (no further bets) seems a reasonable thing to say to a congregation so invested in luck, faith, and contracts. In this secular hall, Lola is rewarded for her own faith, even if it has to be screamed at the top of her lungs.

In contrast to Tagg's observation, Potente/Lola's voice is seldom reverbed or looped on the film's soundtrack. It is not ethereal, but rather grounded, clear, and distinct. The determination engendered by that detail is redoubled by the shift in the lyrics as the film progresses. While "Believe" remains its main musical theme—its "essence," according to the CD liner notes—the lyrics of the tracks move to a greater sense of goal-directedness and determination, as we hear when "I don't believe in ...," moves to "I wish I was a ...," and "I want to." This is not achieved in a direct, linear fashion—most lyrics weave in and out throughout the film—but it is a trend nonetheless. When the subject turns to love, for instance, the music erupts into out-and-out melody: "Love is just the only strain/ that makes me live through all my pain."

Most of these changes occur in "Running Three," which accompanies Lola's final, successful rendering of her twenty-minute challenge whereby she and Manni not only stay alive but also pick up an extra 100,000 marks in the process. This is the version in which Lola's "father," while more sympathetically depicted than in the first two versions, is nonetheless killed off in a street accident that would do Sophocles and Freud proud. And as he dies, Lola restores life to the "good father" figure, the ailing bank guard featured in the ambulance. As if anticipating all of these good things, the music in "Running Three" starts off with a more playful sound and sprightlier beat. A whistle and other sounds are sampled in as Lola whooshes over the animated bulldog; playful piano notes appear with minimal electronic manipulation; even Lola's scene with her father receives this "kinder, gentler" techno, which is nearly inaudible under soft piano music. Still, and no matter how whimsical the piano notes or whistle might be, the ultimately percussive techno of "Running Three" leaves no doubt: this is music with a goal.

Potente's delivery here remains about as robotic as it was at the beginning, but now she's answered. First is the female singer refashioning the same lyrics and then (especially in the related track "Wish/Komm zu mir") male voices like that of German performer Thomas D, who urges the character to "go, go, go, do the right thing, never letting go, never giving up, never saying no, just go, do the right thing," and then, "Komm zu mir." This brings extensive new material into the mix and introduces a sense of emotional dynamism and exchange that had been missing from the vocal parts up to this point. If techno cannot achieve resolution in the way that standard tonal music does, in *Lola rennt* it is able to establish a kind of musical denouement much in keeping with the narrative one, for after two deadly outcomes, Lola and Manni come together in the story line, just as male and female voices come together on the soundtrack. In both cases, the happy ending is laden with self-consciousness and the sense of having been more or less forced into being.

This is not to argue that the film is ironically reflexive about its upbeat resolution. Actually, in terms of its own faith in the power of love sub-tending its happy, profitable finale, *Lola rennt* is quite serious—and con-ventional. The characters' fervent belief in romantic love is articulated right off the bat in the opening segment when a desperate Manni phones her, wailing "but you always said love can do anything." Love becomes an expectation, a right, a law. Yet the film opposes their relationship to the law, or at least to institutionalized representations of it. Here, love is liter-ally up against the clock, the inexorability of time, of fate, of the rules and movements that symbolic law controls. And the law is indeed amply rep-resented in this film (in a story about rebellious energy, it would have to be). It is not by accident that the uniformed bank guard initiates the story in the prologue; kicking the football into the air with a smile, he intones, "Let the game begin."[22] Nor is it by chance that in forcibly restraining Manni, subway police allow the sack of money in the train to begin its journey and thus prompt Lola's. The law is present to maintain order and to ensure that Lola's circularity is repetitive rather than progressive or lin-ear.[23] Thus, even though these various uniformed guardians *initiate* the film's story and appear throughout (in SWAT teams, in police cars, at banks), they also work to *impede* or defer the love story that runs around in it, reminding us that this kind of love is ultimately unobtainable (in Lacan's famous formulation, "impossible"). And so the law is placed in opposition to faith, love, and belief, even as it requires them. Ostensibly, it is Lola's irrational, religious belief in love that enables her to succeed at the casino, to breach the law her father represented, and even to break the law of the lawbreakers by being able to get the money to Manni. Small wonder that "Believe" is the central musical theme of the film.

Another law operates just as forcefully in the text and is scarcely vio-lated at all. Perhaps in the end, this road movie could not be satisfactorily resolved until the couple is saved as proof that "love *can* do anything." It is as if the falsity of that romantic, heterosexual premise were acknowl-edged by its extravagantly impossible success at film's end.[24] In this vein, the incantatory nature of Potente's vocal delivery (suggestive of trance music) shows the preplanned, familiar nature of the game to which her character and the film's promotional campaign were subjected. In short, the laws of love and emotion are as standardized or predetermined as the more conspicuous "contracts" upheld by the law, finance, and urban decorum of the film's diegetic world. Tykwer was keenly aware of the emotional contract, telling an American interviewer: "I was always con-cerned people might be afraid while they were reading [the script], that they might think it was a completely technical film with no emotional elements anywhere. I was very sure we would have to avoid this impression of the film."[25] His commentary on the North American DVD states that the bed scenes between Manni and Lola were "the heart of the movie," key to fostering a sense of emotional intensity. Equally critical was Lola and Manni's initial phone conversation: "I wanted people to care for these two characters immediately, and to make this happen in a very short time." To this end, Tykwer shot the two lead characters in 35 millimeter film, whereas cooler video was used for most of the others.

Techno is not the only music that emotionalizes the film. On this count as well, Tykwer seems to recognize techno's limits as an emotional signifier and even fools the critics. As J. Hoberman contended: "*Run Lola Run* is far too businesslike to indulge anyone's romantic fantasy. There is not a single musical interlude to tweak the viewer's nostalgia."[26] To be sure, scenes of extreme emotional intensity are shot either without music, as when Lola has a gun to her father's head in the second version, or with hardly any sound at all, as in the fatal endings of the first two stories when we hear only the distorted, reverbed thud of a dropped gun or sack of money. Yet after the conspicuous silence of the first story, we hear strings, played softly and very slowly. Barely audible, the underscored violins, viola, and violoncello recall the typical instrumentation and functions of classical Hollywood's scoring practices: strings, played slowly, enhance emotional content. And to be sure, the music *does* bestow considerable emotional impact to the characters' otherwise absurd deaths. The music is the opening fifteen measures of Charles Ives's 1906 *The Unanswered Question*, famous for its quiet, brief nature. Both its title and Ives's programmatic notes are relevant to Tykwer's film. For Ives, the string quartet represents "The Silences of the Druids—who Know, See, and Hear Nothing." After the brief appearance of these "silent druids" is a muted trumpet, which for Ives poses "The Perennial Question of Existence." It repeats the theme in the "same tone of voice each time," not unlike the structure of the film. "But," as his program notes go on, as if describing *Lola rennt*,

> the hunt for "The Invisible Answer" undertaken by the flutes and other human beings, becomes gradually more active, faster, and louder through an *animando* to a *con fuoco*...." "The Fighting Answerers" mock the question, but recognize their futility, and when they disappear, "The Question" of the 8-minute piece is asked for the last time and "The Silences" are once again (barely) heard in "Undisturbed Solitude."

The emotional impact of this quick excerpt of Ives's piece is irrefutable, especially since we hear only the strings; Tykwer cuts it off before the trumpet is able to pose its brash, modernist "Perennial Question." What is more, the chord progression sustained through the background of *Lola rennt*'s "Believe" is not altogether unlike the long, slow string orchestra chords of Ives's work, although, as with Peter Gabriel, it is hard to say definitively whether Ives is sampled in or not.[27] The title of Ives's work alone makes it an obvious complement to a film that is constantly posing questions and riddles, something particularly evident in the bedroom sequences after the deaths, in which one character asks endless questions of the other (What if you hadn't met me? What if I died?) or the prologue in which the voice-over ponders: "People are mysterious.... Where are we going? What do we believe? Answers give rise to new questions. And isn't it always the same question in the end?" Can Ives be far off?

VI

Critics have relished engaging in a "spot the clues" analysis of Tykwer's movie: Where *was* it filmed? How many of those inside references to German film history can *you* identify? What do they mean? At the risk of entering into that game, it is worth noting *Lola rennt*'s debt to the tradition of the "City Symphony" film, most famously, Walter Ruttman's *Berlin, Symphony for a Great City* (1927). And then there is the title. Like its own thrice-told story, Tykwer's "Lola" is the third significant rendering of the famous German cinematic export, following von Sternberg's *The Blue Angel* (1930) and Fassbinder's *Lola* (1982).[28] These female characters (along with others similarly named, including Ophuls's *Lola Montes*)[29] are known for changing the economic and sexual course of individual men's lives. Lola was certainly an overdetermined figure by the time Tykwer's film came out,[30] but she always had been, even in 1930, when she was a variant of Franz Wedekind's notorious Lulu. Like her predecessors, Tykwer's Lola changes the economic fate of her man (whose familiar and generic nature is evident in his name, Manni), but *unlike* them, she does so for the better. In the process, perhaps she is helping more than her boyfriend-in-a-booth. According to Margit Sinka, Lola pushes for a youthful, energetic "reworking" of post-Wall, post-Kohl Berlin. Perhaps we are to read Lola's character, an overdetermined German icon/body/allegory, as Germany coming to its own rescue, running quickly past Helmut Kohl. Or perhaps the film restages its own "Economic Miracle" by having Lola save Manni from Ronni, the hip U.S.-style gangster, enabling the two of them, like the film, to walk off with double the money they thought they would receive.

Smaller, but no less recognizable, markers of German film culture include a visual reference to Fritz Lang's *M* (1931). Manni's phone booth faces the Spirale, the store he wants to rob. Mounted on the outside wall of the store is a spiral in constant motion, in sharp contrast to Manni who, of course, is told to "stay still"—not an unreasonable request, given the trouble he gets himself into whenever he travels in the first two sequences. Even the fact that Manni has run-ins with both gangsters and police officers calls to mind *M*'s famous equations between lawmakers and gangsters both eager for Peter Lorre's hide. (Another reference to *M* is the intervention of a blind bystander changing the course of events.)[31] In Lang's film, the moving spiral comes into play as Lorre gazes into a store window full of toys; here, as in *Lola rennt*, it adorns a façade, a place of commerce, a site of enticing, mesmerizing promise, of lure as much as of looming madness. It visualizes a repetitive circularity out of which there is no egress, unlike the three versions of Lola's breakneck run, which are not only narratively altered but formally varied, changed by camera angle here, revised flash-forward there.

Even more obvious is Lola's scream, which, like that of Oskar Matzerath in *The Tin Drum* (1979), shatters mirrors, windows, and the nerves of anyone within earshot. The famous scream of Grass/Schlöndorff's Oskar was of a boy/nation that refused to grow up; Lola's, by contrast, is that of a character who refuses to *give* up.[32] The film's allusions to non-German cinema are equally numerous, from Mack Sennett (the gag with the pane of glass) to Hitchcock's *Vertigo* (1958), whose opening credit sequence is mimicked in *Lola rennt*'s, and whose star, Kim Novak, is visually alluded to in the casino in an odd portrait of the back of a blond woman's head, painted at the last minute to resemble what *Lola rennt*'s art director could evoke of the actress.

But why, of his own admission, would Tykwer strive to make Berlin as "unrecognizable as possible"?[33] On the one hand, the choice extends a sort of challenge to German audiences or to other viewers familiar with Berlin, who could enter into a "game" precisely *of* identifying locations. In her analysis of Lola's trek, Sinka notes the impossible nature of the character's disjointed trajectory through Eastern and Western neighborhoods; city locations are jumbled, a fact that bothered local critics. Sinka argues persuasively that it doesn't matter—for her, Lola/*Lola rennt* is a vitality and energy that carries the promise of self-renewal, risk-taking, and the idea of not being punished for failed efforts, a contemporary "agent of change." For Sinka, this film/figure is unquestionably German,[34] constructing Berlin, however abstracted, as a half-finished space of possibility for domestic filmgoers.

Compelling as this reading certainly is, Tykwer's efforts to strip Berlin of identifiable markers of place remain stubbornly present, especially considering the international success of the film. Berlin becomes a somewhat nonessential, generic urban place, a reading Tykwer encouraged from foreign audiences. Is this Berlin, or is this Anywhere? Its streets are curiously depopulated. A similar absenting of place—or at least its extreme abstraction—is announced before the credits even begin. The opening shot shows a large, Gothic clock/amulet, whose swinging pendulum wipes away credits. Placed against a black, spaceless screen, history seems to be literally suspended, even though time itself remains in motion.

The reluctance to confer national and historical specificity in a German-language film informs the dialogue, of which there is little. The pragmatic benefits of this are obvious. Like your standard-issue action film not contingent on dialogue, the film is easy to dub or subtitle, and hence easily exported. What dialogue there is tends to recede in the face of *Lola rennt*'s spectacular soundtrack, stunning visual effects, clever narrative structure, and sense of games and chance. That most of the lyrics of the techno score are in English serves further to denationalize the film, offering a variation of what Birgit Richard and Heinz Hermann Kruger have argued: "The neutral matrix of electronic sound which is the basis of Techno means that it can be understood in any culture or language. Different national scenes are then able to add their own interpretations to this internationally recognizable basic style—usually in the form of voice samples from their own language."[35] In one of the soundtrack's few non-techno pieces, Dinah Washington's version of "What a Difference a Day Makes," along with the Ives, helps establish the United States as cultural and marketing reference point. There is a certain irony in this, given how in some ways the film tries to define itself against American filmmaking. Tykwer delivered strong pro-Europe comments on the topic in early press conferences, such as the 1998 Toronto Film Festival, where *Lola rennt* had its international premiere.

It is impossible that Tykwer was unaware of these kinds of formal and marketing matters. Consider his remarks contrasting his film's style to that of music videos:

> There are some really good music videos, but ninety percent don't get rid of the problem that they are meant to be advertisements. When some are really interesting, *they still have some relationship to the song they are selling....* It is always frustrating to hear [critics say that] *Lola rennt* is just a big video clip. Just because it uses visual methods that are completely normal to us now and works in the present tense doesn't mean that I'm just trying to imitate advertisement noises.[36]

To be sure, *Lola rennt* is not advertising anything except itself. But that it does in abundance, and abundantly well. Tykwer's soundtrack has proven indispensable to that project, epitomizing the concept of synergy common in U.S. film and soundtrack marketing since the 1980s and successful in recent German cinema as well.[37] The CD has been a key factor in the film's financial success. In the United States, its sales were $7 million and in Germany the equivalent of US$14 million in its first year alone. (It was made for DM 3 million, about US$2 million.)[38] The North American release of the CD was carefully timed to follow the theatrical release of the film and precede DVD and VHS release by several months in order to maximize sales of the products.

Both the choice of techno and its predominantly English lyrics give the score a certain deterritorialized, transnational appeal. Reflecting the film's nonspecificity, at once German and non-German in its cinematic references, Berlin and not-Berlin in its representation of space, the use of techno, especially at that point in its history, functions as an Americanized form of Esperanto,[39] poised for the global market just as surely as Lola was positioned to run from her domestic environs at the beginning of each version of the story.

Ironically, as mentioned at the outset, that very internationalism obliges a contemporary and hip musical form to perform a conspicuously traditional function—that of working as "international language," a border-breaking phenomenon with which all of humanity may identify. Romantic love occupies much the same large space in the Western ethos. In all, the film's quirky, romantic "tourism" uses placelessness as a marker not of alienation but of transnational markets and global opportunities. While some audiences have come to expect this sort of transcendence from Wim Wenders, with his endless quest for just the right blend of "world musics," humanizing a patently antihumanist aesthetic form such as techno is no small feat. But *Lola rennt* seems to do just that, in the brightening, stabilizing effect of moving from minor to major modes and by incorporating more organic sounds, with male voices urging and merging with female ones.

In this way, techno—that artifice-laden dance music—serves a commodifying function as well as a humanizing one. What is more, that Tykwer used his *own* music for his *own* film, as well as his *own* lyrics and his *own* screenplay, shows that ultimately the music is perhaps less an "extension of Lola" availed by the soundtrack than an extension of *Lola rennt*, as film, as commodity, and perhaps even of Tykwer as its producer.[40] *Lola rennt* thus carries the triple imprimatur of an "auteur-creator," just as techno asserts its impossibility. Tykwer's overdetermined auteurism in *Lola rennt*—as self-taught director/writer/composer—was precisely one of the film's selling points. In this regard, techno or no, it would seem that the economic value of authorship is as powerful as ever.

Lola rennt was clearly marked and marketed for international distribution from the start, something evident in its style more generally, with its snappy, quick editing, the combination of live action with animation, its clever flash-forwards, and its varied repetitions all having a certain payoff. Less than a year after its domestic release, Tykwer had a deal with Miramax that granted him final veto power over any American remake. He told an interviewer: "You have to challenge coincidence, and there is a path to take. All odds are against Lola, and at the end, it shows it's not by chance that she changes fate, it's really her passionate, possessive desire to change the system that she is stuck in. And the system is time."[41] Lola is obsessed with tackling these systems, with beating the clock, with beating the odds. But despite her partnership in an "outlaw couple" whose botched contract must be redressed, she is part of another couple with a similar contract to fulfill: financial gain. And there it seems Tykwer left little to chance.

Notes

I wish to thank James Reel and Diane Wiener for their research assistance. Thanks also to Klaus Phillips for inviting me to Hollins University for the German Film Conference in April 2000 to present an early version of this essay and to Robert Riemer for his comments there. I am also grateful to Tim Anderson for bibliographic suggestions.

1. Corey K. Creekmur, "On the Run and on the Road: Fame and the Outlaw Couple in American Cinema," in *The Road Movie Book*, ed. Steve Cohan and Ina Rae Hark (London: Routledge, 1997), 90–109.
2. That sense of coupling is enhanced by the fact that Tykwer and Potente were romantically involved at the time.
3. If *Lola rennt* is a road film in which techno music establishes external space, it is worth noting that Muzak makes *enclosed* space a desideratum. As one critic notes, "I always liken curvilinear streets to Muzak: vaguely pleasant but nothing you can remember," as if its own looped structure has a tidy, urban equivalent. Quoted in Joseph Lanza, *Elevator Music: A Surreal History of Muzak, Easy-Listening and Other Moodsong* (New York: St. Martin's Press, 1994), 4.
4. Detroit techno, to take a prominent example, developed out of an especially interesting aesthetic-racial-social phenomenon: blacks there retained the rhythmic, synthetic sound of disco long after white music critics had hailed "Death to disco" in the mid- to late 1970s. Detroit has had a long-standing connection to industrial musics (e.g., MC5) and to heavily produced, nonnatural music such as the "Motown sound," which could plausibly be read as an aesthetic, social, and/or economic reaction to the bogus discourse of virile white authenticity associated with so many rock performers. (Ironically, some of techno's continental versions had to "white it down" to make it danceable for nonblacks.) It is no coincidence that in the United States, techno emerged in the industrial Midwest and that in Germany, it also developed out of industrialized regions such as the Ruhr.
5. In Germany, for instance, trance and heavy forms such as *bretter* were popular over the early and mid-1990s. As a noun, *bretter* connotes a hard board; as a verb it means "to beat."
6. Older scholars often streamline techno's archaeology by describing it as a form that channels punk's rebellious energy into disco's repetitive structures.
7. For a discussion of this and of other aspects of contemporary popular music that is sensitive to questions of geographical, ethnic, and political difference, see Peter Wicke, "The Role of Rock Music in the Political Disintegration of East Germany," in *Popular Music and Communication*, ed. James Lull (Newbury Park: Sage Publications, 1992), 196–206; Dietmar Elflein, "From Krauts with Attitudes to Turks with Attitudes: Some Aspects of Hip-Hop History in Germany," *Popular Music* 17, no. 3 (1998): 255–65; Mechthild von Schoenebeck, "The New German Folk-Like Song and Its Hidden Political Messages," *Popular Music* 17, no. 3 (1998): 279–92; and Fred Ritzel, "Was ist aus uns geworden?—Ein Häufchen Sand am Meer: Emotions of Post-war Germany as Extracted from Examples of Popular Music," *Popular Music* 17, no. 3 (1998): 293–309.
8. Antonio Melechi, quoted in Simon Reynolds, *Generation Ecstasy: Into the World of Techno and Rave Culture* (New York: Routledge, 1999), 238.
9. Reynolds, *Generation Ecstasy*, 364.
10. Ibid., 48.
11. Russell Potter, "Not the Same: Race, Repetition, and Difference in Hip-Hop and Dance Music," in *Mapping the Beat: Popular Music and Contemporary Theory*, eds. Thomas Swiss, John Sloop, and Andrew Herman (London: Blackwell Publishers, 1998), 31–45; here 36.
12. Philip Tagg, "From Refrain to Rave: The Decline of Figure and the Rise of Ground," *Popular Music* 1 (1994): 209–22.
13. Achim Szepanski, quoted in Reynolds, *Generation Ecstasy*, 363.

14. Caspar Pound, quoted in Reynolds, *Generation Ecstasy*, 128.

15. Reynolds, *Generation Ecstasy*, 5.

16. Ibid., 85. Derived from the Greek *ekstasis*, originally *existanai*, the word "ecstasy" means a "standing outside of oneself," as well as "delirium." (It was the German pharmaceutical giant Merck that actually patented Ecstasy—as an appetite suppressant before World War I.) Significantly, *Lola rennt*'s diegetic world is bereft of drugs. Lola's incredible energy comes "from the heart," from a superhuman body whose abilities include, in addition to running endlessly, the power to halt and even change action by screaming (the casino scene is particularly relevant here), and the ability to restore, through a laying on of hands, the endangered life of the bank guard, who suffered from a heart problem himself. (This same person had told her that "a little bit of anger is good for the heart.") The film has Lola's adrenaline thus coming from the heart, the emotional center of the body, from her love for Manni. The heart trope occurs repeatedly throughout the film: in the first ending, that is where she is shot. There is the red blood, Lola's red hair, the red-tinted scenes in bed, and, not unlike Roeg's *Don't Look Now* (1973), there is red in nearly every shot. The beat of a heart is sampled into the score at one point, and lyrics include "I wish I was a heartbeat, that never came to rest."

17. As Margit Sinka notes, the director's domestic interviews stress instead the geographical importance of the city to the film, wanting it, among other things, to alter American and other foreign images of Berlin from pre-*Wende* films such as Wenders's *Himmel über Berlin* (1988). From "Tom Tykwer's *Lola rennt*: Why Doesn't Lola take a Taxi?" Hollins Thirteenth Colloquium, Hollins University, Roanoke, Virginia, April 2000.

18. When asked to comment on the somewhat modest length of the film (81 minutes), Tykwer responded that it "gives you an injection … and an inspirational blow [to the brain]." Ray Pride, "Run, Lola, Run: Speed for Life," *Filmmaker* 7 (1999): 56–58, 89.

19. *Lola rennt*'s range is from 120 to 140 bpm.

20. Murray Smith, "David Lynch's *Lost Highway*," presented at the Society for Cinema Studies, Chicago, 2000.

21. Tagg, "From Refrain to Rave," 214–15.

22. The bank guard is a complex, intriguing character, given his clear affection for Lola and the possibility of his being her biological father. His heart symbolically seizes up during the second story when Lola robs her father, landing him in the ambulance in the third, in which he is magically revived. His character moves easily across different spaces, going from inside and outside of the bank, to outside the diegesis (in the film's prologue). He is a liminal and very mobile figure.

23. The character most fully subjected to this law is Lola's astrology- and alcohol-obsessed mother, the only figure shot identically in all three versions. Significantly, she remains indoors and never moves out of her chair.

24. For an outstanding analysis in this regard, see Robert Lapsley and Michael Westlake, "From *Casablanca* to *Pretty Woman*: The Politics of Romance," *Screen* 33, no. 1 (Spring 1992): 27–49. See also Lynda Hart's excellent queer reading of *Thelma and Louise* in *Fatal Women: Lesbian Sexuality and the Mark of Aggression* (Princeton: Princeton University Press, 1994).

25. Pride, "Run, Lola, Run."

26. *The Unanswered Question* (see discussion in referenced paragraph) does not appear on the CD soundtrack. J. Hoberman, "So Long a Go Go," *Village Voice* (June 1999): 16–22. Reprinted on http://www.villagevoice.com/issues/9924/hoberman.shtml.

27. Thanks to James Reel for this observation.

28. In contrast to Tykwer's character, the earlier Lolas are constantly being posed. Iconic figures, they are characterized by their *lack* of movement. This is particularly the case with Dietrich.

29. In Fassbinder's 1969 *Gods of the Plague*, the protagonist enters a bar called the Lola Montes, the neon name of which is highlighted by a quick tilt of the camera.

30. The Lola figure is everywhere, even on the Internet. In an early Web search about the film, the first match that came up concerned a car-racing team named Lola.

31. The bystander is played by Monika Bleibtreu, mother of Moritz Bleibtreu, the German star who portrays Manni.

32. The two share another trait. Oskar, as he tells us in the film, was born under the sign of the Virgin, "between faith and disillusion." Lola plays out a similar tension between faith and disillusion, evident in some of the lyrics to "Believe."

33. In his review, J. Hoberman states, somewhat erroneously, that the film takes place "in a nondescript residential district in summery Berlin." Hoberman, "So Long a Go Go," p. 2.

34. As Margit Sinka has documented, the film's impact on Berlin ranged from the removal of municipal trench-coated guards in the underground system to a 1999 mayoral campaign in which a conservative candidate borrowed posters from the film to show him "running" for office, to the understandable rage of the director, who sued. The following year, Michael Naumann, minister of culture, went so far as to morph his head onto Lola's body in a campaign poster. Sinka, "Tom Tykwer's *Lola rennt*."

35. Birgit Richard and Heinz Hermann Kruger, "Ravers' Paradise? German Youth Cultures in the 1990s," in *Cool Places: Geographies of Youth Cultures*, ed. Tracey Skelton and Gill Valentine (New York and London: Routledge, 1998), 161–74, here 165.

36. Pride, "Run Lola Run," 89 (emphasis added).

37. Ute Lischke-McNab discusses the importance of music to the newer, faster-paced German films of the late 1980s and 1990s. Using *Maybe ... Maybe Not* as her case study, in remarks with obvious relevance to *Lola rennt*, she writes that if "directors have learned how to 'pace films for success,' the pace, in turn, is controlled by the music. The songs move the film along from sequence to sequence and sustain the rhythm of the film. Nondiegetic instrumental music dominates the soundtrack." Ute Lischke-McNab, "Gender, Sex, and Sexuality: The Use of Music as Collateral Marketing Device in *Maybe ... Maybe Not*," in *Queering the Canon: Defying Sights in German Literature and Culture*, ed. Christophe Lorey and John L. Plews (Columbia, S.C.: Camden House), 403–19, here 415.

38. German figures are from Pride, "Run, Lola, Run," 56; U.S. figures from www.the-numbers.com/movies/index1999.html. *Lola rennt* was completely German-produced by Tykwer's X-Filme Creative Pool, a company formed with other young German directors and producers, and other agencies.

39. Significantly, the soundtrack was recorded in Santa Barbara, California.

40. Tykwer: "I couldn't ever be this kind of director who looks in sometimes in the editing room and comes back for mixing. I'm present at every level, and I love post-production." Pride, "Run, Lola, Run," 89.

41. Ibid.

Part V

MEMORY, MUSIC, AND THE POSTMODERN

Chapter 14

"HEINER MÜLLER VERTONEN"
Heiner Goebbels and the Music of
Postmodern Memory

David Barnett

I

"Setting Heiner Müller to music? Even as a composer I would initially say: no."[1] So spoke the German composer and musician Heiner Goebbels at the beginning of a speech he gave at the *Experimenta 6* in Frankfurt in 1990. That his musical career has featured work associated with Müller at almost every turn,[2] and that he has been fêted with many prizes for his efforts, exposes the question as a rhetorical one.[3] This essay will examine Goebbels's musical relationship with Müller in the light of both Goebbels's theoretical musings and the practical ways in which they have manifested themselves in four central pieces. The focus of this inquiry is whether the aural dimension expands or diminishes Müller's problematic texts in performance, a question that raises issues concerning Müller's as well as Goebbels's aesthetics.

When asked which productions of his plays he most enjoyed, Müller replied with wry irony, "[N]one really."[4] This comment may reflect a belief that the huge wealth of material in the texts was never allowed the space on stage required to do it justice. The antinaturalist language, extreme density of speeches, frequent refusal to attribute character, and broad appropriation of intertext point to a maze of dramaturgies irreducible to a single approach. Production styles have to transcend a director's (or an actor's) "interpretation" because of the attenuated implications of the term. Müller has criticized such approaches in the past: "They say Müller is a Communist, therefore he thinks Capitalists are evil, so that's how they should be portrayed. Those are the so-called political productions which simply destroy all the material in the text."[5] The idea of "material"

is central to Müller's understanding of the role of the dramatic text in performance. The power of a text is its ability to connect with itself and its
audience in a series of ways that are unknowable, even to its own creator.
"Metaphors are cleverer than the author," Müller claims.[6] Those planning
to stage the texts, be they directors, actors or composers, must, therefore,
understand the postmodern stance of the "dead" author, to quote Roland
Barthes.[7] Once the words are committed to paper, they occupy a realm in
which polyvalence trumps authorial authority.

The mode of theatrical and musical communication consequently has
to be broadened to one that seeks the form of multilayered experience.
This may entail a confrontation with the material in as many of its facets
as possible. The notion of experience takes pride of place in the reception
of the Müllerian text. Experience implies that understanding, that most
prized of Western values, defers to a realm that does not surrender its
secrets to the faculty of rational thought so easily. Experience takes the
world in all of its complexity and contradictions as its source, and it is here
that the concept of "landscape" emerges. To Müller and many other postmodern writers, the world and its inhabitants are beyond rational exegesis; they are permeated by too many sensual and irrational impulses. The
expansiveness and limitlessness of that which confronts us suggest the
metaphor of the landscape, in which elements indifferent or hostile to
human reason reside. Landscapes do not yield to the machinations of
human beings without a fight. The resistance Müller finds in the landscapes of our experience also become political: "My most defining experience in the USA was the landscape.... It was really strange, this capitalism
with edges. It doesn't have edges in Europe any more, or it's quite hard to
see the edges. In America ... the edges are where there's life.... Landscapes
aren't house-trained."[8] From his earliest plays, Müller pits human subjects
against the landscapes of memory, history, and geography. In his later
works, the battle lines become more blurred in dramaturgies that dissect
the human subject and contrast its desires with those more unwieldy than
its own. The rationalist and instrumentalizing will to dominate a landscape has to defer to a strategy of accommodation. Experiencing Müller is
a lesson in humility that profoundly alters the business of theatrical and
musical communication.

Goebbels treats Müller's idea of text as landscape, incommensurable
and potentially fatal, as a useful metaphor for his own endeavors. The
ramifications of the trope also extend to the listener's role. The landscape
will not fulfill its potential if it is approached by a consuming tourist; on
the contrary, the landscape must activate the listener so that the enterprise
becomes an expedition.[9] The question, then, arises as to how music and
text combine to enable a galvanizing experience of this type.

Goebbels's theoretical approaches to Müller's dense and expansive texts
share many of the latter's own predilections. Goebbels's understanding of
the status of words in Müller's theatre stresses their inviolability: "[Müller]

writes for the theatre, but not for a theatre of character, rather for a theatre of texts; texts which can appear on the stage as literature, but which do not require illustration, that is: when other media are added (set, music, actors, light, space, etc.), they have to be autonomous or at least open the autonomous space between text and potential."[10] Elsewhere, Goebbels criticizes Wolfgang Rihm's setting of *The Hamletmachine* because the music is too busy competing with the power of the words rather than creating its own dimension.[11] The autonomy of the elements is crucial in Goebbels's conception of the role of music in Müller's theatre. The dialectical components of the piece[12] must be held in tensions that resist synthesis, otherwise the composer is depriving the listener of his or her role in the process of generating meaning.

Yet Goebbels's ideas on experience and meaning require more careful study. Unlike Barthes's pluralistic poetics, Goebbels insists on a structural and thematic integrity in his work that seeks to constrain total interpretive freedom. The seemingly contradictory nature of his approach is summed up in the following quotation:

> I try to describe a sort of democratic experience. My idea is not to open the material up to a liberal experience where everyone can think what they want to.… In my work I open up a text at different levels of understanding; it doesn't make the text more deliberate or redundant, it makes it more precise. If you are able to experience the different levels of the text or of the speaking voice yourself, you get closer to the truth of the text than if you receive it in a political package. It's not that anything goes. I show and offer the necessary elements of a subject, of a piece. If the elements are precisely chosen, the experience of an audience is able to combine these elements in a subjective, very different way; but the final experience will be hopefully more precise and complex.… Even when you make the structure more transparent by deconstructing a sentence, even if you look at one single word, you still have the connection; it's never a Dadaist text.[13]

Goebbels treads the line between generating and withholding meaning that strikes at the heart of the postmodern work's dynamic. On the one hand, the idea of experience contains ideas of bypassing the rational faculties and reintroducing the body into the reception of and engagement with the work of art. The result of the experience is unknowable on two counts. First, to experience something is not the same as to know something. The body does not speak the same language as the rational mind. Second, each listener processes experience subjectively, without a transcendental key. One's own memories and associations prevent uniform conclusions from being drawn. On the other hand, Goebbels is keen to retain a constellation of possible meanings and flirts with the idea of the text's "truth." This conservative hermeneutic turn may not, however, prove quite as limiting as it seems. Later in the above transcript, Goebbels says: "I choose my pieces, my subjects, because I don't understand them, and I try to offer my experience with the material to the audience."[14]

Goebbels is attempting neither to communicate a "message" nor to allow a listener his particular reading of Müller's texts. On the contrary he is trying to facilitate a set of experiences. To Goebbels, though, these experiences are the product of an associative engagement in which music and sound are used as complements for the text. They neither interpret nor illustrate but run concurrently with the material as a possibility for a sensual response to the text as a whole.

Consequently, one may conclude that Goebbels has a more ambivalent attitude toward meaning. His musical output is constructed with precision; its elements are designed to convey meaning through his associations with the material. Yet the nature of the elements, the text, the music, and the sounds are too diverse and contradictory to be reduced to a "message." As Goebbels puts it: "[T]o say 'this is the message' would not be true. You refuse the message, because the message is a complex experience."[15] The experience, then, is the site of meaning, yet experience cannot be commensurate with rational understanding. Goebbels is assaulting the listener with works whose compositional logic is tight and rigorous, in which each moment is constructed with care and attention. The meanings generated are many and varied, and depend on the experience of the listener, but there are still themes and topics that are being dealt with that limit a Barthesian infinity of interpretations. Goebbels seems to be aligning himself with Stanley Fish and his idea of "interpretive communities."[16] Goebbels sets apart the middle ground between the myth of perfect reception and the expanse of boundless meaning, and offers a take on Müller's material that is designed to facilitate a very different sort of understanding.

II

One of the corollaries of "text as landscape" is the effect it may have on the speaker(s) within it. In Müller's note to *Waterfront Wasteland Medeamaterial Landscape with Argonauts* he asserts: "[J]ust as in any landscape, the 'I' in this part of the text is collective."[17] A brief survey of character construction in Müller's later work explicates this seemingly cryptic remark. Müller's "I's" explode the limits of the bourgeois individual—they are suffused with intertext and experience that destroy a "realist" interpretation of the speaking figure. Instead, the subject on stage suggests a collective voice, one that aggregates many individuals as a means of approaching the multifaceted landscape. Goebbels takes up Müller's challenge and strives to decenter the speaker in his work, adopting a variety of approaches in the process.

One of Goebbels's earliest attempts at Müller is his *Waterfront Wasteland* (1984).[18] The 17:26 recording is made up primarily of the voices of Berliners, recorded by Thorsten Becker in streets, pubs, amusement arcades, and the Zoo U and S Bahn Station. The piece contains a mere thirty-four lines of text as its verbal material and contrasts them with a range of aural responses.

The work opens with slow, deep, repeated synthesized sounds that suggest a large organism, the waterfront wasteland. Electronic whistles join in before a selection of voices starts to read, repeating the scene's title. The rest of the track oscillates between the interplay of found voices and the synthesized riverbank.

The voices are "spontaneous" in that they are reacting to their first encounter with an unfamiliar text. Incomprehension, misreadings, improvisations, slips, and attempts at interpretation inform the recording throughout. The refusal to engage with the text is as important as the serious efforts to deal with it. The rich, the poor, the old, the young, the native, and the foreign, all appear to be featured, separated by their disparate subjective experiences. Each voice suggests a different history and treads an awkward tightrope: all are undoubtedly individuals, yet their common task, location, and language construct a collective voice. Goebbels questions the category of the individual and makes identity a central theme in the work.

Goebbels could not be accused of illustrating the text here, either with the looped organic patterns of the waterfront, the use of sound effects (such as the S-Bahn or the tunes of arcade machines), or the arrangement of the found voices. Nothing is "explained" as such; rather, Goebbels, like Müller, manufactures a gamut of possible connections. What emerges is indeed a collective voice, but one that maintains its elements at the level of connotation rather than denotation. The collective voice cannot be reduced to a war cry, a "voice of the people." It can, however, be mobilized as a dynamic snapshot, an aural picture of the interaction between human subjects, their histories, and their memories. It is not by chance that Berlin is the locus of the work. Müller's riverbank is on a lake near Strausberg, a satellite of the capital. The setting generates the confrontation of humans, the city, and the past. The preponderance of impressions and the relentless rhythms provided by both Goebbels and the sound effects raise more questions than they could possibly answer. The continual buffeting by the text forces the listener to confront its many textures, as slivers of meaning emerge only to be subsumed within the broader dialectic of the landscape.

Goebbels reuses the technique of taking text from the street in the project *SHADOW/Landscape with Argonauts* (1990).[19] In a work that seems to be a continuation of *Waterfront Wasteland*, Goebbels sallies forth to Boston, Massachusetts, for his material. This time around, he plays off the assemblage of found voices with a musical version of Edgar Allan Poe's "Shadow—Parable."

It is surprising how different essentially the same strategy can be. The American voices are more individuated and are, at times, given more space to "tell their own stories." For example, in the fourth track of the work, entitled "2 Dollar," we hear a black man's voice haggling for a fee before reading the text. There are more extra-textual comments, too, which on occasion seem to point just a little too transparently to the problems of the text. Track three ends with a voice asking, "What the fuck is this?" and the final *Landscape* section, track 15, ends with "All right now, what is it all about?" It is possible that these additional lines are commenting on a particularly American experience of the foreign, of the unknown, of the poetic. Alternatively, they can be construed as illustrative, in that they focus the listener's attention on the difficulties of the text, patronizing him or her by highlighting an obvious problem.

Musically, there is more happening that could also be accused of illustrating or overly contextualizing the voices. To take "2 Dollar" as an example again, the voice, having been cheaply bought, reads the opening lines of *Landscape* with rhythm and pace. Goebbels adds a rap-style beat that only seems to strengthen the voice rather than to challenge it or add tension. The practice occurs elsewhere on the recording, too. A difference in the style of voices, however, may account in part for this practice. Often, but not exclusively, the voices betray a performative quality, showing that they are aware that they are speaking to a microphone. Goebbels highlights the more conscious approach of his American voices by allying the voice with the performance style it quotes. The heightened media awareness of the Bostonians marks an important contrast with the Berliners.

The *SHADOW* sections change the timbre of the piece and are inserted, for the most part, between the *Landscape* tracks. The Iranian singer Sussan Deihim gives a focused and subtle performance as she mainly sings Poe's text. Partly as the performer of a religious ritual, partly as a cabaret singer, partly as a deliverer of text, Deihim evokes gravitas and lightness. The tale stands as a counterpoint to the voices of Boston. The narrator tells the story of a group of friends at a funeral wake in ancient Greece who are visited by an apparition, Shadow. But his voice is not that of their departed comrade; rather, it has the sounds of the many thousands of the dead. The collision of the tale with the many voices of Boston throws them into relief and picks up on a set of ideas that pervade Müller's writing.[20]

For Müller, the function of examining history and the landscapes of memory is to remember the dead: "[A] task of the theatre and of tragedy was always to raise the dead.... It is time to fetch the dead back up from under the carpet and to put them on stage.... The dead have to be buried before things can progress."[21] In this reading, the dead are bloody reminders that have to be dealt with in order to address the problems of the world. Every death that has been repressed poses a question to the contemporary order of things. The imperative to remember and to process the past thus signals Müller's as a memory theatre par excellence. Goebbels's employment of *SHADOW* contrasts the search for identity and the catastrophic description of contemporary Western consumer culture in *Landscape* with the mountains of bodies generated along the way.

The collective voice in *Landscape* is qualitatively different from that of *Waterfront Wasteland*. It is more distilled and processed. Fleeting impressions in Berlin give way to fuller articulations in Boston. *Landscape* resembles a sociological survey that aims to contextualize its objects of inquiry more firmly in social and cultural frames. Breadth is exchanged for depth. The more kaleidoscopic slices of individuated lives in *Landscape* reveal a different type of image, against which *SHADOW* becomes even more radically defined. The good people of Boston mark a shift in the collective voice, one that threatens to destroy the fragile collectivity of *Waterfront Wasteland*. Consequently, the evocation of the masses of the dead in *SHADOW* provides an even greater foil; the exhortation to remember is all the more pointed.

The development in the two projects signals important social, geographical, and historical changes. The breakdown of the collective voice (and its musical emphasis) forms a critique that runs parallel to the content of the *Landscape* text. Poe becomes the provocative corrective. Individualism is contextualized politically within the contemporary United States and is contrasted against the backdrop of history. The bridge between the two is memory, the category that can connect the listener to the present and the past.[22]

III

Realizing text as landscape is, of course, not only limited to the complex reworking of found voices. Goebbels also works with voices in the studio that have the express task of performing Müller's texts. In this section I shall be looking at Goebbels's two settings of the fragment "The Man in the Elevator" from Müller's play *The Task*. Goebbels's first deployment of the text was in his version of another Müller fragment, "The Liberation of Prometheus," taken from the play *Cement*. The second was in his full-scale reworking of "The Man" in the complete work *The Man in the Elevator* (1988).[23]

Goebbels's *The Liberation of Prometheus* (1985) takes the figure of The Man as a possible modern incarnation of the Prometheus of Müller's text. His is a compromised figure, like so many in Müller's plays: he has given human beings fire but has not taught them how to use it against the gods because he has also dined at the gods' table. He appears on tracks 4 and 5 of the radio play. Goebbels's task here is to locate the fragment within the larger structure of *The Liberation*.

The texture of the two tracks is distinctly dream-like. A looped synthesized harpsichord, soft and persistent, dislocates the listener from the "Liberation" text that precedes it. The "quoted" sound and its incessant repetition introduce a hypnotic, temporally ambivalent and unreal feeling to the text that complements the neutral reading of "The Man" by a male voice. The booming brass that is heard in the background is unpredictable and formless, signifying a realm beyond the control of the conscious mind. Its sudden swelling or unexpected meandering is divorced from the text's semantic turns during the reading. The reintroduction of the "Liberation" text midway through "The Man" seems to return the listener to the structuring narrative of the work, but the persistence of the harpsichord and brass undermines the idea of a simple transition. The reliability of the "Liberation" text as some kind of anchor is also called into question by the many voices that speak it. Müller's own, ironized by the clichéd sound of a Bavarian "oom-pah" band, is replaced by a different voice before a babble of speakers takes over. The collective voice is thus activated once more before the "Elevator" stops at Peru. In Peru, the classical sounds of the harpsichord are missing, and the music of the unconscious, the brass, is missing, too. The mild shock of the geographical transplant (signaled by short pauses in the reader's still neutral delivery) gives way to the measured tones found earlier. The speaker is nonetheless interrupted by a welter of other noises. They begin with a regular "ping," like that of an ECG machine. This is also the same "ping" that begins the radio play as a whole, which makes the demarcation of textual elements all the more problematic. The assault by the many slices of sound presents a peculiar tension in the track. One is left to ask where the sounds are coming from and whether the speaker is aware of them. His dogged adherence to his narrative may suggest fortitude—or foolhardiness. By the end of the section, when the first lines of the text are spliced in with the last, the narrative creates its own ironic closure by pointing to its circularity. The dream-like text becomes the mark of an obsessive projection, condemned to repeat itself until it has finally confronted its own experiences. The text attains the quality of a memory that the speaker has not been able to process fully. Just like the dead that Müller exhorts us to bury, the memory endures until the collective Prometheus figure is able to lay it to rest.

Goebbels's second treatment of the "Elevator" material lasts for almost forty-three minutes and uses only the "Elevator" text (with the exception of two songs, tracks 5 and 11). Three voices give The Man a split form. Müller reads in his usual distanced and precise manner. Ernst Stötzner, whose versatile vocal talents also feature in a range of guises on *The Road to Volokolamsk*, provides a variation that injects a more "human" slant, while still conveying distance, as if he is reporting his impressions. His changes in expressive register give a sense of one's own possible reactions, yet it would be difficult to assert that Stötzner ever really approaches naturalism. Don Cherry, the famous jazz trumpeter, is the only American voice. He sings and narrates, sometimes combining both in a loose and casual style. His laid-back manner is dreamy and comforting. The three voices evoke a complex sonic image of The Man. Müller sets down the narrative in its bare bones, allowing the text the space and freedom to generate meanings away from the exigencies of an interpretation. Stötzner and Cherry add layers of differentiation, but neither is reducible to a pat psychological reading. The narrators' varied styles, radically aestheticized subjective responses to the text, frustrate a listener's possible attempts to extract linear meaning.

The music that accompanies the voices switches between a jazzy, relaxed sound and the violent insistence of heavier guitar-driven rock, although the two styles do coalesce, only to diverge again, in the course of the piece. In addition, Arto Lindsay, a singer and musician raised in Brazil, contributes two songs. At the point when the speaker decides to leave the elevator, Lindsay's "No Taboleiro de Baìana" (The Market Stalls of the Women of Baìa) hints at the Peruvian encounter that is still ahead of The Man. Stötzner's voice and the drum machine underneath it can still be heard for most of the track until Lindsay is finally allowed to perform solo. The Man's reality returns as a distorted guitar resumes during Stötzner's narrative in the next track. Lindsay also suggests Peru in the eleventh track, "Fito nos meus Olhos" (Tape on My Eyes), a track that comes just before The Man's decision to leave the elevator. Lindsay again does not appear as a "pure" fragment. He is initially faded in against the sound of percussion. His song is then allowed to proceed without additional instrumentation until a synthesizer accompanies the last minute of the song.

At the end of the recording, Stötzner and Cherry both read lines from earlier "Elevator" text that muse on how one fulfills an unknown task. Linearity, as in all of Goebbels's settings, is jettisoned in favor of the foibles of the speaking subject. In this version of the "Elevator" text, Goebbels constructs the dream state once more, but this time uses the material as an investigation of the landscape of The Man's consciousness. The split voice, with its implicit distance pitched at three different levels, presents but deliberately fails to comment on the experiences of the speakers. Müller, the voice that gives space for the listener's own thought processes, does not compete with the subjectivity of Stötzner or Cherry; rather, he becomes an equal partner in the aural economy of the work.

IV

In all of his works, then, Goebbels explores a variety of strategies that open up the text for the listener in a fashion that echoes Brecht. The listener is no longer a consumer, but rather an active participant in the creation of meaning. Goebbels arranges the elements to encourage the possibility of connections. This does not, however, take the listener's work away from him or her by reducing the material through musical or vocal interpretation. Goebbels plays with Müller's post-Brechtian dramaturgies by constructing a complex dialectic in which competing elements never gain primacy, holding each other in a dialectical check. Goebbels's montage technique marks a shift away from the high-modernist stance taken by, for example, Sergei Eisenstein.[24] Although Goebbels encourages the construction of meaning from the many montage elements, he denies the existence of a priori knowledge. Landscapes of history, memory, and geography confront the listener with no detectable set of rules for how they should be addressed or processed. The sensual relationship between the listener and the many collective voices is unknowable. Goebbels has attained an expansive quality throughout his work, one which probes Müller's fragments for their potential. He asks questions that do not surrender rational answers and phrases them in forms that resist their reduction.

Notes

1. Heiner Goebbels, "Heiner Müller vertonen. Beitrag zur Podiumsdiskussion anläßlich der *Experimenta 6*, Frankfurt 1990," 10 May 2003. http://www.heinergoebbels.com/deutsch/writings/vertonen.htm.
2. In addition to the works I shall be discussing in depth in this chapter, Goebbels has also used texts either by or adapted by Müller in the following projects: *Life of Gundling Frederick of Prussia Lessing's Sleep Dream Cry* (1979), *The Hamletmachine* (1985), *Maelstromsouthpole* (1987), *Heracles 2* (1992), *Medeamaterial* (1993), *Or the Hapless Landing* (1993), *Surrogate Cities* (1994), *Der Horatier – Chien Romain – Roman Dogs* (1995), *Black on White* (1996), and *Nightplay* (1998). The major project *The Road to Volokolamsk* (1989) has been omitted from this current essay for reasons of space. I have, however, discussed it in *Literature versus Theatre: Textual Problems and Theatrical Realization in the Later Plays of Heiner Müller* (Frankfurt am Main: Peter Lang, 1998), 152–57.
3. Among others, *Waterfront Wasteland* won the Karl-Sczuka-Preis der Donaueschinger Musiktage 1984; *The Liberation of Prometheus*, the Hörspielpreis der Deutschen Kriegsblinden 1985 and the Prix Italia 1986; *The Road to Volokolamsk*, the Preis der Publikumsjury, Akademie der Künste, West-Berlin 1989, the Karl-Sczuka-Preis der Donaueschinger Musiktage 1990 and the Prix Futura 1991 for its fifth part.
4. David Barnett, "'Ich erfinde gerne Zitate': Interview mit Heiner Müller," *GDR Bulletin* 22, no. 2 (1995): 9.
5. Heiner Müller, "Ein Grund zum Schreiben ist Schadenfreude," *Gesammelte Irrtümer. Interviews und Gespräche* (Frankfurt am Main: Verlag der Autoren, 1986), 114.
6. Heiner Müller, "Fatzer ± Keuner," in *Heiner Müller Material*, ed. Frank Hörnigk (Göttingen: Steidl, 1989), 31.
7. Roland Barthes, "The Death of the Author," in *Modern Criticism and Theory*, ed. David Lodge (London: Longman, 1988), 167–72.
8. Heiner Müller, *Krieg ohne Schlacht* (Cologne: Kiepenheuer & Witsch, 1992), 284.
9. Heiner Goebbels, "Text als Landschaft," 10 May 2003 (http://www.heinergoebbels.com/deutsch/writings/landscha.htm).
10. Goebbels, "Heiner Müller vertonen."
11. Heiner Goebbels, "Expeditionen in die Textlandschaft," in *Explosion of a Memory. Heiner Müller DDR. Ein Arbeitsbuch*, ed. Wolfgang Storch (Berlin: Hentrich, 1988), 81.
12. All of the works discussed in this chapter are designated radio plays, not merely music for Müller's texts. Goebbels presents a fixed and recorded musical text for each setting.
13. Heiner Goebbels, "Opening up the Text," *Performance Research* 1, no. 1 (1996): 55.
14. Ibid., 57.
15. Ibid.
16. Stanley Fish, *Is There a Text in This Class? The Authority of Interpretive Communities* (Cambridge, MA: Harvard University Press, 1980).

17. Heiner Müller, *Verkommenes Ufer Medeamaterial Landschaft mit Argonauten*, in Heiner Müller, *Herzstück* (Berlin: Rotbuch, 1983), 101.

18. All references taken from Heiner Goebbels, *Verkommenes Ufer*, on Heiner Goebbels's recording, *Hörstücke nach Texten von Heiner Müller*, ECM 1453, 1994.

19. All references taken from Heiner Goebbels's recording, *SHADOW/Landscape with Argonauts*, ECM 1480, 1993.

20. Goebbels reports, in a short piece written shortly after the death of Heiner Müller in December 1995, that it was Müller who initially recorded *SHADOW* for him. Heiner Goebbels, "Against the Vanishing of Human Beings," *ECM Newsletter* 1 (1996).

21. Heiner Müller, "Für ein Theater, das an Geschichte glaubt," in *Gesammelte Irrtümer 2. Interviews und Gespräche* (Frankfurt am Main: Verlag der Autoren, 1990), 136. This is but one of many places Müller takes up this idea.

22. See Simon Ward, "Wolfgang Koeppen and the Bridge of Memory," *German Life and Letters* 52, no. 1 (1999): 97–111, for a more detailed discussion of this metaphor.

23. All references taken from Heiner Goebbels, *Die Befreiung des Prometheus*, on Goebbels, *Hörstücke nach Texten von Heiner Müller*, ECM 1452, 1994; and Heiner Goebbels, *The Man in the Elevator*, ECM 1369, 1988.

24. See, for example, the assertion that "the basic characteristic of a montage sequence is its suggestiveness." Sergei Eisenstein, *Towards a Theory of Montage*, ed. Michael Glenny and Richard Taylor (London: British Film Institute, 1991), 150. Eisenstein stresses that meaning *can* be reassembled after concessions are made to modernist ideas of the multiple perspective.

Chapter 15

THE TECHNOLOGICAL SUBJECT
Music, Media, and Memory in
Stockhausen's *Hymnen*

Larson Powell

I

The inevitable aging of musical modernity, prematurely diagnosed by Theodor W. Adorno in the 1950s, appears now to have been effected retrospectively by the distancing vacuum of the end of the twentieth century. For the first time in European musical history, no new generation arose in the space of over a quarter of a century to dispute or continue the accomplishments of its predecessors. Compared to the surge of productivity, the consensus around which polemics took place, of the 1950s and 1960s, the last three decades of the twentieth century now appear as a time of eclectic disorientation.[1] Not one of the musical movements then launched—whether neo-Romanticism, minimalism, or the opportunistic blending of high and low forms—has retained much sense of necessity for the present. In the wake of this, 1950s and 1960s modernity is at once closer and also further removed from the present than any other art. Perhaps Adorno's aging of modernity is in itself less tragic than his contemporaries feared; what matters is only a rendering-conscious of that age in critical resistance to the reactionary amnesia beneath which so much of modernity is now buried.

Few modernists have been subjected to this amnesia more than Karlheinz Stockhausen, once so much a household name that even pop musicians referred to him in an attempt at legitimation.[2] While Arnold Schönberg seems still not to have achieved the canonical status of James Joyce and Pablo Picasso (particularly in the United States, where even Freud is hardly accepted), the post-1945 musical modernists appear to have passed into complete oblivion in the domain of public concerts and radio broadcasting, the university setting being an exception. The 1960s are the hinge on which the end of modernism turns. If the phenomenological sobriety and constructivism of the 1950s have been received and canonized with slightly greater ease, the theatrical spectacles and neo-Dadaism of the 1960s have worn less well.[3] The embarrassment now often felt when reviewing some films of Jean-Luc Godard, or when rereading the heady blend of Maoism and Derrida of the Tel Quel group circa 1968, is paradigmatic here. It is not only the questionable wisdom that nothing dates faster than yesterday's utopias; it is the inherent fragility and ephemerality deliberately risked by much 1960s art that has not always aged well. Adorno saw this and sought heroically to defend it:

> Those works which apparently hasten to their doom often have better chances of survival than those that, for the sake of an ideal of security, elide their temporal core and, empty at their center, become as if in revenge victims of time.... It is conceivable that what we now need are works of art which consume themselves through the temporality at their heart, offering their own life to the moment of truth's appearance and then vanishing without a trace while remaining completely undiminished in the process. The nobility of such an attitude would not be unworthy of art.[4]

It is not always remembered that this reduction of art to its transient minimum is a gamble that might fail. Stockhausen's work participated in this tendency as no other. The question of its survival, however, must be asked of individual works and not just of a larger tendency. The historical decay of the "-isms" (or of what Bloch called "Tendenzen") not only makes the text into a cipher[5] but also constitutes it, almost in spite of itself, as a work. One is forced by historical distance to interpret. The following analysis will thus seek to coordinate elements of hermeneutical close reading with a broader perspective informed by discourse and media theory.

II

Arguably a high point in Stockhausen's electronic career, *Hymnen* (1966–67) is a sustained meditation not only on nations and nationalism but also on German memory and the public spaces of music. The work is built out of an abstract electronic recomposition of at least forty national anthems, loosely grouped into four "Regions" corresponding obliquely to the four movements of a symphony or the four operas of Richard Wagner's *Der Ring des Nibelungen* tetralogy. This earned the composer the sobriquet of being, together with Hans-Jürgen Syberberg, Anselm Kiefer, Joseph Beuys, and Heiner Müller, one of Germany's late-modern Wagnerians.[6] As in the *Ring*, Stockhausen's work concludes with an apocalyptic fantasy of the world's destruction and renewal, a matter given particular portent by the work's historical context of the Cold War arms race. Eschatological perspectives had been part of electronic music and musique concrète (concrete music) at least since Edgard Varèse's *Poème Électronique* of 1958; as Friedrich Kittler has pointed out, electronic music technology had its origins in "the abuse of military equipment,"[7] and *Hymnen* has in consequence the horizon of warfare written into its internationalist plea for peace.

War defines that temporal horizon at both ends, not only as imagined future but also as remembered past, as a trauma to be worked through. In Region II—the German region—Stockhausen directly quotes from the "Horst-Wessel-Lied" and then cuts to his own voice in the electronic studios of Cologne Radio, reflecting on the associations of Nazi music: "Otto Tomek [director of the radio studios in Cologne] said that there was bad blood associated with the Horst-Wessel-Lied. But—I didn't mean it that way. It was only—a memory."[8]

Political quotation in German music dates back at least as far as Schumann's slyly anti-Metternichian reference to the then-tabooed "Marseillaise" in *Faschingsschwank aus Wien* (1839). Yet Stockhausen distances himself from this tradition by the phenomenological neutrality of the word *Erinnerung* (memory), implying that even the "Horst-Wessel-Lied" is only so much raw material to be reworked in an abstract composition, in an epically distanced chronicle of modern life. Here the problem of working through the past runs into a contradiction with the aesthetics of the postwar period. Like the *nouveau roman* or even the *nouvelle vague*, Stockhausen's work of the 1960s, which experimented with radio materials and quotation, sought to define a poetics of pure immanence, opposed to linear narrativity. As with his radio piece "Kurzwellen" of 1968, *Hymnen* may be heard as one simultaneous radio broadcast: "What happens consists only of what the world is broadcasting *now*.... *Everything* is *simultaneously* the *whole*. The notion of time is swallowed into the mind's past."[9] The question then arises as to how such phenomenological neutrality and detachment may be mediated with the historical memory of trauma, or whether it does not in fact already bear the latter's signature.

To be sure, music's function as one of the architects of political and national *Öffentlichkeit* (publicness) is here made explicit.[10] Stockhausen has himself noted the defining role played by the omnipresence of Nazi music in his own recollections of the Third Reich (in which both of his parents perished and he himself had to serve as a stretcher-bearer in a military hospital as a very young man). This traumatic memory played a decisive role in the composer's formation, yet it was understood in a sense to be diametrically opposed to Wolf Biermann's understanding of his own childhood experience of the Hamburg firebombing. Biermann retrospectively recalled the war as a source of political legitimacy. He turned it into a mythic family romance constituting socialist subjectivity, a martyred father, and an authentic experience of war. For Stockhausen, the war meant the end both of any traditional ego identifications (dependent on a family structure he had to watch destroyed) and of any political beliefs.[11]

Hymnen thus suggests, but does not work out, a musical anticipation of the New German Cinema's theme of mourning through the image: a musical *Arbeit am Mythos*, a reworking of the raw material of memory, even at its most corrupt, kitschy, and colonized.[12] In 1966, however, the avant-garde was still hopeful about waking up from the nightmare of history: the *Trauerarbeit* (work of mourning) of Kiefer, Rainer Werner Fassbinder, and others is not a factor here.

The relation to film does not stop here. The aforementioned comparison of Stockhausen to Syberberg could be worked out in terms of ironic montage technique (shared also, at the other end of the political spectrum, by the collective film *Deutschland im Herbst,* Germany in Autumn, 1978). Many aspects of classical film theory are pertinent to a description of electronic music: its tendency to flatten out the acoustical depth field into a framed plane; its photographic melancholy of documentation; its "concern with unstaged reality"; its tendency to "stress the fortuitous" and "suggest endlessness"; and its "affinity for the indeterminate."[13] This blurring between media (what Adorno called *Verfransung*)[14] suggests that Marshall McLuhan's thesis of the untranslatability of media is less hard and fast than Kittler would have it. This also suggests that the demarcation between media and art is not so definitive either,[15] a matter that we will return to at the end of the present essay.

Electronic music would ultimately need to be seen, in its institutional and media-historical context, in relation to the *Hörspiel* (radio play), which was, at the time of *Hymnen,* moving into a new phase of technological self-awareness (the so-called *neues Hörspiel*).[16] Like the radio play, electronic music is an "impure" genre. Despite the utopian predictions made by post-Webernists in the 1950s (and still anachronistically held to by Pierre Boulez in Paris today), electronics did *not* result only in pure abstract constructivism freed from all reference, in a technological *scienza nuova* of free aesthetic play.[17] Three of Stockhausen's most important pieces in the medium *(Gesang der Jünglinge, Telemusik, Hymnen)* work with *objets trouvés* (that is, found objects), whether text snippets or quoted musics, as their point of departure; none are created ex nihilo. The reasons why this is so are related to the reasons why the *Hörspiel* could never become a purely self-referential or abstract genre. *Hymnen*'s use of these acoustical found objects thus creates formal difficulties of understanding, for the work has, as it were, two forms: one exoteric-narrative and one esoteric-structural.

On first contact, it is clear that *Hymnen* renders explicit the ideological and historical implications of the national anthems that it reworks in a kind of capsule history of political and public musics from the Enlightenment to the Cold War: the four Regions progress from the "Internationale" and the "Marseillaise" (liberal patriotism and revolutionary internationalism, Region I) through the "Deutschlandlied" (reaction, Region II) to a Cold War conflict of the Soviet hymn and the "Star-Spangled Banner" (Region III) to a close centered on the peaceful federalism of the Swiss anthem (Region IV). The work thus stands in a precarious position between absolute and program music. As Boulez once said of Gustav Mahler, it is an "invisible opera." In its narrative aspect, it is much easier to follow than the abstract works of the still high-modernist 1950s that preceded it. Many of its transformational techniques, as noted, resemble filmic montage cutting more than traditional musical developments of themes, and can thus be more easily followed by the ear than the internal and subjectified thematic logic of Central European music that Adorno defended against Igor Stravinsky's static repetitions (or the distortions of jazz), for instance, the treatment of the "Deutschlandlied" in Region II (1. Zentrum, 11 mins. 52 secs., score p. 14) or the punning combinations of the "Star-Spangled Banner" with scraps of other anthems in Region III (2. Zentrum, esp. at 10 mins. 08 secs., score p. 25).

On the other hand, there are also purely abstract developments, such as Region I's 2. Zentrum (with "Vorsatz" and "Nachsatz," ca. 17 mins. 55 secs. on into the beginning of Region II, score pp. 6ff.), or the "Zweite Transition" after the American section of Region III (13 mins. 24 secs. on, score pp. 27f.), where the ear cannot follow the (presumably) serialized expansions and transformations of the material. Stockhausen himself described Region I as follows: "A rigorous, pointed form develops from an international gibberish of short-wave broadcasts," and appropriately dedicated this Region to the master of such strict forms, Boulez.[18]

Hymnen thus does not simply transmogrify music into film; as the composer insisted in his notes, the work is not a collage, despite its open form. (Like many other works of the period, *Hymnen* exists in different versions.)[19] This is drastically unlike, for instance, the eclecticism of recent "world music," most often an ahistorical musical tourism reproducing only the leveling of globalization and reducing the foreign to an exotic commodity to be given the false aura of studio reproduction. Stockhausen seeks instead to bring his international materials into an internal relation with each other via the compositional technique of post-Webernist serialism. The colorful local musics of the work thus stand in tension with the technological rationality of Western European high modernism, which, as Adorno noted, tended rather to eradicate than to preserve national cultural differences.[20]

The apparent lack of internal relation between form and material remains the work's greatest difficulty. The impression is given that an abstract form has been arbitrarily imposed upon random material. Adorno saw this hermeneutical problem already in Webernist serialism:

> Material and composition remain unrelated to each other, merely opposed. Their internal mediation is not actually taken into consideration. This unrelatedness is manifested in the fading of musical idiom. Formerly, idiom managed something like a reconciliation between composition and material; the more sovereignly the composer operated with the latter, the more predetermined

musical material he eliminated, the more abruptly he would encounter his material. Through this, there entered into the traditional[ist] behavior of the composer, who merely made use of the material, something … comparable to industrial forms of production; a carelessness relative to the material that the musical subject at its height had not known.[21]

One might add that musical subjectivity as such depends on the existence of just this relation between form and material; without the latter, there can hardly be a subject at all.

It would be only too facile to reverse the signs and praise *Hymnen* for just apparent elision of the subject, thereby reading it via Kittler's media theory as an instance of desubjectivization, a direct transcription of the perceptual real. Nothing would do the piece more injustice, for a closer look at *Hymnen* reveals rather a repotentializing of musical subjectivity, thereby drastically giving the lie to Kittler's rhetorical reductivism, his seemingly rebellious stance as a bull-in-the-china-shop of traditional hermeneutics. These implications will need to be drawn out after a closer look at *Hymnen* itself, at how it responds to Adorno's indifference of form and material.

III

Hymnen is not comprehensible without a look backward at the larger context of Stockhausen's entire electronic project, originating in the early 1950s in the Cologne studios. The birth of electronic music was fostered not only by the technological medium of the tape recorder but also by the internal logic of post-Webernist serialism, with its project of a total rationalization both of musical material and of compositional procedures themselves. That project had, however, rapidly reached an impasse by the mid-1950s, an impasse answered in different ways by John Cage, Boulez, and Stockhausen at almost the same time. As is now well known, the aporia of total serialization gave birth to its apparent opposite, the aleatoric music of chance of which Cage was the most drastic exponent and which Boulez and Stockhausen, both of whom were less willing to abandon all compositional rationality to neo-Dadaist "action composition," had then to absorb in a more reflective fashion. The legacy of Cage would continue to occupy Stockhausen into the late 1960s: with *Hymnen* and the live electronic piece "Kurzwellen" of 1968, Stockhausen would finally incorporate into his own work the radios Cage had first used a quarter of a century earlier in *Credo in US* (1942) and his series of *Imaginary Landscapes*.

This development in music may be historically correlated to the then contemporary interest in information theory and machines reflected in Jacques Lacan's work of the period, especially his second *Seminar* of 1954–55. But it is a crude simplification to imply[22] that the discovery of

Turing machines and probability meant a simple elimination of linguistic subjectivity altogether. Lacan himself had no patience for Foucauldian attacks on straw-man humanism and insisted that "le sujet, ce n'est pas l'homme,"[23] that is, psychoanalysis, even at its most decentering, never threw the baby of the subject out with the bath water of ego-centered humanism. In fact, the discoveries enabled by information theory and its "conjectural science" meant rather a redefinition of the subject, now conceived as distinct from any neo-Freudian notions of ego-strengthening. Precisely the same renewal of subjectivity was to take place in post-1945 music.[24]

Stockhausen began his electronic career around 1952–54 with a series of abstract compositions all titled "Etüde" or "Studie." In polemical opposition to the amateurish cut-and-paste illustrations of Pierre Schaeffer's musique concrète, which Stockhausen disliked as much as did Boulez, these works were constructed only of pure studio-produced sine tones, not found objects. As an early text has it: "In general, one can recognize a first criterion of the quality of an electronic composition in the degree to which it is kept free of all instrumental or other tonal associations. These associations distract the listener's understanding from the autonomy of the tonal world being presented to him."[25] Boulez would not have disagreed and has never deviated from this position at all. In contrast to Cage (whose work he found "eher 'exponiert' als komponiert"),[26] Stockhausen was not primarily interested in shock effects: mere "tonal enrichments of our imaginary world are rapidly used up and become ordinary."[27] Yet within a couple of years, Stockhausen had shifted from "pure" electronic composition to the incorporation of recorded speech in *Gesang der Jünglinge* (1955–56). The turn to seeming montage in Stockhausen's works of the 1960s, which surprised many listeners, had in fact already occurred a decade earlier. This was promptly misinterpreted by many as either a concession to popular accessibility or an admission that the absolute ratio of electronic technology was inherently insufficient and needed to be referred back to concrete sounds.[28] In Adorno's terms, total rational integration must produce its opposite; in Kittler's, media must directly inscribe the real.

Neither of these readings is, however, adequate to Stockhausen's project, which will yield itself only to closer consideration. Crucial to the new musical subject that Stockhausen had evolved through his experiments in the electronic studio and to his studies of information theory under Werner Meyer-Eppler was a different relation between subject, material, and time. Stockhausen had become aware of the discrepancy between Schönberg's serialization of pitch and his continued use of traditional rhythms; to this, the attempts by Olivier Messiaen, Boulez, and others simply to transpose the numerical series from pitch to durational values was, at best, an inadequate solution. Working with electronic tapes in the Cologne studio allowed Stockhausen to decompose the internal make-up of individual tones and uncover within it an underlying identity between pitch and rhythm. An individual tone is composed of periodic impulses that the ear synthesizes as an identity bounded in space, pitch, color, and duration. With this, the discontinuous and uncoordinated composition of reified individual "parameters," typical of much Darmstadt School composition, could be overcome in favor of a radical monism, comparable to the unified field theory of contemporary physics. In other words, the material of music is its time.

To illustrate this rather abstract idea more concretely, consider that if one takes a specific pitch and speeds up or slows down its impulse frequency, one may gradually alter not only its register, but also its tone color; one may pass gradually from pitch-defined sound—the traditional material of Western music—to the noise first introduced by Edgard Varese and Cage, for noise is nothing but sound of aperiodic frequency. This transition from high to low pitch or from noise to definite pitch is "demonstrated" by Stockhausen at many points in his electronic oeuvre: one instance is in *Kontakte* (1958–60), about 17 mins. 05 secs. into the piece (pp. 19–20 of the score); another is the bridge passage to the beginning of Region II of *Hymnen*, where swamp ducks are slowed down until they become human voices (p. 12 in the score).

Serial music, Anton Webern's in particular, had already dissolved the traditional minimal unity of European music, the *Einfall* (idea, theme) or *Gestalt* (definite shape).[29] Stockhausen took this still further and dissolved the tone itself into its constituent components. The consequences are very much comparable to those Lacan drew from information theory; the subject is no longer identified with the imaginary ego, with any localizable tonal shape or *Gestalt*. The musical subject is no longer to be located in any definite shape, but only at the latter's margins, in the diffuse synthesis of shapes into statistical fields. (The ear possesses an "aureole of indeterminacy" comparable to that of the eye, in Lacan's well-known analysis.)[30] Stockhausen thus develops a "conjectural science" of the musical subject, similar to Lacan's psychoanalytic model. He differentiates "between the measured quanta-time and the experienced field-time," which must now be composed by "statistical field composition."[31]

This shift in compositional accent was further developed in Stockhausen's work on *Kontakte*, during which "the precise notation of microstructures gives way to diagrams of transformation procedures, like flow charts."[32] Stockhausen has already shifted from composing the "what"— the musical substance or identity—to composing the "how"—the process of transformation itself. From *Gesang der Jünglinge* on, he allows the imaginary—not only the definite referentiality of known sound objects (preeminent among them the human voice) and their attendant implications of communication, but also definite and recognizable *Gestalten*—to reenter his music, no longer excluding that imaginary as he had in the ascetic period of total symbolic rationalization of the early 1950s. Yet that imaginary is now clearly derivative, dependent on larger symbolic processes of structural transformation concealed beneath them. The course of his work in the 1960s would permit ever greater amounts of these definite imaginary shapes, finally breaking through to a reconsideration of tonal harmony in *Mantra* of 1970, which defined the "formula composition" with which he has worked ever since.

It should by now be clear that Adorno's seeming hermeneutic aporia between abstract form and arbitrary quotation mentioned earlier is indeed technically mediated from within the music. With this in mind, the inner form of *Hymnen* may be renarrated one last time, with an eye to its implications for media and music history.

IV

The narrative process of *Hymnen* may be read not only as the world-historical apocalypse and survival of the collective subject of humanity but also as an allegory of its own technological subjectivity as process. The work begins by quite literally plunging into the maelstrom, by switching on the radio to a storm of white noise. The listener senses him or herself already enclosed in an auditory envelope of perception comparable to film's primary identification,[33] yet without any definite object on which to center an imaginary ego. Stockhausen is composing a modern variant of the birth of music from the *Ungeist* of noise that began with the hollow opening string tremolos of Beethoven's Ninth Symphony and was continued by the beginnings of the *Ring* and by most of Bruckner's symphonies. The ear is, at this point, as if directly in Kittler's (and Lacan's) media real. Yet Stockhausen is not Cage (and even Cage—pace his apologists—could not reduce art to nothing more than a direct transcription of the real, which would be a *contradictio in adjecto*).[34] Moreover, the real of noise is itself only an element in a larger symbolic structure. The chaos of the opening begins to alternate, at first with a pair of hovering electronic chords (Harvey aptly calls them "dominant chords"),[35] and then with an uncanny croupier's voice ("Messieurs et Mesdames, faites votre [*sic*] jeux, s'il vous plaît"), crowd sounds and snippets of music.

Hymnen then begins to pass through the political imaginary, which is gently mocked with a neo-Dadaist excursus on the word "red," spoken "fugally" by four speakers in English, French, German, and Spanish. From the "Internationale" and the "Marseillaise," there is the aforementioned bridge of human crowds and swamp ducks to the "Deutschlandlied," and the "Horst-Wessel-Lied" allusion, followed by the studio discussion between Stockhausen and his assistant David Johnson ("Otto Tomek sagte …"). In between these last two events, the African center has already begun.[36] After Region III's vast and brooding Russian adagio, a decentered American montage (the "Star-Spangled Banner" intercut with Japanese, Israeli, and other anthems), and a lightning-fast Spanish section, which is then sped up into high chirping noises, the dark, slow Region IV begins, announced by the Swiss anthem. A section of piercing, physically painful, falling band-noise glissandi ensues, clearly a pictorial imagination of nuclear war. Into the clefts of this violent sound mass one hears the composer's own voice calling out autobiographically referential names, the calls being followed by long echoes. This is one of the most filmic passages in the entire piece, and its composition seems to have proceeded purely intuitively, if one follows the composer's comments to Cott: "At the end of the Fourth Region of *Hymnen* I decided to take the last chord of the Swiss anthem as sung by a male choir and repeat it a few times with an accent on each repetition. I made a tape loop of this single chord. I was so strongly taken by it that I went on listening to it—I didn't know at that time that I'd use it with as many repetitions as I finally did." (One can see here how far Stockhausen's intuitive composition, his working directly in sound material as a sculptor, has taken him from the abstract-suprematist ratio of the 1950s.) "The longer I listened, the more fascinated I was because in my previous work I'd always excluded periodic repetitions. There are a few exceptions ... where the repetitions occurred so fast that they resulted in a continuous sound. But periodicity as such, like ostinato pulses, I'd never used before."[37]

The reader may recall the previous discussion of the internal periodicity of tones. The reasons for Stockhausen's aversion to repetition were, in part, born of the historical trauma of 1933–45; repetition thus becomes a political question. To continue with Stockhausen's comments to Cott: "There has been a lot of music where this periodicity becomes so absolute and dominating that there's little left for what is happening within the periods." (This could be applied to so-called minimalism, but also to the rigid four-bar phases, I-IV-V cadences, and repetitive rhythms of pop.) "You see, marching music is periodic, and it seems in most marching music as if there's nothing but collective synchronization, and this has a very dangerous aspect. For example, when I was a boy, the radio in German was always playing typical brassy marching music from morning to midnight, and it really conditioned the people."[38]

This is why Stockhausen's music has so largely avoided the sort of drumming, hectoring rhythmic rhetoric one associates with Beethoven symphonies (and which is indulged in ad infinitum in commercial pop). Repetitive periodicity is the origin of the musical imaginary, whether that of the bourgeois ego or that of the delirious political collective. In a sense, individual "experience" as such is an imaginary form of periodicity. And as Lacan knew (and Kittler seems to have forgotten), the imaginary can never be simply eliminated without psychosis resulting. *Hymnen* must therefore pass from the real of the opening short-wave radio through the imaginary both of politics and of the composer's individual childhood, before landing in another form of the real at the end.

What remains at the very end of the piece is no more than the sound of the sleeping composer's own breathing (transcribed in the score with a pair of diagonal lines on the XY axes of time and pitch: /\ ). From the real of radio noise, the piece has arrived finally at the real of the composer's body (with which, the score implies, the listener should identify through *Mitatmen*—by breathing along with the music. Breathing—the subject of several important poems in the German tradition (in Johann Wolfgang von Goethe's *Diwan* and Rainer Maria Rilke's *Sonnets to Orpheus*)—is the literal fallout or remnant[39] of nuclear catastrophe. The periodicity of breathing is an exact answer to commercial music's tautological reinforcement of pulse-beats, the disciplinary rituals of aggressive imaginary periodicity.[40] Stockhausen can only return to this real of breathing—on the edge between inner and outer, subject and outer world, "extimate" in Lacan's terms—since his music has taken him outside it: "Almost all the rhythms in Western music are those of the human body—when we march or run or walk or move slowly—the rhythms of our limbs and their subdivisions and multiplications. A work like *Hymnen* incorporates rhythms and durations that are no longer bound to the body."[41] "Western music" (in Stockhausen's view) has been tied to the imaginary, ego-bound, conscious body. The musical world-history of *Hymnen* chronicles the violent self-destruction of that ego and effects a "piercing of the anthropological sound-wall,"[42] breaking normal ego boundaries. Thus, the breath at the end of *Hymnen* is the result of a *nostos*, a kenosis of the subject out of the body. Rather than simply overwhelming the listener with the noise of the insane real (as Kittler would have it, which is an impossibility), Stockhausen's piece has, as Christian Metz wrote of film,[43] inscribed a new area of the real into the symbolic, thereby changing the latter itself.

In its work with media, *Hymnen*—and Stockhausen's other works of the period—are no longer conventionally "classical" music, at least not in its high-modernist form. Alone among the most talented postwar composers, Stockhausen risked the *va banque* gambit of turning to the electronic instruments that the mass public still associates only with pop— even though the latter most often did little more than borrow Stockhausen's technical inventions and incorporate them as decorative, illustrative sound effects over a restoration of tonal harmony at its most symmetrical and repetitive.[44] Nothing could be further from the mark than Kittler's claim that pop and rock are a direct irruption of madness and the real. In fact, in most pop, electronics function as a conventional version of the sublime, with precisely the same disciplinary socialization purpose (spooky horror movie thrills-and-chills). Nor can Kittler's notion that media are opposed to the subjectivity of high art hold up (an idea depending, in fact, on the systematic exclusion of musical modernity from Kittler's historiography).[45]

Admittedly, Stockhausen's ability to carry out the experiments necessary for his work depended, as did the New German Cinema, on state subsidies to protect him from a commercial mass market that would never have allowed him to survive. In the 1960s, the money once spent in the previous decade for lavish orchestral rehearsals at the Südwestfunk and for electronic music began to be diverted to television. New German Cinema was thus, in more than one sense, the heir to the musical school of Darmstadt. That Stockhausen's work has had so few successors depends less on any inherent subjectlessness of media than on a sociology of art music patronage that has yet to be written.[46]

Notes

1. This applies, nota bene, not so much to the continuing work of the 1950s and 1960s modernists—Boulez, Carter, and Stockhausen—as to that of younger composers. The present essay has not space to consider Stockhausen's work after *Mantra* (1970), which includes substantial pieces such as the live-electronic *Sirius* and the dance-performance *Inori* (from the 1970s) and the huge ongoing opera *Licht* (1977–): these works would in any case have to be termed neomodernist (rather than postmodernist).

2. A personal favorite of this writer's would be the ads run by Columbia Records in the *New York Review of Books* showing a student protester marching with a sign reading "Sing Along with Stockhausen." For an instance of the current amnesia, one could scarcely outdo the ignorant Philistinism of Jost Hermand, "Avant-Garde, Modern, Post-Modern: The Music (Almost) Nobody Wants to Hear," in *German Essays on Music*, ed. Jost Hermand and Michael Gilbert (New York: Continuum, 1994), 282–99.

3. Both the total serialism of Darmstadt and the artifice of the *nouveau roman* have been received by the academy, kin as they both were to the "text-immanent" readings of structuralism. As regards neo-Dadaism, see Huyssen on the Fluxus group and this writer's "Zufall und Subjekt, Erwägungen zu Cage," in *Mythos Cage*, ed. Claus-Steffen Mahnkopf (Hofheim: Wolke, 1999), 203–22. For a consideration of the aging of the modern, see Ulrich Schönherr, *Das unendliche Altern der Moderne* (Vienna: Passagen-Verlag, 1992).

4. Theodor W. Adorno, *Gesammelte Schriften* [hereafter *GS*], ed. Rolf Tiedemann, with assistance of Gretel Adorno, Susan Buck-Morss, and Klaus Schultz (Frankfurt am Main: Suhrkamp, 1997), 7:256.

5. Adorno, *GS*, 2:39.

6. Gabriele Forg, ed., *Unsere Wagner* (Frankfurt am Main: Fischer, 1984).

7. Friedrich Kittler, *Gramophone Film Typewriter*, trans. Geoffrey Winthrop-Young and Michael Wutz (Stanford: Stanford University Press, 1999), 97.

8. Karlheinz Stockhausen, *Hymnen*, Deutsche Grammophon Gesellschaft, SLPM 2707039 (1969). It is now CD no. 10 in Stockhausen's own catalogue.

9. Karl Wörner, *Stockhausen: Life and Work*, trans. and ed. Bill Hopkins, rev. ed. (Berkeley: University of California Press, 1973), 69.

10. Hitler himself noted the importance of the acoustical domain in his own recipe for media-based power: "The sound is in my opinion much more suggestive than the image. But it has yet to be learnt to take advantage of the possibilities of radio broadcasting." Ulrich Schönherr, "Topophony of Fascism: On Marcel Beyer's *The Karnau Tapes*," *The Germanic Review* 73, no. 4 (Fall 1998): 329.

11. See the very strange autobiographical essay, "About My Childhood," in Robin Maconie, *The Works of Karlheinz Stockhausen* (Oxford: Clarendon, 1990), 15–23. For the composer's dislike of overtly political music, see his critique of Henze in Jonathan Cott, *Stockhausen: Conversations with the Composer* (New York: Simon and Schuster, 1973), 119.

12. Compare Wenders's famous quote on how images had been "debased as vehicles for lies," cited in Timothy Corrigan, *New German Film: The Displaced Image* (Austin: University of Texas Press, 1983), 25–26. On the politics of the national anthem, see George

Mosse, "National Anthems: The Nation Militant," in *From Ode to Anthem: Problems of Lyric Poetry*, ed. Reinhold Grimm and Jost Hermand (Madison: University of Wisconsin Press, 1989), 86–99.

13. Siegfried Kracauer, *Theory of Film* (Princeton: Princeton University Press, 1997), 15–20.

14. Adorno, *GS*, 10:1.

15. Friedrich Kittler, *Discourse Networks 1800/1900*, trans. Michael Metteer with Chris Cullens (Stanford: Stanford University Press, 1990), 236, 256.

16. Klaus Schöning, *Neues Hörspiel* (Frankfurt am Main: Suhrkamp, 1970).

17. On this, see the first number of the Darmstadt periodical *Die Reihe*, "Elektronische Musik," published by Universal Edition in 1955, especially the articles by Eimert and Stuckenschmidt.

18. Karlheinz Stockhausen, *Texte zur Musik, 1963–1970*, ed. Dieter Schnebel (Cologne: DuMont, 1971), 3:96.

19. Ibid., 98; Wörner, *Stockhausen*, 58ff.

20. Adorno, *GS*, 10:372–73.

21. Ibid., 16:507.

22. As does Kittler, most emphatically in "Die Welt des Symbolischen—eine Welt der Maschine," now in Friedrich Kittler, *Drakulas Vermächtnis. Technische Schriften* (Leipzig: Reclam, 1993), 58–80.

23. See the still unpublished *Seminar XV: L'Acte psychanalytique*, session of 6 March 1968 (unofficial copy published by Editions Schamans, Paris, 198–99).

24. For an analysis of how this change in musical subjectivity affected Cage and Boulez, see Powell, "Zufall und Subjekt," 203–22.

25. Karlheinz Stockhausen, *Texte zur electronischen und instrumentalen Musik: Aufsätze 1952–1962 zur Theorie des Komponierens* (Cologne: DuMont, 1963), 1:143.

26. Ibid., 132.

27. Ibid., 50.

28. Seppo Heikinheimo, *The Electronic Music of Karlheinz Stockhausen: Studies on the Esthetical and Formal Problems of Its First Phase*, trans. B. Absetz (Helsinki: Suomen Musiikkitieteellinen Seura, 1972), 82.

29. The consequences of this are worked out repeatedly by Adorno, beginning with the *Philosophie der neuen Musik:* For a psychoanalytic extension of these implications, see Larson Powell, "Das Triebleben der Klänge. Adornos *Philosophie der neuen Musik* im Lichte der neueren Psychoanalyse," in *Mit den Ohren denken: Adornos Philosophie der Musik*, ed. Richard Klein and Claus-Steffen Mahnkopf (Frankfurt am Main: Suhrkamp, 1998), 117–33.

30. Adorno, *GS*, 7:43, 63. Compare with Jacques Lacan, *Le Séminaire XI: Les Quatre concepts fondamentaux de la psychanalyse* (Paris: Seuil, 1973), part 2.

31. Stockhausen, *Texte zur electronischen und instrumentalen Musik*, 129 and 135.

32. Robin Maconie, *The Works of Karlheinz Stockhausen* (Oxford: Clarendon, 1990), 101.

33. Christian Metz, *The Imaginary Signifier: Psychoanalysis and Cinema*, trans. Celia Britton, Annwyl Williams, Ben Brewster, and Alfred Guzzetti (Bloomington: Indiana University Press, 1982), 56, 96.

34. On this misunderstanding of Cage's work, see Powell, "Zufall und Subjekt."

35. Jonathan Harvey, *The Music of Stockhausen* (Berkeley: University of California Press, 1975), 103.

36. Although the African center is directly followed by the Soviet anthem, there is no overt linking or contrast of African anthems to their European colonial ex-rulers: it would thus be difficult to read much of a postcolonial subtext into the work.

37. Cott, *Stockhausen*, 139–40.

38. Ibid., 27–28.

39. Lacan's terms, it will be recalled, for the *objet petit a* as remnant of trauma, of what cannot fit into the symbolic.

40. Compare Adorno's famous passages on Stravinsky: "The effect envisaged by Stravinsky's music is … [the listener's] being electrified like the dancer.… In the process, this music appeals, as if for legitimacy, to the body—in the most extreme case, to the regularity of pulse-beats"(*GS*, 12:179).
41. Cott, *Stockhausen*, 124.
42. Adorno, *GS* 16:490.
43. Metz, *The Imaginary Signifier*, 3.
44. To multiply examples here would be tiresome, but one might be given: one passage from Region IV, score p. 51, at 18 mins. 04.2 secs., was copied verbatim into the first track of Pink Floyd's *Meddle* (early 1970s).
45. Once again, examples could be multiplied. But when Kittler waxes eloquent about Syd Barrett's having "wild hin und her gedreht" the stereo channels while mixing—in the late 1960s (*Draculas Vermächtnis*, 136)—he seems to forget that Stockhausen and others had discovered the idea of music in space over a decade earlier, and had subjected it to a far more searching and unsettling exploration than the pseudorebellion of "wild hin und her drehen."
46. The composer was kind enough to recommend to the present writer two additional sources: Dr. Imke Misch's dissertation on *Hymnen* (published by Pfau-Verlag) and a special number of *Perspectives of New Music*, vol. 36, no. 1 (1998). Neither had yet appeared at the time of writing. Stockhausen's work had earlier been published by DuMont Schauberg, Cologne (essays), and Universal Edition, Vienna (scores), and has been recorded mostly by Deutsche Grammophon. All of these materials are now available from the Stockhausen-Verlag, 51515 Kürten, Germany.

CONTRIBUTORS

Nora M. Alter is Professor of German, Film, and Media Studies at the University of Florida. She is affiliate faculty in the programs in European Studies, Jewish Studies, and Woman and Gender Studies. Her teaching and research have been focused on twentieth-century cultural and visual studies from a comparative perspective. She is the author of *Vietnam Protest Theatre: The Television War on Stage* (1996) and *Projecting History: Non-Fiction German Film* (2002), and has recently completed a book on Chris Marker (forthcoming, 2005). Current projects include a study on the international essay film. She has been awarded year-long research fellowships from the National Endowment for the Humanities, the Howard Foundation and the Alexander von Humboldt Foundation.

Hester Baer is Assistant Professor of German and Film and Video Studies at the University of Oklahoma. She is currently completing a book, based on her dissertation, about gender, spectatorship, and visual culture in West Germany in the early postwar period. Her new research focuses on discourses of the popular in postunification German literature and film.

David Barnett is a Lecturer in Drama, Theatre and Performance at University College Dublin. He has published a monograph on Heiner Müller (*Literature versus Theatre*, 1998) and articles on twentieth-century German and English drama, including works on Heinar Kipphardt, Werner Schwab, Howard Barker, and Joseph Goebbels. He is currently preparing the first book-length study on Rainer Werner Fassbinder and the German theatre as a Fellow of the Alexander von Humboldt Foundation.

Russell A. Berman is Walter A. Haas Professor in the Humanities at Stanford University. He has received many honors and awards including a Mellon Faculty Fellowship at Harvard University (1982–83), an Alexander von Humboldt Fellowship (1988–89), and the Bundesverdienstkreuz of the Federal Republic of Germany (1997). His publications include *Between*

Fontane and Tucholsky (1983), *The Rise of the Modern German Novel* (1986), *Modern Culture and Critical Theory* (1989), *Cultural Studies of Modern Germany* (1993) and *Enlightenment or Empire: Colonial Discourse in German Culture* (1998). He is currently involved in a project on literary history.

Thomas F. Cohen is Assistant Professor of Film Studies at Rhodes College. He is currently completing a manuscript on the relation between modern experimental music and avant-garde cinema. Most recently, his research has focused on filmmakers and video artists who work primarily in small-gauge or obsolete formats.

Caryl Flinn is the author of *The New German Cinema: Music, History, and the Matter of Style* (2003) and *Strains of Utopia* (1992), and coeditor of *Music and Cinema* (2000). She is the author of numerous articles and anthology chapters on film music, German cinema, sound, and feminist and gender studies. She is Director of Graduate Studies and Professor of Women's Studies and Media Arts at the University of Arizona.

Elizabeth C. Hamilton is Assistant Professor of German at Oberlin College, where she teaches German language, literature, and film. Her areas of special interest include disability studies, New German Cinema, and East German cinema. She is currently completing a book, *Deviant Bodies in German Literature and Film*, that explores embodiment within the Enlightenment tradition.

Christopher Jones is Senior Lecturer in German in the Department of Languages at the Manchester Metropolitan University, England. He teaches German literature and culture at undergraduate level, and German literature at postgraduate level. His research interests lie in the field of popular culture, particularly crime fiction. Recent conference papers and publications have included studies of contemporary Swiss crime fiction, the popular television show *Kommissar Rex*, and violence in female-authored crime novels.

Lutz Koepnick is Associate Professor of German, Film, and Media Studies at Washington University in St. Louis. He is the author of *The Dark Mirror: German Cinema between Hitler and Hollywood* (2002), *Walter Benjamin and the Aesthetics of Power* (1999), and *Nothungs Modernität: Wagners Ring und die Poesie der Politik im neunzehnten Jahrhundert* (1994). Koepnick's current book project is entitled "Framing Attention: Windows on Modern German Culture."

Richard Langston is Assistant Professor of German at the University of North Carolina at Chapel Hill. He is currently working on a manuscript tentatively entitled "Visions of Violence: The Avant-Garde and Trauma after Fascism." He has written, published, and presented on such topics as fascism and the petite bourgeoisie, aesthetic violence, terrorism, decadence, and globalization.

Carl Niekerk, Associate Professor of German, teaches at the University of Illinois at Urbana-Champaign. Research interests include eighteenth- and nineteenth-century German literature and culture, anthropology, (post)-colonialism, psychoanalysis, and comparative Dutch studies. He has authored a book on Georg Christoph Lichtenberg in the context of eighteenth-century anthropology and natural history (2005), and is currently preparing a manuscript titled "Gustav Mahler, the Idea of a German National Culture, and the Avant-Garde."

Brigitte Peucker is the Elias Leavenworth Professor of German and Professor of Film Studies at Yale University. Her most recent books include *Lyric Descent in the German Romantic Tradition* (1987) and *Incorporating Images: Film and the Rival Arts* (1995). She has recently completed *The Material Image: Art and the Real in Film*.

Larson Powell is Assistant Professor of German at Texas A&M University. He has published and presented lectures on Adorno, Lacan, Luhmann, Freud, Bachmann, Doeblin, Rilke, Loerke, and Kraus, among others. His work focuses on music aesthetics (Boulez, Cage, Carter, Stockhausen, Wolpe), comparative modernism (French, German, Russian), and film and media theory. He has completed a book manuscript, "The Technological Unconscious," which examines the persistence of nature in twentieth-century German literature. A second book on music aesthetics is nearing completion.

Frank Trommler is Professor of German and Comparative Literature at the University of Pennsylvania in Philadelphia. In 1995–2003 he was Director of the Humanities Program at the American Institute for Contemporary German Studies in Washington, editing its series on contemporary German culture. He has published widely in the areas of nineteenth- and twentieth-century German literature, theatre, and culture, as well as German-American cultural relations. In 2001 he coedited *The German-American Encounter: Conflict and Cooperation Between Two Cultures, 1800–2000*. Modernism, Weimar culture, and postwar literary developments have been topics of special interest. Recently, he has been working on German culture under—and against—National Socialism.

Nicholas Vazsonyi, Associate Professor of German and Director of the German Studies Program at the University of South Carolina, has published extensively on German literature and culture from the eighteenth to the twentieth century, focusing increasingly on issues of national identity and music. His first book, *Lukács Reads Goethe: From Stalinism to Aestheticism* (1997), was followed by *Searching for Common Ground: Diskurse zur deutschen Identität 1750–1871* (2000) and *Wagner's* Meistersinger: *Performance, History, Representation* (2003). He is currently working on a book manuscript concerning what he terms the "Wagner industry."

INDEX